Psychodynamic Group Psychotherapy

Psychodynamic

Group

Psychotherapy

J. Scott Rutan, Ph.D.

Assistant Clinical Professor of Psychology
Department of Psychiatry
Harvard Medical School

Director, Center for Group Therapy
Massachusetts General Hospital

Walter N. Stone, M.D.

Vice Director and Professor of Psychiatry
University of Cincinnati College of Medicine

MACMILLAN PUBLISHING COMPANY
NEW YORK

COLLIER MACMILLAN CANADA, INC.
TORONTO

COLLIER MACMILLAN PUBLISHERS
LONDON

Macmillan Publishing Company
866 Third Avenue, New York, New York 10022

Collier Macmillan Canada, Inc.

Collier Macmillan Publishers • London

International Standard Book Number: 0-02-404930-1

Library of Congress Catalog Card Number: 82-73289
Printing: 3 4 5 6 7   Year: 7 8 9 0 1 2 3 4

Contents

Preface

The idea for this book took form in 1981 when we were cochairmen of the American Group Psychotherapy Association's Institute Committee. The Institute is a remarkable event that occurs each year prior to the Association's annual conference. The purpose of the Institute is to enable mental health professionals to learn about therapy groups by participating in experiential learning groups. During the many years we were associated with the Institute, we had the marvelous opportunity of meeting, observing, and appreciating the skills of the Institute faculty—men and women from around the world who practice a wide variety of types of group psychotherapy.

Out of this experience we learned a great many things. We learned anew how very powerful groups are as change agents. We also learned that therapists with widely diverse philosophical, theoretical, and technical points of view can be immensely helpful to their patients.

As psychodynamic psychotherapists, we were particularly impressed with the differing approaches that live under the rubric of psychodynamic group therapy. Some practitioners focus on the dynamics of the group itself, rarely speaking to individual members. Others rarely seem to note the group processes, choosing to focus on the specific interpersonal interactions. We found that some of our colleagues listen only for material relevant to the group, while others are avidly curious about members' personal histories or their out-of-group lives. There are leaders who love a good dream, and others who view dreams as resistances. It became difficult to determine what might represent an orthodox psychodynamic approach to groups!

This led us to the realization that, though there are many fine books on group therapy, there is no book dedicated to a consistent, thoroughgoing psychodynamic approach to group therapy. That is what this book is about.

We begin with broad philosophical considerations, speculating about the place of group therapy in today's society. We move then to a history of small groups and of group therapy. From that foundation we explicate a theoretical basis, a road map the clinician can use in traversing the complicated terrain of a therapy group. After the theoretical section, we move to quite pragmatic material. We have sprinkled the book liberally with clinical examples in an attempt to bring the material alive. It is our goal that a mental health professional who reads this book can, with appropriate supervision, be a therapeutic agent as a group therapist.

For literary purposes we have used primarily the masculine form. We hope this is not offensive to any readers.

Were we to mention by name all the people to whom we are indebted for their assistance in this work, the acknowledgment section would be far longer than the book itself. But we would be remiss if we did not give special thanks to some. First and foremost, we are grateful to our patients, our finest teachers. Second, we were moved by the willingness of our colleagues and friends to offer their expertise and time to help us refine this work. Anne Alonso, Ph.D., Martin Keller, M.D., Cecil Rice, Ph.D., Robert Kunkel, M.D., Edward Klein, Ph.D., Esther Stone, M.S.W., and Katherine Stone read and reread various versions of the present book, and their contributions are inevitably woven into the present text. Furthermore, this book would never have reached fruition had it not been for the diligent and compassionate assistance of our editor, Sarah Boardman, and of Collamore's production manager, Merle Schlesinger. Because the secretarial assistance that goes into the writing and rewriting of any manuscript should never go unrecognized, we wish to thank Natalie Reynolds for the willing and patient work she so admirably performed. Finally, we are grateful for the loving forebearance given us through this arduous process by our wives, Jane and Esther, and our children.

Human beings are group-oriented. We begin in the small groups known as families and thereafter live our lives in various groups. The formation of our personalities is predicated upon our experiences with the different groups in which we interact, and the opportunities for modification and change of our personalities are very much affected by the groups we are involved in. As Harry Stack Sullivan maintained, it takes people to make people sick, and it takes people to make people well again.[1]

The premise of this book is that groups are uniquely important today because of the structure of modern society. By extrapolation, group therapy is a uniquely important therapeutic modality in our twentieth-century world. To understand this proposition we must examine some of the differences between Freud's Victorian age and our twentieth-century culture and how each age affects the lives of those who live within it.

Culture and Mental Illness

Pathologies confronting modern clinicians seem to be different from the pathologies that confronted Freud. In Victorian times Freud analyzed the pathologies of members of the society in which he lived, and through that examination he made revolutionary discoveries about the formation and complexion of human personality. The pathology that most fascinated Freud was hysteria. This disorder became the lens through which he focused his conceptions of individual psychodynamics. In modern times classical hysteria is not the pathology around which theory is being built. Masterson, for instance, noted that today's patients usually come to psychotherapy, not "with a specific discrete symptom picture, such as an obsession or a phobia, as was reported in Freud's time. Rather, their complaint is more general and vague—of getting too little satisfaction in their lives."[2] The cutting edge of modern psychoanalytic thought has to do with narcissistic and borderline conditions, character disorders where pathology is manifest in a disturbed quality of relationships with other human beings.

These "new" pathologies have been accompanied by other post-

Freudian developments in our understanding of psychopathology and our practice of psychotherapy. Giovacchini observed that as psychoanalysts began to treat character-disordered people, this "shifted our focus from a predominantly id-oriented psychology to an ego psychology. . . . It highlighted the importance of early development. The subtleties and vicissitudes of early object relationships have assumed paramount importance."[3] These developments themselves nest within larger contexts.

The etiology of psychopathology is multidetermined. Elements of temperament, genetics, and biology go into the human experience along with the intrapsychic and interpersonal forces that are the province of psychodynamic theorists.

The search for a link between cultural factors and mental illness has significant roots. As early as 1897 Durkheim[4] wondered about a connection between suicide and social conditions. In the 1930s Faris and Dunham[5] suggested a causal relationship between schizophrenia and the living conditions in Chicago slums. Leighton et al.,[6] in their well-known Stirling County (Nova Scotia) study, documented both an overall correlation between mental illness and social disarray, and correlations between specific sociocultural settings and particular types of psychiatric disorder. Dohrenwend and Dohrenwend[7] have found that while schizophrenia seems to be present in all cultures, there is considerable discrepancy in the types of schizophrenia that dominate in different cultures. Likewise Cohen[8] demonstrated cultural factors in the etiology of depressive reactions. Eisenthal[9] has summarized the studies just mentioned, as well as a substantially larger sampling of the literature on this subject.

Thus the notion of a connection between cultural factors and the formation and expression of mental disorder has already been examined in some depth by other authors. For our purposes it is of particular relevance that cultures and ages have their own characteristic and dominant pathologies. In our modern world, for example, there is great evidence of individuals having difficulty in obtaining and sustaining intimate interpersonal relationships even though our culture emphasizes individual gratification. We shall pursue these ideas by comparing the cultures, focal pathologies, and psychodynamic formulations of Freud's day and our own.

Victorian Culture

The Victorian era was stressful and comforting to people in specific ways. Victorian society offered many fewer choices than does twentieth-century America. Although vastly more open than the societies that preceded it, its members were nonetheless born into role expectations largely defined by class, ethnicity, and sex. There was little opportunity to go beyond those expectations, so that hopes and aspirations were sources of frustration. On the other hand individuals were spared the burden of ambiguity and choice. Acceptable behavior was highly codified, typically by a strong Church morality, with the result that sexual drives in particular were restricted. (The presence of the Victorian pornographic literature indicates that the drives were not thwarted altogether.)

In that society individuals had a definite place, though not necessarily a place they chose or relished. Concomitantly, individuals had an identity that was clear. Relational patterns were set within the framework of the Church, the neighborhood, the extended family, and the work world, all of which provided most people with natural sources of support and stability.

Individuals in Victorian times were presented with many fewer choices about how to live their lives and with whom to live them. There was less ambiguity and uncertainty. This is not to imply there was an absence of frustration and pain. If few complained about being "bent out of shape" it was because being shaped was so universal. It is within reason to suggest that the restrictiveness of that society might lead to pathologies that express conflict between individuals' powerful innate impulses and the introjects of a restrictive society.

Victorian Psychopathology: Hysteria Revisited

Freud's theories developed as he treated his patients, many of them neurotic hysterics. Students of Freudian theory are familiar with the case of Anna O., the young woman Breuer treated from December 1880 until June 1882. She suffered from classic hysteria, or "conversion reaction." In the course of nursing her dying father she had developed paralysis of three limbs, contractures and anesthesias, a nervous cough, and other symptoms. Breuer conducted his first analysis on Anna O., using hypnosis throughout the treatment. In the course of the treatment it was discovered that Anna O. had two quite distinct personalities. Further, during the course of that treatment Anna O. developed what later became known as a transference love for Breuer.[10]

Freud and Breuer often discussed this case, and out of this discussion came many of Freud's formulations about the existence of unconscious material and the structure of personality. Shortly after this, Freud saw Emma von N., and in this case he had the opportunity to observe firsthand the strange behaviors present in hysteria.

Freud postulated four major premises about personality: First, all behavior is determined, not random. Second, there are unconscious urges, memories, wishes—a vast reservoir of information outside the individual's awareness. Third, human behavior is purposeful and geared toward the protection of the self ('der Ich'), with even the most bizarre symptoms serving such an adaptive/compensatory purpose. And fourth, Freud eventually suggested that there are two basic drives within human personality, the libidinal (pleasure) drive and the aggressive drive, with personality formed in the thwarting and harnessing of these two drives. These four postulates are, of course, a most summary attempt to distill the essence of Freud's theories.

Do psychotherapists see patients like Anna O. in our offices today? Probably, though certain aspects of her pathology, such as the conversion reactions, are much rarer now, and when they do appear they are more likely to be seen by our colleagues in neurology or even internal medicine. Perhaps more telling is the likelihood that a patient like Anna O. would be diagnosed differently today, probably with a label like "borderline personality." Why the difference in diagnosis and understanding of psychopathology?

Freud utilized the models implicit in the society, technology, and theories of his day; he attempted to view personality in terms of energy and structure. The Victorian era was a time of rapid and monumental change, as industrialization and mass production changed the fabric of society and created a new world order. The people of that era had the conviction that "structure" could harness the very forces of nature, and their convictions seemed borne out by their unprecedented productivity, wealth, population growth, and hegemony over peoples of a more "primitive" nature around the globe. It is little wonder that Freud began to hypothesize about the "parts" that make up personality.

The theory that resulted is to a great extent that of an order based on structure, an organization of parts. As we will note below, modern pathologies—and theories about them—refer not so much to faulty parts as to dysfunctional relationships and dissatisfying ways of living. Modern conceptions of pathology are cast less in terms of mismatched, unmeshed parts than in terms of disrupted developmental processes.

Whereas modern theorists chart the evolution of personality through social systems, Freud viewed the ego as essentially the product of intrapsychic conflict. Though individual personality was seen to be affected by interactions with significant others (especially the mother), it was nonetheless not seen as predominantly formed in those interactions. Rather, human personality was understood to be the result of thoroughly inward processes. The ego was viewed as a rational, unemotional arbiter between the instinctual urges common to mankind and the acceptable mores of the society in which man found himself. And the superego was the "alien *it* which tyrannizes the ego."[11]

It is difficult to criticize Freud for this focus, given the genius required to hypothesize as much as he did about human development. Rather, we should simply understand that he did not have time or opportunity to expand all his observations to their logical conclusions. Indeed it was later authors who elaborated on Freud's observations about the impact of human interactions and developed theories about personality as a product of interpersonal transactions. This now represents the hallmark of modern theory of human development. The object relations theorists maintain that it is the craving for human relationship, not the power of instinctual urges, that is primary in human development. If, indeed, this is an important component of modern psychopathology, then a therapeutic modality that utilizes the interactions of networks of individuals should be especially capable of altering disturbed or disturbing relationships and producing a more satisfying existence.

Modern Culture

In modern culture the traditional sources of identity and continuity are gone or waning. It is as if, on many important axes, the Victorian and the modern era are opposites. Mainstays of the community and identity such as the extended (and even nuclear) family, the neighborhood, the church, and the ethnic group, are all diminishing in stability and dependability. The rate of change is so enormous that generations begin to have their own "cultures." Mass media and transportation diminish and collapse distinctions of time, place, and social situation that once gave people a sense of themselves.

There was a certain dependability about the future in Victorian times. If a goal could not be attained in an individual's lifetime, there was always the reasonable expectation that it might be attained in one's children's or grandchildren's lifetimes. This is not the case today. With increased technology, change is exponential, occurring at a faster pace than at any time in history. If that were not enough, we live under the realization that mankind now, for the first time, has the capacity to destroy all life on this planet in a matter of moments or months. And there is little in human history to inspire confidence that men will be able to avoid using this awesome capacity. The value of working for and investing in future generations seems thereby diminished. The press to "live for today" finds external validation.

Further, modern individuals are confronted with a bewildering array of critical choices new to this era (see Alvin Toffler's *Future Shock*[12]). We can choose our profession, our mate, our geographic location, our educational level, and even our gender. And while it is true that each of these choices is relative and within limits, nonetheless they are real. With the presence of such a proliferation of choices, modern individuals must also accept a new and more pervasive type of ambiguity and uncertainty. Each choice involves the quality and type of relationships each of us will have with others.

There has been a strong trend in modern society to value happiness *now* at the expense of deepened relationships and firm foundations.[13,14] "Doing your own thing" is no longer counterculture ethos. It has become part of the value system in all sectors and strata of society. The ready option today is to change relationships rather than resolve conflicts. This tendency has become both the cause and the effect of the dramatic instability of modern marriages and family life. (The present odds of a marriage ending in divorce are approaching one in two.)

Modern Psychopathology

The ability to enter into cooperative, loving, interdependent relationships with other human beings is a sign of psychological maturity and health. It is particularly a sign of health in this day and age. Indeed a rough but accurate indicator of psychopathology is the degree to which individuals allow themselves to know how important others are to them.

Given the changes that have occurred since Freud's day, it is quite understandable that the stereotypic pathologies of today involve the ability to effect, experience, and enjoy intimate and sustaining relationships. Whereas in Victorian times individuals had primarily to struggle with internal conflicts about wishes which that society would not allow to be fulfilled or even experienced (notably aggressive and sexual urges), modern individuals have much more permission to experience those wishes, and even on occasion to act on them. There are many more things that modern individuals may try, but there are fewer and fewer things upon which we can rely. Specifically, people today have fewer "guaranteed" relationships and sources of identity. The neighborhood is usually transient, the Church is less cohesive than in past times, and the extended family and even the nuclear family has developed porous boundaries.

Thus the modern psychopathologies written about most extensively are the narcissistic and borderline conditions, both having to do with an impaired ability to gain authentic relationships. Fairbairn[15] was among the first to state the view that it is the relationship with the object (another human being), and not the gratification of an impulse, that is the fundamental fact of human development. Modern patients who enter the offices of psychotherapists do not disable physical "parts" of themselves, as Freud's patients did, nearly as often as they disable their relationships (as Otto Kernberg would suggest) or find their capacity to relate to be inadequate (as Heinz Kohut would maintain). The development of object relations theory and self psychology represent not only further refinements of psychoanalytic theory, but also a modification of that theory which is mandated by the differences in culture between Freud's time and our own.

Group Therapy

Our understanding of the structure, functioning, and objectives of therapy groups is consistent with our description of modern society and the pathologies it fosters.

Freud's patients lived in a structured and mechanistic world. This both affected the ills that beset them and determined the focus and the form of cure that would work for them. As to focus: Freud's hysterical patients needed abreaction, catharsis, access to their repressed wishes and memories. As to form: one-to-one treatment served very well. Patients did not lack social connectedness. The social element was, in a sense, all too present.

The situation is typically reversed today. Individualism is so dominant that social connections are not formed or, if formed, soon unravel. The requirements and goals of psychotherapy are thus necessarily different. Modern patients need authentic human relationships, the skills for building them, and the ability to make the compromises necessary to live intimately with other persons. Modern man needs help not so much with the structure of his being but with the process of relating and acting. From this perspective the benefits of group therapy, of a therapeutic community geared to assist patients in exactly these areas of individual and cultural deficit, become clear.

Therapy groups are supportive yet, in a way, restrictive communities. They are restrictive in that their cultural expectation is akin to that of the Victorian age. Individuals are brought into groups and are expected to *work at* their relationships with the other members of the group. The easy out of changing relationships is highly discouraged in favor of resolving conflicts.

Put another way:

Group therapy, by its very format, offers unique opportunities to experience and work on issues of intimacy and individuation. In such groups the community is represented in the treatment room. It is usually impossible for individuals to view themselves as existing alone and affecting no one when in a group therapy situation over any significant period of time.[16]

Group therapy would seem to be a natural antidote to many of the predominant disorders of our age. Because therapy groups focus on individuals as relational beings and rely on relationships for growth, learning, and change, they offer a response to modern mankind's fragmented ability to relate.

If modern society promotes precocious and excessive independence, group therapy may provide just the necessary corrective emotional experience—of supported but not forced dependency and of responsive but not invasive interdependence. The group setting offers the hope of relatedness in the context of appropriate limits, and opportunity to gain independence, not at the expense of intimacy, but *through* intimacy.

References

1. H.S. Sullivan, *The Collected Works of Harry Stack Sullivan* (New York: W.W. Norton, 1953), pp. 372ff.
2. J.F. Masterson, *Psychotherapy of the Borderline Adult* (New York: Brunner/Mazel, 1976), pp. 10–11.
3. P. Giovacchini, *Treatment of Primitive Mental States* (New York: Jason Aronson, 1979), p. 3.
4. E. Durkheim, *Suicide: A Study in Sociology*, translated by J. Spaulding and G. Simpson, edited by Simpson (Glencoe, Ill.: Free Press, 1951). Originally published in 1897.
5. R.E.L. Faris and H.W. Dunham, *Mental Disorders in Urban Areas: An Ecological Study of Schizophrenia and Other Psychoses* (Chicago: University of Chicago Press, 1939).
6. A. H. Leighton, *Stirling County Study of Psychiatric Disorder and Sociocultural Environment: My Name Is Legion*, vol. 1, *People of Cove and Woodlot*, vol. 2, and *The Character of Danger*, vol. 3 (New York: Basic Books, 1959).
7. B.P. Dohrenwend and B.S. Dohrenwend, "Social and Cultural Influences on Psychopathology," *Annu. Rev. Psychol.* 7, no. 25 (1974):417–452.
8. Y.A. Cohen, *Social Structures and Personality* (New York: Holt, Rinehart and Winston, 1961).
9. S. Eisenthal, "The Sociological Approach," in *Outpatient Psychiatry: Diagnosis and Treatment*, edited by A. Lazare (Baltimore: Williams and Wilkins, 1979), pp. 73–115.
10. S. Freud, "Analysis Terminable and Interminable," in Standard Ed., vol. 18, 1937, pp. 316–357.
11. W. Binstock, "The Psychodynamic Approach," in *Outpatient Psychiatry: Diagnosis and Treatment*, edited by A. Lazare (Baltimore: Williams and Wilkins, 1979), p. 56.
12. A. Toffler, *Future Shock* (New York: Random House, 1970).
13. P. Marin, "The New Narcissism," *Harpers*, October 1975, pp. 44–56.

14. C. Lasch, *The Culture of Narcissism* (New York: W.W. Norton, 1979).
15. W.R.D. Fairbairn, *Psychoanalytic Studies of the Personality* (London: Tavistock, 1952).
16. J.S. Rutan and A. Alonso, "Group Therapy," in *Outpatient Psychiatry: Diagnosis and Treatment*, edited by A. Lazare (Baltimore: Williams and Wilkins, 1979), p. 612.

History of Small Group Theory and *Practice*

Differences between the way individuals behave when alone and when in groups have interested observers for many years. LeBon and McDougall, both in 1920, were among the first to write about the impact of groups on the behaviors of individuals. Freud, F.H. Allport, Sullivan, Lewin, and Rogers are just a few of the well-known authors who have written about group psychology.

It is important to examine the historic interest in the effect of groups upon individuals if we are to understand more fully the possible ways in which groups currently are thought to be curative.

Group Therapy Theory

Aristotle referred to man as a "social animal," and he considered man's affiliative needs to be a source of strength. Rigorous scientific exploration of the effects of grouping upon individuals began as early as 1895, when Gustav LeBon, a French social psychologist, referred to the phenomenon of the "group mind." As with the other early authors in this field, LeBon was concerned with groups of very large numbers. Having been impressed by the primitive nature of crowd behavior, he used the word *foule* 'crowd,' to denote the object of his study. LeBon hypothesized that a type of hypnotic power engulfs individuals and causes behavioral change once individuals become part of a crowd. Individuals lose their sense of responsibility, and a group mind assumes control.

LeBon's main thesis was that something different occurs to individuals when they are in groups. The result, in his estimation, was a diminishing of human functioning. He described large crowds as regressive, primitive, and uncivilized. He stated:

> By the mere fact that he forms part of an organized group, man descends several rungs in the ladder of civilization. Isolated he may be a cultivated individual; in a crowd, he is a barbarian—that is, a creature acting by instinct.[1]

LeBon accounted for this change by three factors. First, he believed individuals in groups experience a sense of *increased strength*, even invincibility, by virtue of their group membership. Second, he spoke of the *contagion* that occurs in groups. He described contagion as akin to a hypnotic state induced by the group on its members. Finally, and for LeBon the most important, he felt *suggestibility* was greatly increased in groups.

> We see, then, that the disappearance of the conscious personality, the predominance of the unconscious personality, the turning by means of suggestion and contagion of feelings and ideas in an identical direction, the tendency to immediately transform the suggested ideas into acts; these we see are the principal characteristics of an individual forming part of a group. He is no longer himself, but has become an automaton, who has ceased to be guided by his will.[2]

This is not an auspicious or optimistic appraisal of the potential benefits of groups for therapeutic purposes! But succeeding authors have more and more postulated that the power of groups can be effectively turned to therapeutic use.

William McDougall,[3] an Englishman, published *The Group Mind* at the same time that LeBon published his work. As the title suggests, McDougall had come to the same conclusion as LeBon regarding the premise that something additive occurs when individuals find themselves in groups. However, McDougall contributed an important new notion, for while agreeing that groups have the potential for degrading the level of civilized behavior of individuals, he also saw the potential of groups to enhance individual behavior. McDougall is perhaps the first theorist to see the potential of groups as a means of helping persons change their behavior for the better.

The key for turning the power of groups into a positive force, according to McDougall, is *organization*. Of unorganized groups he was no more optimistic than LeBon, thinking them "excessively emotional, impulsive, violent, fickle, inconsistent, irresolute, and extreme in action." But, he stated that his book would

> show how organisation of the group may, and generally does in large measure, counteract these degrading tendencies; and how the better kinds of organisation render group life the great ennobling influence by aid of which alone man rises a little above the animals and may even aspire to fellowship with the angels.[4]

McDougall further stated that clear goals and purposes are essential to the effectiveness of a group.

There is . . . one condition that may raise the behavior of a temporary and unorganized crowd to a higher plane, namely the presence of a clearly defined common purpose in the minds of all of its members.[5]

Thus two of the earliest authors on the impact of groups upon individuals identified several important phenomena: the power of groups to affect the behaviors of individuals; the presence of "contagion," or the capacity of groups to fill each of the members with affects; and the importance of organization, contracts, and goals.

Sigmund Freud added a great deal more. He was intrigued by the effect of the group on the individual, and his study of group dynamics was a step in his further conceptualization of the superego, which had been thought of as the ego ideal. As he considered what constituted a group, in contrast to a collection of people, Freud posited that group formation necessitates having a sense of purpose (a goal) and the emergence of clear leadership. Using the theory available to him at the time, Freud suggested that groups form when members develop libidinal ties to the leader and to one another.

The nature of the ties of the members to one another and to the leader differ. Freud speculated that group members identify with one another as a result of their libidinal ties to the leader. He used the example of the army to illustrate his hypothesis: "It is obvious that a soldier takes his superior, that is in fact, the leader of the army, as his ideal, while he identifies himself with his equal and derives from this community of their egos the obligation of giving mutual help and for sharing possessions which comradeship implies."[6]

Inherent in these formulations of identification between members is a regression and dedifferentiation of each individual, who is no longer seen as having individuality except to meet a common goal. This phenomenon helps explain some of the attraction as well as some of the fears explained in entering group life.

A second dynamic emerging from Freud's formulations concerned the process by which an individual relinquishes his ego ideal and accepts instead the group leader's goals and ideals. Freud compared the members' relationships to the leader with being in love, a situation in which the loved one is overvalued and idealized. He suggested that "when we are in love a considerable amount of narcissistic libido over-flows on to the object. It is even obvious in many forms of love-choice that the object serves as a substitute for some unattained ego-ideal of our own."[7] This mechanism linked individual psychology to processes operating in groups and offered an explanation of the behaviors observed by LeBon and McDougall.

Freud pointed the way toward resolution of the regressive phenomena occurring in groups in his frequently quoted reference to empathy. He wrote, "a path leads from identification by way of imitation to empathy, that is to the comprehension of the mechanism by means of which we are enabled to take up any attitude at all towards another mental life."[8] This pathway suggests that individuals, following the initial regression associated with group formation, can reverse the process by learning to identify emotionally with others temporarily. This process, empathy, enables a redifferentiation of each individual to occur and, for the purpose of group therapy, to learn about one's own emotional life and the emotional life of others.

The closest Freud came to conducting an actual therapy group was probably the famous Wednesday Evening Society, which met in the first decade of this century. This group of analysts interested in psychoanalysis met regularly and discussed the theoretical concepts of psychoanalysis, with highlights from their work with patients. Early analysts such as Adler, Andreas-Salome, Federn, Graf, Reik, Nunberg, Sagner, and Wittels attended regularly. The group was initially an educational group; however, the founder of the group, Wilhelm Stekel, had been a patient of Freud's, and thus the legacy of using Freud for therapeutic purposes was built into the fabric of this group. The members regularly engaged in mutual personal sharing, with Freud remaining in the role of group leader. Ultimately, as documented in the minutes of the Vienna Psychoanalytic Society, the meetings became exceedingly affective and passionate. The group ceased meeting when the conflict between Adler and Freud reached its crescendo.

Group Therapy Practice

While scholars were theorizing about how groups affect individuals, practitioners were already experimenting with the use of small groups as therapeutic agents.

Joseph Pratt, an internist in general medicine in Boston, is widely credited with being the founder of group psychotherapy. In July 1905 he established a group of fifteen of his tuberculosis patients. While the format of this class was primarily lecture presentations, it was nonetheless a therapy group for two reasons. First, it is the initial known attempt at having patients discuss and learn about their common problems in a small group setting, and, second, it involved a contract that each member had to make before being allowed to join the group. Each participant had to agree to give up working and to live essentially out of doors as part of the treatment. Pratt reported very positive results from this new type of treatment.[9]

Other early pioneers who experimented with the effectiveness of small groups for therapeutic purposes included Edward Lazell, the first to see psychiatric (largely schizophrenic) patients in groups, which he did at St. Elizabeth's Hospital in Washington, D.C., in 1919; Tigrant Burrow, who saw neurotic patients in groups in 1920; Alfred Adler, whose theories about man's being entirely a social creature led him to use groups with patients as early as 1921; Julius Metzl, a pioneer in group techniques for alcoholics, began using groups by 1927; Cody Marsh, who presided over lecture-type groups in New York City in 1930; Rudolf Dreikurs, who, in 1930, conducted the first private therapy groups; J.L. Moreno, who used groups in psychodrama in the 1930s; and Sam Slavson, an engineer by profession who at the same time began seeing disturbed children in "activity group" therapy.

It is evident that small group psychology bears a strongly American flavor. Not only was America receptive to the use of groups, but adverse conditions in Europe at this time meant that many eminent Viennese psychologists immigrated to America, bringing with them their interests in small groups. Julius Metzl, who was doing innovative work with alcoholics, and Rudolf Dreikurs, who was experimenting with small groups for psychotherapy, represent but two of these Viennese psychologists.[10]

History of Sensitivity Groups

The sensitivity group movement, developing roughly parallel in time with the development of group therapy, is another wellspring of theory and experimentation about the potential uses of small groups for purposes of human growth and education. Kurt Lewin is the man most responsible for using small groups where alleviation of pathology was not the goal.

In order to place Lewin's contributions in context, one must understand the scientific tenor of the time. This was an era in which scientists were severely questioning the reductionistic model of scientific investigation. As smaller and smaller units of matter were discovered, it was postulated that the universe might not be nearly so ordered as had been previously assumed. A specific example is found in the theory of light.

Newton's time-honored corpuscular theory of light had originally won favor over a wave theory proposed by Huygens because it seemed to explain more of the characteristics of light. However, in succeeding years scientists discovered increasing evidence in support of *both* the diverse theories. Planck finally offered a resolution by formulating quantum theory, which conceptualized light not merely in terms of waves or corpuscular units, but in terms of both. He spoke of a *field* of forces.

Lewin, along with Freud and others, applied the concept of a field of forces to personality development. Just as in the physical sciences it is too restrictive to posit simple one-to-one causal relationships in most instances, Lewin maintained that in personality development we must consider whole fields of influences that touch upon each person. Perhaps the most important forces in each person's field are other persons.

Given this interest it was natural that Lewin would become interested in the interaction of people in small group situations. During World War II he was heavily involved in small group work with soldiers, especially concerning himself with the effect of small group experiences on individual effectiveness and morale. Lewin's goal was to increase effectiveness within "normal" populations.

After the war Lewin continued his work at the Massachusetts Institute of Technology, Research Center for Group Dynamics, the first agency specifically designed to study the dynamics of small groups. In 1947 he initiated a series of workshops at Bethel, Maine; this series of workshops culminated in the formation of the National Training Laboratories (NTL), the first of the sensitivity group, or T-group, organizations.

Another school of small group practitioners was being developed concurrently by Carl Rogers at the University of Chicago. This project began as a means of training counselors for the Veterans' Administration shortly after the war. A major difference between Rogers' and Lewin's groups was in their goals: "The Chicago groups were oriented primarily toward personal growth and the development and improvement of interpersonal communication and relationships, rather than having these as secondary aims. They also had more of an experiential and therapeutic orientation than the groups originating in Bethel."[11]

Thus by the 1940s the sensitivity group movement can be identified as a separate entity with at least two distinct traditions: the tradition that uses the small group as a forum for improving individual and task effectiveness and traces its roots back to Kurt Lewin; and the tradition that uses the small group as a primarily emotional education for individual growth and traces its roots to Carl Rogers.

Modern Theories of Group Therapy

In the beginning group therapy was conducted on a trial-and-error basis, with practitioners trying to meld together the observations of LeBon, McDougall, Lewin and others on how groups function with the individualized theories of psychotherapy, notably Freud's. However, a satisfactory integration was not forthcoming, and theorists varied in their emphasis. Some focused on the individual, while others examined groupwide phenomena. Imbedded in the theories was the proposition that multiple interpersonal transactions could illuminate the individual's inner conflicts or expose groupwide processes. Although we still have not achieved a unitary theory, over time therapists have come to use a combination of group dynamic, interpersonal, and intrapsychic psychodynamic theories as the foundation of group psychotherapy practice.

Group-as-a-Whole Approaches

Bion: Group-as-a-Whole. Wilfred Bion, whose name has become almost synonymous with one theoretical view of groups, made his contributions from work during and after World War II, a time of extensive attention to small groups by many great thinkers. Although the groups he ran were composed of colleagues interested in learning about group processes, not patients in psychotherapy, his influence has nonetheless been enormous.

Bion[12] conceptualized every group as having two levels. At the overt level groups have a purpose and a task, and the group works toward that end. The leader is not the only one with skills; he leads only as long as he can serve the task of the group. The members are discreet individuals who contribute to the task and, in short, operate at a level of secondary process. Bion referred to this as a *work group*. This level is rare, and Bion's theory has primarily to do with the other level of group functioning, the *basic assumption group*.

Bion posited that all groups operate on fundamental unconscious assumptions, as if they are meeting in order to fulfill emotional needs and/ or avoid dreaded relationships. Bion hypothesized three basic assumption groups.

1. In the *dependency group* behavior is *as if* the members can gain security and protection from one individual, the leader, who is omnipotent and omniscient. Although this fantasy is unrealizable, the members act *as if* they really can create a situation that will conform to their wishes.
2. In the *fight-flight group* behavior is *as if* the members gain security and preserve the group through battle or escape. Action is essential and the individual needs may be sacrificed in order to preserve the group. This is a group that may "fight" the ideas of self-examination; the group may flee the therapeutic task by engaging in trivial talk. Members may demonstrate other overt flight behavior such as lateness, absence, or even premature dropping out of the group.
3. The *pairing group* operates *as if* it were to produce a Messiah. The discussion often appears intimate or sexual and is future

oriented. Two people create something in the future; the hope is that what is produced will save the group from intense feelings in the present.

These are the basic assumption groups Bion observed, but he indicated there may be more.

Bion utilized two additional concepts to account for group interaction. One concept is *valency*, which refers to an individual's primary tendency to enter into group life with one of the basic assumptions mentioned above. Individuals differ in their valency to the three basic assumptions, with some entering into a dependency basic assumption and others entering into the others. However, the concept implies the instantaneous and involuntary nature of each individual's tendency. A second concept follows from the application of Melanie Klein's idea of *projective identification*. Bion, who was analyzed by Klein, makes use of this concept in his understanding and interpretation of unacceptable wishes or impulses being disowned and poured into other members or the leader.

Bion visualized group life as alternating between basic assumption group and work group status. The therapist is seen as sitting on the group boundary. This theoretical orientation results in a particular style of leader intervention that has the flavor of noninvolvement punctuated by mystic pronouncements. In the Bion tradition leaders attempt to make interpretations aimed primarily at helping the group members examine the manifestations of the basic assumptions under which they are functioning. Probably no group therapist functions exclusively in this pattern, but Bion's influence on understanding the unconscious aspects of group life has had a major effect on therapists utilizing group-as-a-whole concepts. Furthermore, Bion's work illustrates the group processes that are at work in all groups. Some therapeutic styles opt not to focus on these process issues, but they exist and are at work nonetheless.

The therapeutic goal for Bion was to enable people to learn about their earliest problems with authority, to free individuals from their historic bonds, through an understanding of their natural valences and basic assumptions, and subsequently to enable individuals to enter into more satisfactory peer relationships.

Ezriel: Psychoanalytic Group Therapy. Henry Ezriel[13] became interested in groups through his conversations with Bion. Ezriel began with the hypothesis, derived from object relations theory, that individuals seek to reinforce repression and avoid contact with frightening unconscious fantasies. The reinforcement is accomplished through the development of object relationships that help deny the unconscious fantasies; such relationships are labeled the *required relationship*. In this view such "roles" or transferences take place in many situations and are not a developmental process, as in classical transference. The required relationship is precisely that, required, in order to bypass the *avoided relationship*; entry into the avoided relationship would result in a calamity (the *calamitous relationship*). These three object relationships constitute the tripartite model associated with Ezriel's work.

A common group tension (which is unconscious) emerges as patients try to express the three relationships. Since no two patients have identical intrapsychic conflicts, each "tries to express something different and impose his own pattern on the group." Tension at a latent level then develops among the group members. As a structure develops in the here and now of the meeting, the group therapist demonstrates the common group tension and each individual's contribution to it. Essential to this approach is the idea of "communication by proxy," by which Ezriel meant that a patient may not say anything, but unconsciously or silently identifies with another patient.

Ezriel stated that no interpretation is complete without elucidation of all three relationships for the group-as-a-whole, and, in addition, as thoroughly as possible for each individual. For example, if a group were involved in highly intellectualized discussion about there not being enough emotion shared in the group, Ezriel might suggest that the group is talking about there being too much analysis and not enough feeling (the required relationship) in order not to criticize directly the therapist, who represents the analytic point of view (the avoided relationship) because they fear that he will not feed them or care for them (the calamitous relationship). Ezriel would then elucidate how each member's personal conflicts were woven into the discussion. Ezriel preferred a group size of five patients.

All interpretations are rooted in the here-and-now; and the therapist restricts his activity solely to interpretations. Indeed he may remain silent until he is able to clarify the common (unconscious) group tension and the individual's contribution to it. A successful interpretation frees the individual so that he can face more successfully the avoided relationship, and then memories and associations from the past will spontaneously emerge. However, Ezriel also believed that avoidance of the past may be used as a defense, since revelations of past conflicts might expose an avoided relationship in the present.

In this purist approach, Ezriel has no contact with patients outside of the group meeting and limits himself entirely to interpretive comments. Other interventions are conceptualized as gratifying the required relationship, lowering anxiety, and undermining the work of the group. The therapist is central in this approach, and peer transference is viewed as a displacement from the therapist (rivalry among group members is required because to struggle with the therapist could be calamitous). The interpretations are made to the group-as-a-whole, at the level of the common group tension and to each individual member. Overall, this method attempts to integrate object relations theory with group-as-a-whole concepts.

While Ezriel has many fewer followers than Bion in contemporary group therapy, he remains important as one of the first within the group-as-a-whole tradition to pay attention to the individuals within the group as well as to the group itself.

Foulkes: Group Analysis. Group analysis is the name applied to the therapeutic approach of S.H. Foulkes,[14] an English analyst who finished his analytic training in Vienna in the 1920s and who wrote his text on group analysis in 1948. Foulkes was heavily influenced by classical Gestalt psychology, and from that source he maintained that the group is more than the sum of its parts. For Foulkes, the group is primary, not the individual. No individual can be studied successfully in isolation, since individuals exist only in networks (including families). Pathology occurs when an individual ceases being the nodal point of a network and becomes the focal point of a network problem. Utilizing the Gestalt notion of figure-ground, Foulkes maintained that individual pathology would appear as the figure in the midst of the group's ground.

The group therapist (or "conductor") is concerned with helping the group perform its natural healing functions. The focus of the therapist's attention is not interpretation of individual behaviors, but rather it is the analysis of the here-and-now group process, thereby exposing the individual pathologies of the members who compose the group.

Foulkes had absolute confidence in the group's capacity to help the individuals within it. Unlike Bion, who was more concerned with analyzing the group itself, Foulkes's analysis of the group process was based on his conviction that this was the most powerful way to fully understand the individual.

Carrying this notion to its logical extension, most supervision of group analysis occurs in small groups of therapists, where the supervisory group itself is analyzed in order to gain insight into the groups that each therapist is conducting.

Whitaker and Lieberman: The Group Focal Conflict. The group focal conflict approach is an integration of the work of Thomas French[15] and group dynamic theory. First described by Whitman and Stock[16] in 1958 and elaborated in a monograph by Whitaker and Lieberman[17] in 1964, the central notion suggests that all or almost all of the verbalizations and behavior of patients in a session can be understood as efforts to solve an intragroup conflict. By definition, the focal conflict is closest to the surface (i.e., preconscious) and will account for the observable data. The theory further posits that as conflicts are integrated, deeper material becomes exposed for interpretation, enabling patients to learn about themselves.

In this approach it is postulated that a wish (the disturbing impulse) becomes generated in the group but cannot be directly exposed for fear of some negative consequence (the reactive motive) and therefore is expressed in a compromise fashion (the solution). Focal conflicts may be elaborated into themes, which may then be expressed over a series of sessions, or certain solutions in themselves may stimulate further conflicts. After conflicts are actively clarified and worked through, the group may enter a conflict free period during which more personal material can be examined, responded to, and worked on without stirring unmanageable anxiety or resistance.

An individual patient may or may not respond to any particular conflict; however, as in other theories, the notion is advanced that silence is not lack of interest, but is often a cover for significant emotional participation. Therefore the therapist may make appropriate groupwide interpretations that would affect each member, including the member who seemed not to be participating in the conflict.

Notions derived from group dynamics include those of the group culture, which are used in this context to describe how the group deals with the focal conflicts—that is, either by enabling or by restrictive solutions. The enabling solutions allow the group greater safety so that conflicts can be worked through at greater depths. If conditions become unsafe for the individual, he or she may attempt to alter the group culture through habitual defensive maneuvers, thereby setting in motion another focal conflict. An enabling group culture provides the patient an arena in which it is possible to understand and relinquish habitual maladaptive patterns.

In utilizing the group focal conflict model the therapist is in emotional touch with the group but stands apart where he can interpret it. The therapist observes the group process and attempts to interpret restrictive group solutions. The framework (as in other such theories) is interpretation of the disturbing motive (the wish), the reactive motive (the fear), and the solution.

Successful interpretation alters the group solution and increases the safety of the group culture, which in turn will benefit the individuals within the group. Whitaker and Lieberman considered the use of individual interventions when the therapist is aware that particular conflicts are related to a patient's personal history. However, they caution that the therapist needs to be aware of the potential effects, both negative and positive, of such interpretations, and they lean toward proscribing individual inter-pretations. Their main point of view is that all therapists' interventions have an impact on the group process. Awareness of response to interpretation enables the therapist to follow the group struggles toward new and hopefully enabling solutions to focal conflicts.

Interpersonal Theories

Irvin Yalom, in *The Theory and Practice of Group Psychotherapy*,[18] elu-cidates his theory of interpersonal learning as it occurs in group therapy. Yalom trained in the Sullivanian tradition, and many of his notions derive from that interpersonal orientation. He believes that the major therapeutic thrust for change occurs in the group interaction as it takes place in the here and now. He does not preclude discussion of outside ideas or events, but the main arena for learning is the therapy group. With proper struc-turing this evolves into a social microcosm, a miniaturized representation of each patient's social universe.

Through repeated experiences in the group setting, patients learn about their maladaptive interpersonal transactions and their perceptual (parataxic) distortions that elicit negative or undesirable responses from others. The mechanisms involved in helping patients learn are feedback from others (consensual validation) and self-observation. During this process patients learn that their fears may be groundless in the present and that their anxieties arise from perceptual distortions. As patients learn about their behavior patterns in the group, they become more able to observe comparable behaviors in the outside world. Finally, patients are encouraged to try new behaviors, both inside and outside the group, thereby increasing their ability to manage themselves successfully. The ultimate responsibility for change rests upon the patient. Increased insight alone will not guarantee change.

Interpersonal learning takes place at several levels, according to Yalom. As in other theories the therapist is a representative of prior family (parental) relations, and the group members represent both authority and sibling relationships. Transference and insight are considered aspects of interpersonal learning, but they are considered of less therapeutic value than the "corrective emotional experience" of the authentic human inter-actions that occur in the group. Transference is understood, in the Sulli-vanian tradition, primarily as an interpersonal perceptual distortion, and the work of the group involves working through these distortions. Insight is categorized as learning at four different levels: (1) how others see the patient, (2) what the patient is doing in relationship to others, (3) why the patient might be doing what he is doing, and (4) genetic insights.

For most patients Yalom feels that the first three levels of insight are sufficient for change. He suggests that intellectual understanding (insight) is a critical element for change, but he does not feel that this must extend into the patient's past in order to be useful (depth of interpretation and insight is not correlated with potency).

The therapist's role in this model is that of a real person whose tasks include the creation of an appropriate group culture where interpersonal behaviors can be examined. The group therapist, by attending to development of group cohesiveness and appropriate norms, shapes a social system. Particularly in the early group sessions, the therapist must be attentive to tardiness, absences, subgrouping, extragroup socializing, and scapegoating. The therapist's task is primarily as gatekeeper, and he shapes the norms of the group through his use of authority and by the presentation of a rationale for his work. At various stages in the group the therapist utilizes different techniques. The therapist models the group's behavior by offering feedback, by clarifying the concept of responsibility, by disconfirming fantasied disastrous consequences, by reinforcing generalizability of learning, and by encouraging risk taking. Thus Yalom does not exclude group dynamics and group-as-a-whole phenomena, but he relegates them to a secondary position. He maintains his focus on the interpersonal interactions and transactions within the group setting.

Intrapsychic Approaches

This approach to group therapy emphasizes the principles of intrapsychic conflict and the translation of the psychoanalytic model into the group therapy situation. The paradigm is that of an individual-within-the-group—psychoanalysis in a group setting. Group dynamics in their pure state are seen as resistances and interferences with the basic therapeutic task. This orientation was central to the work of Sam Slavson.[19] Alexander Wolf and Emmanuel Schwartz[20] give a scholarly exposition of this position. Theoretically the group provides a situation where regression takes place and allows for elucidation of transferences and resistances that then become available for interpretation. The presence of other members enhances the possibilities for exposing a variety of relationships, thereby broadening the context in which the patient's intrapsychic problems can be examined. The group provides unique opportunities for development of parental (vertical) and sibling (horizontal) transferences. The value of the peers includes not only their representation as siblings, but also as parental transferences. Initially peer displacements may be easier to analyze than more commonly identified therapist-parental transferences. Furthermore, the presence of peers means more affective stimuli to elicit associations, memories, and affect.

There is controversy as to the depth of the regression and transference that can occur in group psychoanalytic therapy. One end of the continuum maintains that group provides a special matrix in supporting the individual and creating a safe environment, which along with all the stimuli of the other members enables an in-depth regression. Alternatively, the presence of others and the need to share time is seen as a significant limitation to the depth of regression. Either possibility may account for the differences in transference and resistance observed in group and in dyadic therapy. However, the basic premises remain that significant transferences develop, and through interpretation of these transferences neurotic conflicts and character styles can be analyzed.

Exploration of genetic material is seen as crucial in helping patients develop thorough self-understanding. According to Wolf and Schwartz, the group analyst is not "concerned so much with the collective effort as he is with the emerging wholesome individual ego. He is not preoccupied with how the mystique of the group feels, an irrational projection, but with how the individual within the group thinks, feels, fantasizes, dreams and behaves."[21] Thus, for those authors the therapist in group psychoanalysis helps patients explore the latent motivation behind their current interaction: the here-and-now is suffused with the there-and-then, and the interpersonal is translated into the intrapsychic.

The group psychoanalyst interprets the nature of the unconscious processes among patients and between therapist and patient. The patients learn to understand the latent meaning of their interactions and make interpretations among themselves, thereby acting as auxiliary therapists. The therapist does not allow any single member to become the sole focus of the analytic action but shifts attention from one member to another. The analyst searches for transferential material or defensive operations he believes to be appropriate to work on at a certain time. He exercises judgment in these individual choices and pays less regard to the reactions of others. As Wolf and Schwartz state, "If he didn't, he would fail to function effectively as an analyst."[22]

Most contemporary psychoanalytic group therapists do not adhere exclusively to this individual-within-the-group model but utilize their awareness of group dynamics to help explore issues that may be relevant to more than one individual.

General System Theory

In the past decade many practitioners and theorists have found an incompleteness in psychodynamic theory and have explored a broader theoretical basis for understanding human behavior. This has led to the application of General System Theory (GST) to group psychotherapy. The work of von Bertalanffy[23] served as the foundation upon which to build a new theory for the practice of group psychotherapy. This theory provides a model for examining the interrelationships among the intrapsychic, interpersonal, group-as-a-whole, and social aspects of the therapy group.

A number of important assumptions make GST an attractive conceptual model. For example, GST maintains that though a wide diversity of form and behavior are exhibited by systems, fundamentally all systems possess a common underlying structure, *isomorphy*. Additionally, there are similarities in organizing processes, which are conceived of as self-organizing and are labeled *living structures.*[24] Further, GST holds that transformation or change takes place across boundaries that each system or subsystem can autonomously control.

GST is a growth or change theory, not a conflict or deficit theory. In GST transactions are seen as occurring across boundaries. The nature of these boundaries is a critical concern for GST.[25] It is at the boundary level, whether it be between group members and group members, group members and the leader, or even boundaries separating aspects of an individual, that attention should be paid. Boundaries must be permeable enough to take in and give out what is necessary, and yet impermeable enough to offer protection and separation. The opening of boundaries (for example, to allow a transfer of information or emotion) is essential for the system (individual or group or any structure) to survive. Gaining the capacity to open and close boundaries appropriately is an important goal for members of groups. Thus group therapists should focus their attention on various levels of boundaries, depending upon which boundary is the focus at any given moment in the life of the group.

The therapist in GST is seen as a boundary regulator (though not the exclusive regulator—a group member could take on this role as well) and a boundary observer.[26] The therapist monitors boundaries and makes interventions that are appropriate to his diagnosis about the permeability or impermeability of boundaries.

Clearly, from this perspective the precise level at which the therapist opts to intervene is related to his conceptualization along the lines described by the other psychodynamic theories. But GST provides a unifying approach that does not require a major shift of conceptual levels when moving from intrapsychic to group levels of inquiry and observation.

One of the problems tackled by GST theorists is that of energy exchange. The transmission of information and emotion across boundaries implies a shift of energy. Systems, in order to remain alive, must counter entropy, the process by which systems gradually become disorganized. Negentropy, the inherent self-organizing activity of systems, counters entropy and is fueled by energy shifting across boundaries. Although this aspect of the theory is incomplete, it suggests an avenue for exploring the flow of emotions that occurs in group situations.

Recent Integrative Advances

Originally, group therapy was founded on established psychodynamic theories. However, those theories were based on dyadic practice. A great deal of attention has been given to the task of finding an authentic integration of individual and group therapy theory.

Group Psychodynamic Formulations

Efforts at integrating group and individual processes and theories are exemplified in the work of Helen Durkin[27] and Henrietta Glatzer.[28] These authors focused upon the transferences and resistances in group psychotherapy, utilizing the interactions that emerge to help clarify those phenomena. They took individual psychoanalytic theory and made initial inroads in establishing a real integration with group therapy and practice. According to these authors, in addition to transferences to individuals, transferences to group phenomena exist as well. An example of the latter would be a situation where one patient is the focus of attention, which stimulates rivalrous feelings in other members. Analysis of the transference or the resistance to this sibling transference becomes the focus of the group's inquiry.

Group-as-a-Whole Integrative Theory

Integrative efforts have also been approached from the perspective of group-as-a-whole theorists. Kernberg,[29] who was heavily influenced by Bion's concepts about object relations, suggested that group-as-a-whole interventions address one developmental level of psychopathology—that of preoedipal development. In contrast, more individual transferences (and resistances) are at a higher level of object relations development, representing dyadic (jealousy, envy) and triangular (oedipal) conflicts. Thus Kernberg posited that the group therapist may choose the intervention most appropriate to the group and individual levels of functioning.

Hierarchical Integration

A third integrative effort has been suggested by Horwitz.[30] Trained in a group-as-a-whole tradition, Horwitz modified his position and suggested that the group therapist conceptually must maintain a hierarchy of group-as-a-whole to interpersonal to intrapsychic formulations. With this in mind the therapist assesses the group members' abilities to examine their functioning within a group. Horwitz suggested that in most instances group members are emotionally able to understand comments about themselves before understanding comments relating to their relationships to the groupwide issues. This approach represents a technical advance because it highlights the need for collaboration and alliance between the group therapist and each individual group member. The more traditional group-as-a-whole approach does not sufficiently value or utilize the importance of therapeutic alliance.

Conclusion

In general, group-as-a-whole theorists have highlighted authority (parental) relationships in contrast to the interpersonal theorists who have paid closer attention to peer (sibling) transactions. Relationships with both authorities and peers are obviously very important considerations in psychotherapy, and most patients referred to group psychotherapy have difficulty in each sphere. Therefore an integrative conceptualization is necessary for the psychodynamic group therapist.

The social structure of the group and the impact of the social forces must be kept in mind at all times. Just as in the world at large, individuals in groups exist within social systems, complete with leaders, followers, and colleagues. Furthermore, not only do the social forces affect and impact upon each individual in the group, but each individual in the group affects the group-as-a-whole. Thus the group therapist has the considerable task of keeping complex, interacting forces in mind. Sometimes the group-as-a-whole factors are the most significant (as, for example, when a new member enters a group), because whenever the group's basic boundaries are changed or endangered, the entire group reacts and individuals are best helped by careful attention to the group-as-a-whole process. At other times the group-as-a-whole processes may fade into the background, though never disappear. We must always remember that, despite the powerful influence of the group dynamics, the job of the group therapist is to treat individuals who are seeking help, not groups. We choose to utilize the forces within social systems in order to maximally assist our individual patients. The uniqueness of each individual should not be lost in our eagerness to understand the workings of the group. The purpose of this book is to help the group therapist understand and harness the forces at work in a therapy group in order to move effectively across boundaries from group-as-a-whole to interpersonal to intrapsychic foci with proficiency, thereby taking advantage of the therapeutic power residing in therapy groups.

There will continue to be innovations and shifts in emphasis as long as our understanding about human beings is broadened. Three primary considerations emerge from examining the diversity of approaches subsumed under psychodynamic group psychotherapy. First, there is an emphasis on the individual's internal life (the *intrapsychic*). This component examines the patient's character formation, typical defenses, problem-solving techniques, internal object relations, and so on. The second component is the *interpersonal*, which gains information from analyzing relational styles and deducing what internalized conflicts are replayed in the interpersonal field. This component includes inquiry about individual role, style, and externalization of the internal role through projection and projective identification, or in Sullivan's term, "parataxic distortions." Finally, the *sociopsychological* component is the broad context in which the group occurs, including but not limited to the social structure of the group. In this component the group-as-a-whole dynamics are explored, including group norms, values, assumptions, and restrictions.

References

1. G. LeBon, *The Crowd: A Study of the Popular Mind* (New York: Fisher, Unwin, 1920), p. 36.
2. *Ibid.*, p. 35.
3. W. McDougall, *The Group Mind* (New York: G.P. Putnam's Sons, 1920), p. 28.
4. *Ibid.*, p. 28.
5. *Ibid.*, p. 67.
6. S. Freud, *Group Psychology and the Analysis of the Ego* (Standard Ed., vol. 18, 1921).
7. *Ibid.*, p. 56.
8. *Ibid.*, p. 66.
9. J.H. Pratt, "The Home Sanatorium Treatment of Consumption." Speech delivered before The Johns Hopkins Hospital Medical Society, January 22, 1906. In H.M. Ruitenbeek, *Group Therapy Today* (New York: Atherton Press, 1969), pp. 9–14.
10. For a more complete discussion of these preconditions, see *Group Dynamics*, edited by D. Cartwright and A. Zander (Evanston, Ill.: Row, Peterson, 1960), pp. 9–30.
11. C. Rogers, *Carl Rogers on Encounter Groups* (New York: Harper & Row, 1970), p. 4.
12. W.R. Bion, *Experiences in Groups* (New York: Basic Books, 1960).
13. H. Ezriel, "Psychoanalytic Group Therapy," in *Group Therapy: 1973*, edited by L.R. Wolberg and E.K. Schwartz (New York: Stratton Intercontinental Medical Book, 1973).
14. S.H. Foulkes, *Introduction to Group-Analytic Psychotherapy* (London: Heinemann, 1948).

15. T.M. French, *The Integration of Behavior*, vols. 1, 2 (Chicago: Univ. of Chicago Press, 1952).
16. R.M. Whitman and D. Stock, "The Group Focal Conflict," *Psychiatry* 21 (1958): 269–276.
17. D.S. Whitaker and M.A. Lieberman, *Psychotherapy Through the Group Process* (New York: Atherton Press, 1964).
18. I.D. Yalom, *The Theory and Practice of Group Psychotherapy* (New York, Basic Books, 1975).
19. S.R. Slavson, *Analytic Group Psychotherapy* (New York: Columbia University Press, 1950).
20. A. Wolf and E.K. Schwartz, *Psychoanalysis in Groups*. (New York: Grune and Stratton, 1965).
21. *Ibid.*, p. 246.
22. *Ibid.*, p. 269.
23. L. von Bertalanffy, "General System Theory and Psychiatry," in *American Handbook of Psychiatry*, edited by S. Arieti (New York: Basic Books, 1966), pp. 705–721.
24. J.E. Durkin, "Foundations of Autonomous Living Structures," in *Living Groups: Group Psychotherapy and General System Theory*, edited by J.E. Durkin (New York: Brunner/Mazel, 1981), pp. 24–59.
25. A.K. Rice, "Individual, Group, and Intragroup Processes," *Human Relations* 22 (1969): 565–584.
26. B.M. Astrachan, "Towards a Social Systems Model of Therapeutic Groups," *Soc. Psychiatry* 5 (1970):110–119.
27. H.E. Durkin, *The Group in Depth* (New York: International Universities Press, 1964).
28. H. Glatzer, "Handling Transference Resistance in Group Therapy," *Psychoanal. Rev.* 40 (1953):36–43.
29. O.F. Kernberg, "A Systems Approach to Priority Setting of Interventions in Groups," *Int. J. Group Psychother.* 25 (1975):251–275.
30. L. Horwitz, "A Group Centered Approach to Group Psychotherapy," *Int. J. Group Psychother.* 27 (1977):423–440.

Group Development   **3**

A neophyte group therapist observing two groups, one having been in existence for three or four sessions and another for several years, would quickly be able to distinguish between their functioning. What development has occurred that accounts for this change? Understanding the predictable broad outlines of group evolution, complete with the tasks involved in the various stages of that evolution, provides an anchor for the therapist. Just as a knowledgeable individual therapist can gain a deeper understanding of his patients' ideas and associations by having an appreciation for the developmental levels and the associated tasks for individuals as they grow, so group therapists are helped by an understanding of the usual stages of group development.

Like individuals, groups do not move forward in a linear fashion; they are subject to forward and backward movement. Furthermore, these fluctuations do not take place automatically or by any set timetable.

Group development is a product of the individual members, their interactions among themselves and with the therapist. Nonetheless, accurate assessment of the developmental level can aid the therapist in attempts to notice shifts in groupwide functioning. In some situations, patients with preoedipal conflicts or with significant developmental arrests may make major therapeutic gains while working on the early issues of joining and belonging to a group. These patients derive the most therapeutic benefit when the group members are examining aspects of building trust and belonging. For patients who have conflicts at a more advanced individual developmental level, there is less therapeutic gain at early levels of group development. If a group is composed entirely of patients with preoedipal problems, that group will likely remain at early levels of development for prolonged periods, which would be quite beneficial to such patients. On the other hand, if healthier patients remained stuck in an early stage of development for a prolonged period, this would constitute either a case of misdiagnosis or significant problems of transference or countertransference.

As discussed in Chapter 2, some therapists reify group development and focus on little else, as, for example, the strict followers of Bion. The stages of development are indicators that help the therapist more fully understand what is going on in the group. One stage is not inherently more valuable than another. A common misconception among therapists is that in order to have a "good" group, it is imperative that the group must attain and maintain the most advanced developmental level. For many patients, this would be asking the impossible. Rather, there should be a reasonable fit between the level of group development and the dynamic issues salient for the members.

A major portion of the knowledge about group development emerged from studies of time-limited, closed-membership groups.[1] Generalization of these ideas to ongoing, open-membership psychotherapy groups has often been done indiscriminately. There is overlap, but the two situations are not identical. For instance, a psychotherapy group has only one actual beginning. Yet, with the additions of one or more new members there are modified new beginnings repeatedly, each usually accompanied by the reemergence of themes and modes of relating similar to those at the time of the initial sessions. Similarly, events inside or outside an ongoing group may set off recrudescences of power struggles characteristic of the second phase of development. The repetition of various developmental phases provides an opportunity to rework previously traversed ground, sometimes in greater depth and with increased insight, and therefore has considerable therapeutic potential. Keep in mind the reality that these are schematic presentations; only the careful study of processes in each particular group, as well as the individuals involved, will provide the base for meaningful therapeutic change.

Not everyone endorses the concept of development within groups. Slavson[2] attempted to expunge group processes from psychotherapeutic groups; he focused instead purely on interpersonal interactive processes. Slavson's position represents an effort to transpose classical dyadic psychoanalytic concepts (transference and resistance) into the group psychotherapy setting. By linking group interaction closely to dyadic therapy, Slavson and others[3] stressed the continuity of psychodynamic/psychoanalytic concepts. This historic bridge made group therapy acceptable, if not attractive, to the mainstream of the American psychotherapeutic community.

Gradually the tradition of linking individual psychodynamics to group psychotherapy included the transposition of individual developmental stages to groups. Group development came to be seen as replicating oral, anal, and phallic stages.[4,5] Using such traditional analytic metaphors does not do justice to the complex phenomena observable in groups; an expanded perspective that encompasses the more complex data of individual and group interactions is necessary. Within the group matrix are a variety of relationships—among the members, between the members and the leader, and between the members and the group-as-a-whole. These patterns develop in a rather characteristic fashion.

One of the tasks for members is to determine what will make their efforts in the group most useful. When a new group forms, these tasks are unknown, and the members, through trial and error, discover what are helpful tasks, roles, and norms. That learning becomes reflected in shifts in how the members relate and examine themselves and their relationships to each other and the leader.

Thus far no schema describing group development has been able to do justice to the complexity of internal fantasies and behavioral transactions that occur when a small group of individuals organize and begin to work together.[6] However, two elements are always present in successful groups: accomplishing the goal and simultaneously attending to the emotional needs of the members. In group psychotherapy, where the goal is improved emotional functioning of the members, the overlap with the group task is extensive. Nonetheless, the components can be separated, and it serves a heuristic purpose to do so.

An individual's attainment of goals and fulfillment of emotional needs are central considerations in group development and can be seen as occurring in three phases: the first phase consists of the reactions to joining and forming the group, the second phase consists of the reactions to feelings of belonging, and the third phase is the stabilization of the mature working group. In the third phase the members have a consistent image of what is necessary to attain therapeutic goals. It is important for therapists to remember that the ultimate goals of therapy—improved intrapsychic functioning and self-learning—can occur during any of these three stages.

Stage 1: Group Formation

There have been a plethora of contributors to understanding group formation. Yalom labeled this first phase "orientation, hesitant participation, and search for meaning."[7] Fried[8] and Schutz[9] have stressed the issue of inclusion. Those espousing a psychoanalytic framework[10] emphasize the dependency aspects in this initial phase. Saravay[11] likened this early phase to that seen in the childhood progression of oral drives. Day[12] emphasized both the patients' dependency needs and their inevitable competition with one another during this initial phase. Slater[13] suggested that the main concern of the new group is the fear of being controlled or engulfed by the group, and thus he viewed the deification of the leader as the normative and characteristic response. Common to all these contributors is the notion that a series of expected processes routinely take place in a new group, processes involved in the task of joining and forming a group.

The major task facing patients entering into group therapy is forming a group. In the case of newly formed groups this is obvious, but it is equally true when a new individual joins an ongoing group. When any new member joins, a new group must be formed. Belonging implies that a level of agreement has been reached regarding common goals, ways of relating, and ways of resolving problems. A member must loosen personal boundaries in order to emotionally enter this larger collective labeled "group." This task must be accomplished in the face of stranger anxiety.

Every member approaches this task with his or her own personal history, developmental needs, and conflicts. Still, there are some common experiences in our culture. Growing up has provided each person with prior experiences in small groups, beginning with the family and then continued in schools and a host of religious, business, or social institutions.

In group therapy, particularly the relatively unstructured situation in dynamic group psychotherapy, clues regarding how to proceed are minimal. Members have to orient themselves through trial and error to see what will work, and they go about those tasks in a variety of ways. The ambiguity of the situation stimulates regression. Each member tends to regress to a personally important developmental stage, and his response in the group may represent either a successfully or an unsuccessfully completed task. That situationally induced regression is clinically useful to the therapist in gaining understanding of a member's manner of managing anxiety.

While it is expected that patients will regress when they join a group, it should not be expected that all patients will respond to this regression in the same way. For some this is a time for gaining insight into the nature of their relationship to their parents, since many patients respond to joining primarily in terms of feelings of dependency, helplessness, and confusion. Those patients often replicate important aspects of their relationships to their parents and demonstrate important transferential reactions to the therapist. Others regress to developmental stages of fear, self-dissolution, annihilation, or intense desire for merger and engulfment, along with the consequent responses of fight-flight behaviors. Still others might turn away from the therapist and approach peers in their efforts to determine the best way to proceed. These patients are often labeled counterdependent by theoreticians who emphasize the regression to dependency upon the leader.

It is hard to join a group "wrong," since whatever happens becomes a part of the group history. And whatever a new member does in an attempt to join is clinically relevant because it represents an opportunity for learning. No patient generates totally new behavior just for this situation.

Whatever the level of regression, a tension soon develops, stimulated by the members' respective needs and defenses. This tension sets in motion the important process of belonging to an organized group having a common task.

During group formation, conscious and unconscious responses are activated in the members. As a result, subliminal agreements are reached that help members contain their fears and anxieties. These agreements become the group norms and standards.

Typically, new members look to the therapist to determine how they should proceed, what they should talk about, what behavior is "good" group behavior. Common questions are addressed (though not always overtly): What information is relevant? Are past events significant or do we just focus on what happens in the meeting? How do my outside relationships fit in with what is happening here? How far can we take these relationships after the therapy hour ends? Am I expected to share all my secrets with these people? These and many other questions generally produce interaction among members, stimulating a variety of opinions and conflicts. Affects are stirred, and how these affects are managed becomes embedded in the group norms as well as providing valuable therapeutic information. Members may not be ready to face angry encounters and therefore may establish a norm, "Let's be friendly and not angry." One individual may aid in maintaining the norm by joking whenever angry feelings are likely to erupt. Another might shift the topic of discussion. Allowing these patterned distractions by the other members indicates that a group norm is operating.

Patients not only ask questions, they also tell about themselves and their experiences. Under the pressure of getting to know one another, and the anxiety about how to proceed, patients usually "tell their story," including informing the group about why they have come and what they hope to gain. This may take the form of a "go around" with one member acting as the conductor. Patients experience intense pressure to conform, and seldom will they refuse to tell something about themselves. They might tell about anxiety laden or frustrating situations they have encountered or are encountering. These stories also should be heard as unconscious metaphors for the individual's experience of being in the meeting. The therapist, acting to help establish the most therapeutic environment, may choose to translate the metaphors into the here-and-now of the meeting, with the goal in mind of establishing a norm of examining the in-group transactions and affects. Since this implies more openness and directness, the norm becomes fully established only as it is experientially validated—as members gain real help by examining their in-group interactions.

The emotional position of the members in a newly formed group, or of a new member joining an ongoing group, is analogous to that of meeting strangers. Rarely are first encounters anxiety free, but when the task at hand includes sharing the most intimate details (and secrets!) about one's life, the stakes are very high. All the usual concerns about trust and safety, quite appropriately, are central in the minds of the participants. Gustafson and Cooper[14] have pointed out that members enter a group planning a series of tests. These tests, containing both conscious and unconscious elements, revolve around the individual's anxiety: will he or she again be traumatized by the group as happened in early childhood or with significant others in the past? Added to this formulation is the important idea that patients are not only testing, they are actively trying to master and resolve earlier conflicts around trust and safety.

The very processes that set regression in motion also contain the seeds for solutions. The anxiety and apprehension regarding the formation phase also represent the first commonly shared experience of the group. Everyone (including the therapist) approaches the unknown with his or her own internal fantasies and his or her own mechanisms of defense and mastery. This situation is particularly true before the first meeting of a new group. Since there is no reality for this group as yet, there can only be fantasies. The sharing of anxieties represents the first in-group experience of being involved and less isolated; and it represents a beginning step for experientially based group cohesion. For the individual joining an ongoing group, the same is true because the veteran members observe and perceive the new member's anxiety and are reminded of their own initial anxieties upon entering the group. They also have their own anxieties about meeting a stranger. As those anxieties are shared, a common beginning point is again forged.

The overriding characteristic of the formative phase is the members' unique responses to the emotional and work aspects of group formation. Within expectable variations, members try to orient themselves to the task of learning the ground rules for making group therapy work. The themes then revolve around gaining information—asking the leader or inquiring amongst peers to see if there is an expert in the group. When such information is not readily forthcoming, which it never is, self-protective mechanisms and reactions to frustration are manifest. The frustration and ambiguity inherent in the task exert a regressive pull upon the members. The emotions stimulated by this situation then dovetail as all the members struggle to form a group that feels safe enough for them to do their work.

A Clinical Example

> *A group that had met only a few weeks began one meeting with a period of silence. The silence was broken by one member telling about a recent vacation in which he was learning to ski. He had found it a frightening experience, both because of the novelty of the sport for him and also because of the various stories he had heard about skiers breaking bones. Moreover, he was quick to point out, the instructor had given them too difficult a slope to begin with, and in general had done such a poor job that many of the class had quit.*

This vignette highlights the anxiety of the new group enterprise, adding the specific fear of being injured. The blame for this traumatic experience is placed directly on the instructor/therapist's shoulders for picking too difficult and dangerous a task and for not instructing them properly in advance. An implicit threat to quit was present. One could imagine a new group getting caught up with such a story and giving advice such as "change instructors" or "choose a less steep hill." Indeed advice giving is a characteristic of early group formation. Yet another response from the group might have been for the other members to begin associating to similarly harrowing experiences in their own lives, or comparable times of insufficient instruction or assistance. If the members were particularly insightful, they might see the metaphorical aspects of the story and begin discussing their fears in the group and their concern with the amount of preparation and help they were or were not getting from their therapist.

Different group therapists might handle this early group vignette quite differently, depending upon their theoretical orientation. A therapist who wants the norm to be that the member will examine *only* the in-group interactions might point out that the member had taken the focus outside the room. For this therapist the member's story is a resistance, and he would exert pressure for members not to talk about events outside the group itself.

A psychodynamic therapist, on the other hand, might welcome such a sharing as a metaphor for the patient's feelings within the group itself, complete with references to the perceived danger of the new venture and questions about the skill of the leader. By linking the story to possible groupwide feelings, the therapist helps set the norm of curiosity about potential deeper meanings of communications, placing out-of-group and in-group events in juxtaposition with each offering possible elaboration and insight into the other. Yet other therapists, still within a psychodynamic frame of reference, might understand the member's sharing in the manner suggested but decide to make no comment at all. That approach serves to enhance the members' dependence upon one another for input and sharing, and, by keeping the overt input of the therapist to a minimum, enhances the opportunities for the patients to draw conclusions about the therapist's point of view out of their own history and basic assumptions.

The therapist's role in the formative stage, as in all phases of group development, is to help establish useful norms so that the members feel safe enough to be spontaneous in their participation. Then his role is to help them learn from their feelings, behaviors, reactions, and memories so that they may resolve their interpersonal and intrapsychic difficulties.

Stage 2: The Reactive Phase

In the second phase of group development, members are more focused upon their reactions to belonging to the group. In the formative phase, the focus was on joining and finding commonalities. In the reactive phase the individuality of the members becomes more apparent and important. Some authors[15] have suggested that rebellion is characteristic of this phase. Schutz[16] noted that individuals seem to share a common purpose of maintaining control, and he labeled this phase as one of "power." Authors[17] emphasizing the comparison between group and individual development refer to the anal quality of the transactions during this phase; that is, transactions are characterized by alternating withholding and outbursts. Tuckman[18] succinctly labeled this the "storming" phase.

Descriptively, this phase is characterized by emotional outbursts and unevenness of commitment to the group. The norms that arose in the initial phase are now tested and modified. The contract will be tested. This is a time when members often arrive late or not at all, threaten to quit or actually do so, or become tardy in payment of their bills. Emotionality is rampant, making it difficult for members to think clearly and rationally; obvious distortions in perception occur and members experience transactions within the group as controlling, demanding, or otherwise injurious. Anger and sadness, two of the affects most accepted in our culture, are expressed and shared.

The tasks of this phase revolve around moving from a sense of "we-ness" to a sense of belongingness that includes "I-ness." As with the growing child, members often react as if they are saying "Me do it!" Yet, just as with the child, this should never be interpreted as a wish to no longer belong to the family. Members are freeing themselves from the enthrallment with the therapist and the group. The honeymoon has ended. Early norms are now experienced as rigid and inflexible. Members try to exert their individual mark upon the group by testing how far they can bend, break, or more constructively alter the norms. Other individuals are not seen as having their own needs or wishes but are viewed as exerting control and power. It is during this phase that many patients experience their presenting problems most powerfully within the sessions. This is often a painful reality for the patients, and we frequently hear comments such as, "This group is no different from my family!" or "Why should I stay here? I have as much trouble talking in here as I do in the world outside!" It is important that therapists help patients understand that the change in attitudes about membership during this phase is most helpful for their therapy, since therapy groups are much more effective when individuals are actually experiencing their problems within the group itself.

The reemergence within the therapy of early internalized styles of object relationships enables individuals to learn a great deal regarding their developmental problems and tasks. There can be very important congruences between individual development and group development, and the growth potential stimulated in this rebellious/differentiation phase is very important in helping individuals resolve comparable problems in their individual development. Fried[19] distinguished among various types of anger shown in groups. One type is the anger shown in response to disappointment and hurt. The other, very salient to this developmental phase, is the equivalent to normal assertiveness.

Patients' historic patterns of handling angry feelings, originating either within themselves or coming from others, are characteristically exposed during this phase.

Not all patients experience or demonstrate overt anger, rebelliousness, or assertiveness. For some the emotional response is withdrawal, passivity, and compliance. Many patients do not have direct access to more active forms of aggression and use passive aggression instead. For these individuals crucial developmental tasks may be accomplished during this phase as they learn to balance anger and withdrawal with assertiveness and compromise. Such affect-laden tasks are neither quietly nor permanently achieved, but as groups move back and forth through this phase the individuals within them are provided repeated opportunities for mastering their particular developmental tasks.

Powerful group processes impact upon individuals in this phase. The rebellion or hostility may be concentrated exclusively in one or two "difficult" individuals, and the remaining members seem peaceful and even scornful of the troublesome ones. Often the difficult member is the spokesperson for similar affects felt by others, and the therapist must never assume that quieter members do not share the affects verbalized by the more overtly troublesome member. Indeed the hostility may be increased or aggravated in the rebellious member as the others unconsciously project their feelings into him and disown the feelings themselves. This is the commonly observed process of projective identification. A converse situation arises when the anger is not universally shared. In order to maintain the appearance of togetherness, thereby protecting against retaliation or rejection, angry members try to recruit others to their point of view. Powerful forces for conformity are unleashed under these conditions. This is also a time of conflict among members, and some of their fighting may be a displacement of anger felt toward the leader, because in our society hostility and assertiveness is more condoned when directed toward peers than toward authorities.

Not every group has a volatile storming period, just as not all two-year-olds are "terrible two's." Theories of development offer guidelines based upon common behaviors seen in many groups. But groups go about the tasks involved in development according to the unique mix of individuals, not according to an inexorable set of unvarying steps. If a group were not experiencing the storming phase overtly, its therapist would be mistaken to persist in viewing this as a sign of grave dysfunction.

Nonetheless, most groups do seem to move from a stage of giving information, advice, or opinions to a stage of exploring emotional reactions within the meeting. They seem to move from a stage when the members are preoccupied with belonging, of developing we-ness, to being preoccupied with themselves as individuals, competing to have their needs met. In the emotional transactions that occur in this period, members bond to one another in much more authentic ways than had been possible before. This is vitally important if groups are to gain maturity, where the curative factors are predominantly within the membership and not the leader.

A Clinical Example

> A group of eight members had met for an extended period. They had made progress in their capacity to experience a feeling of belongingness and inclusion, but they had remained stuck in that comfortable stage for many months. The underlying themes of competitiveness between members and concern about the power of the therapist began to emerge initially through a seemingly innocent argument about whether or not a window should be opened! Some members wanted the window opened, while others did not; and all seemed quite concerned with the therapist's opinion in the matter since they feared his power and did not want to offend or anger him by their actions. In the middle of this debate, as fate would have it, the therapist canceled several meetings in order to fulfill various professional obligations. Finally, concerned about the number of sessions missed, the therapist suggested that the group meet for a double session to replace one of the missed sessions (see Chapter 11 for a discussion of a variety of responses to leader absences). This offer was

experienced by the group as an effort at control and domination by the therapist. "You just need our money, Doc!" was the way one irate individual put it. The initial intense rejection of the idea of a double session was modified because the group was quite cohesive and members found it pleasant and helpful to meet. Moreover, the members were trying their best to understand their feelings and reactions rather than simply acting on them.

In the discussion prior to the proposed double meeting, one member abruptly announced that this was to be his last meeting. "My insurance has been discontinued for some time, and I've been thinking about stopping treatment," he said by way of explanation. In reality, he held a relatively high-paying job, lived alone without undue overhead, and could easily have managed the financial obligations. The remaining members were enraged, but they neither could help him explore the meaning of this sudden flight, nor could they deter him from actually terminating. One of the primary interpretations the group offered this member was the notion that his sudden desire to leave was directly in response to his feelings about the power and control of the leader.

The theme of power and control was also evident in another way just prior to the double session. The members joked about the extended session; and they explored the need for an intermission, for bringing in food, and for allowing time to feed parking meters (despite the fact that the group met at night, when the meters did not require feeding). There was also sufficient feeling of belongingness and togetherness among the remaining members to stimulate curiosity regarding their worries about what might happen in the longer session.

The remaining seven members all appeared on time for the three-hour session. The meeting was characterized by considerable fear of overinvolvement, which dominated the first ninety minutes (the usual length of the group). Within five minutes of the halfway point, one man ostentatiously juggled his coins and left the room to buy a cola. Upon his return two men in succession left the room, announcing they were going to the bathroom. When all the men were back in the room, the group discussed these events, and the exploration clearly showed both conscious and unconscious rebellion by the men who left. As one man said, "I sit through business meetings and sporting events that last three hours or more without having to go to the bathroom." Moreover, the group began to recognize that there was subtle encouragement by the women. One woman, for example, said, "I saw him get those coins, and I hoped he would get up and leave."

In this instance a change in format provided an opportunity to bring simmering rebelliousness into the open. In the context of the emerging conflicts, this rebellion was not a protest against the loss of a maternal object (the therapist), but rather an opportunity to test one's own power to control his fate. The members' fear of the strength and power of the therapist, along with their wish to take him on, was manifest in their responses to the double session. The terminated member's rebellion was clearly echoed in the less self-defeating rebellions of the remaining members.

Stage 3: The Mature Phase

The mature group is a performing, working entity. In the schema used here, this phase represents the apex of group effectiveness. Since a number of authors have contributed to our understanding of this developmental stage, we will first review selected formulations.

Review of the Literature

In the group-as-a-whole tradition, Bion[20] refers to the mature stage as the *work group*. Some of the characteristics of a work group are a goal-directedness, an ability of the individuals to cooperate in an activity, and an ability to relate to reality. For Whitaker and Lieberman[21] group maturity is attained when no focal conflict is evident and group members work on their problems in a concerted fashion. This is rare and appears to coincide with a culture that "provides the patient with a special form of safety which guarantees that certain damaging or disastrous results will not occur when he relinquishes the personal habitual solutions heretofore regarded as essential to his existence. Under these special conditions of safety, the patient may take steps to test the necessity of maintaining his old maladaptive solutions."[22] Tuckman labels this the *performing* stage.[23]

J. Durkin[24] has attempted to describe optimal group maturity in the more recent terminology of General System Theory. He considers the mature group as having a balance between open and closed boundaries. Boundaries that are too open do not protect the individual sufficiently, and boundaries that are too closed stop the necessary exchanges of information and feeling. Durkin suggests that maturity coincides with the establishment of semipermeable boundaries that allow new information to be processed appropriately. H. Durkin[25] maintains that this strictly systems point of view is incomplete without adding a psychodynamic understanding of the individual. In an earlier work, contrasting individual psychoanalysis and ordinary living, she suggested that the former almost completely cancels reality and focuses on transference, whereas the latter obscures transference in the reality interchange.[26] Group therapy falls in the middle, where reality is present but diminished, and transference is present but available for examination. Mature groups for both Durkins are those in which free interaction is made possible by a permissive and safe atmosphere, and this free interaction is the basis for the development of multiple defenses and transferences that are then analyzed and understood.

Gustafson et al.[27,28] have drawn another parallel between group and individual development. Utilizing Mahler's[29] stages of separation and individuation, these authors suggest that a mature group is like the practicing toddler: members periodically return to the leader for reassurance and support, but they can continue practicing on their own and do so with increasing effectiveness. With their attention to cooperation and clashing of interests, Gustafson et al. maintained that members' ability to tolerate differing points of view and conflicting feelings are signs of a maturing group.

Day[30] has introduced the concept of the group working within an envelope, by which he means that a symbolic membrane has developed. This state is characterized by the members' mutual appreciation of one another and trust for one another. In turn members gain the flexibility to understand themselves more completely in relation to the other members and the leader; they become able to process rather than merely experience transferential relationships.

Garland[31] defines a working group as one in which the members have become less interested in the problems that they came to the group to solve, and more interested in the group interactions that were initially viewed as *not* a problem—the nonproblem. This essentially means that the norm of focusing on the here-and-now interaction has been firmly established as part of the culture. Within such an environment patients are able to expand their views of their respective problems to include elements of their lives that they did not know were problems, but that in fact are essential in understanding the initial problem.

Indications of a Mature Group

With this general review, we can more closely examine some of the indicators of a working group environment.

1. Mature, working groups emphasize the intragroup responses and interactions as the primary source of learning and cure. A sense of history develops so that current episodes are linked to prior events, and members become sensitized to repetitive patterns in themselves and other group members.

2. Despite the primacy of in-group interactions, flexibility develops that allows discussion of relevant outside events in the members' lives. Groups develop the capacity to distinguish between outside events brought into the discussion as resistances and outside events discussed as part of the therapeutic quest. Where possible, members seek to bring such outside material into the group in order to clarify issues. For example, an individual who complains about his interactions with a significant person in his life might be helped to understand his contributions to the problems if members are able to link the outside problem with their in-group awareness of the individual's behavior.

3. In mature groups the members develop a more collegial relationship with the therapist. The therapist is viewed as an authority and expert, but he is demystified and not imbued with magical powers. In other words a therapeutic alliance has been established that allows for a more realistic appraisal of the leader as well as a more complete conviction that he is an ally in the therapeutic venture. While transference reactions are still operative, members are able to help one another gain objectivity on distorted perceptions of the leader and each other.

4. Members have developed confidence in their ability to tolerate anxiety and to examine problems themselves. They no longer look solely to the therapist as the primary source of caring, concern, guidance, and understanding. They have learned that no permanent harm will result from intense affective interactions, and they do not consistently interfere with heated exchanges. The members are more able to trust that it is helpful to share spontaneously the affective responses they experience during the meetings without undue regard for politeness, rationality, or embarrassment. At times individuals remain unable to tolerate specific affects, but such instances are utilized as opportunities for self-understanding. Members have developed a sense of distinction between expressions of feelings and destructive attacks.

5. Through repeated experiences members gain a deep understanding and appreciation for one another's strengths and weaknesses. Compassion and tolerance are founded upon the knowledge that unconscious factors operate for everyone and often adversely affect interpersonal relationships. Members in these groups have also learned that the most abrasive aspects of behavior are often defenses designed to protect against pain, not indications of inherent malice in the individuals in question. Members have an appreciation of the unconscious, even if they do not understand its sources, and they attempt to understand the behavior of their fellow members as well as their own. Similarly, the therapist's strengths and weaknesses can be appreciated or accepted without overwhelmingly intense or prolonged affective swings.

6. Finally, members have learned that transactions inevitably involve two distinct components—the interpersonal and the intrapsychic. They know that behavior is not always what it appears to be, and that there are personal meanings that might produce particular behaviors. They further appreciate that identical behaviors might have very different meanings for different individuals. Members strive in a consistent manner to respond to behaviors from two perspectives—as the recipient of behaviors (external observer) and as the empathic understander of the more personal meanings of the behaviors (internal observer).

Successful Termination of a Member

One vital aspect to the development of group maturity is the successful termination of a patient. In the early months members struggle with their fears that this treatment might not be truly therapeutic. Indeed the first terminations usually are therapeutic failures—patients who flee the group prematurely. It is often quite a long time before any patient successfully completes the work he or she set out to achieve and leaves with a sense of well-being and accomplishment. It is not unusual that members will refer to such a patient for many years, using that memory as an antidote to doubts and worries about the effectiveness of the group. Successful terminations are harbingers of hope for other members. Mature groups almost invariably have had at least one termination that was perceived as successful by the great majority of the members.

New members also become symbols of successful or unsuccessful treatment because new members fill seats formerly occupied by individuals who have terminated. Groups develop oral legacies, whereby history is remembered a long time. The ways in which various members leave take on powerful meanings for groups. During a period when an undue number of members leave unhappy and unfulfilled, the sense of confidence and maturity in the group is dramatically affected. On the other hand, when there are a number of primarily successful terminations, the optimism and maturity is raised greatly. Perceptions of new members are obscured by the shadows of the members who left before. A new member who happens to fill a seat occupied by a member who left prematurely is greeted differently than someone who fills the seat of an honored member who left with work completed. Both situations have their problems. Examination of the impact of terminations on feelings about the replacement member or the group-as-a-whole provides one more opportunity for members to differentiate reality from the affective response, which contributes considerably to group maturity.

An Illustration of the Effects of Group Development

Repetitive events may be handled differently at different stages of development. In order for the therapist to maximize learning, it is important to understand the differences in how groups respond to similar events at different developmental stages.

Throughout the life of a group, individuals will from time to time break the contract regarding prompt attendance to all meetings. Such breaches are inevitable, but members use those breaches for learning in quite different ways, depending upon the stage of group development.

In the formative stage lateness is often ignored or only cursorily addressed. Commonly, reality reasons are offered to explain the tardiness, and these reasons are quickly accepted by the others. Thus a late member might casually announce, "The bus was late," or, "My boss kept me in a meeting," or even, "I misplaced my car keys." Such explanations, accompanied by a sincere apology, are usually satisfactory to the others, and the attention of the group moves on to some other subject. These responses are multidetermined. At one level members do not know how to explore or appreciate such behavior. Sometimes members offer advice about how to avoid such situations in the future, but there is little permission in the group to express feelings about such situations. If a member has an intense affective reaction, such as anger, it is usually kept under wraps out of an even more pressing need for acceptance. Furthermore, members at this stage seem to view the lack of condemnation or attack from the therapist as a sign that they, too, should offer no strong response to the tardy member. They are still looking to the therapist for direction about how to behave. Finally, there is a powerful but subtle unconscious pressure *not* to comment upon breaches in the group boundary, since at this stage of development members may feel a need to employ the same behaviors. It is as if no one wants to bolt the door too securely lest they, too, be forced to stay in the group and experience intense emotions.

As the members develop a sense of belongingness, and thereby move to a different stage of development, there is usually increasing pressure to arrive on time, as well as to honor the other rules. Lateness now occurs in the face of potential censure from one's peers, and it may represent either a displaced expression of dissatisfaction with the developing norms or a more direct expression of rebelliousness and assertiveness. Whereas lateness in the forming stage may represent some response to anxiety about joining, such as a fear of being engulfed or becoming dependent, lateness now represents a move toward individualizing, of fighting for fulfillment of one's own goals potentially at the expense of the others. Often the rebelliousness begins as an attack on the leader, and this can include overt and covert collusion by the other members. Patients in this mode may pay no more attention to lateness than patients in the earliest stage of development, but in this case the affective tone is quite different. Whereas in the initial stage the nonattention is out of naiveté or unwillingness to try to understand a defense that others might want to employ, now the unwillingness is an angry, belligerent struggle with the leader and his rules. As one patient angrily expressed it, "Russ comes for eighty minutes. Why focus on the ten minutes he *isn't* here?"

Given that norms are often very rigid during this stage, the affective responses to the perceived or actual tyranny of the group are understandable. A member's breach in the contract frequently produces strong emotions, which then are directed either toward the offending member or toward the leader. At the same time recognition is dawning of the existence of underlying, or even unconscious, motivation for lateness. No longer would the excuse "I misplaced my keys!" be accepted without question. Following the lead of the therapist, and by now having had occasion to see the fruit such inquiries have borne in the past, members begin to explore lateness for hidden meanings. They are freer to communicate emotions, not just thoughts, and they have begun to internalize the curiosity about behavior as a means of learning very important information about themselves and their colleagues.

In mature groups the members have begun to examine the meaning of breaches of the contract, both for the individuals who come late or not at all, as well as for themselves. Such behavior is understood as potentially powerful communication. The members may still be enraged by the fact that an individual arrives late or occasionally does not come to the group at all but have begun to accept that not all individuals are the same, and that absolute conformity is neither just nor fair. Thus members can utilize such interactions to study both their own external and internal responses and concurrently the inner meanings for the latecomer. Finally, members begin to explore the possibilities that such behavior on the part of one individual member is in fact a group event. The latecomer might be the "voice" of the whole group. It is commonly observed that lateness and absenteeism tend to increase as a therapist's vacation approaches, and these breaches of the contract are in fact a groupwide commentary about the therapist's impending absence.

Many variations on this example occur, but common to mature groups is the capacity of the group to establish a norm of viewing behavior as communication and therefore one more pathway to knowledge. Understanding the multiple determinants of behavior, along with exploring the reactions various individuals have to that behavior, becomes a powerful therapeutic tool when the entire group becomes attuned to exploring these arenas.

Group Development: Culture, Norms, and Individual Roles

Group Culture and Norms

In the course of group development, particular ways of handling conflicts or affects become ingrained within the interactional patterns. Groups develop particular kinds of culture, which help define what individuals can and cannot do as well as how they express themselves or deal with a variety of affects. In the beginning phase some groups look to the therapist for solutions to the problems of joining, whereas in other groups members talk primarily to one another and ignore the therapist. These represent two differing group cultures; members are negotiating the task of joining and forming a group but are doing so in different ways.

The study of a group culture helps define how the members relate to one another, to the therapist, and to the group. It is a way of viewing the organization of the group. Each group develops norms (both conscious and unconscious) regarding appropriate behavior. These norms begin with the expectations of the members and the therapist.

The therapist serves as a regulator of the group boundaries and tries to help define what is in and what is outside the interest of the group.[32] For leaders who focus on the here-and-now and the affects raised in the therapy room, a description of a childhood event would be a distraction; and soon, members would no longer relate childhood events. For therapists who value the metaphorical value of a childhood story, such a memory might throw light on group dynamics in the immediate setting. For a therapist who values the place of genetic exploration, this might represent an important piece of personal work. Since the therapist is a potent initiator of group norms, reinforcement through his interest or noninterference serves to establish appropriate ways of interacting within the group. There is often a dichotomy between therapists who emphasize transferences to the leader, thereby helping individuals learn about their relationships with authority and the functioning and meaning of these inner fantasies, and therapists who focus on peer transactions, which highlight the learning of social skills and the giving and receiving of feedback but diminish exploration of the unconscious.[33]

The therapist is not solely responsible for normative behavior and the subsequent group culture. The individuals who constitute the group are constantly changing and altering ways in which norms are expressed, although usually these are not major changes because, once established, norms are rather difficult to alter. In a study of T-groups, Lieberman, Yalom, and Miles[34] found the expectations that members brought with them were a powerful set of constraints that were unlikely to be reversed in the actual state of affairs. Furthermore, in determining eventual outcome, the impact of the individual upon the group norms is as potent as the leader's. Since this was a study of groups limited to thirty hours' duration, the opportunity to alter the norms through analysis of groupwide and individual resistances was diminished. Recognition of norms and the resultant group culture provides another perspective for the therapist to begin exploration of the individuals within the setting as well as to understand differences in group development.

Individual Roles

Individuals exhibit patterns of behavior that fulfill their own personal needs and that interact with the group culture and norms. These behavioral patterns are labeled *roles*. When the concept of role is used to describe behaviors in a therapy group, it is important to distinguish between specialized functions within the group itself and characteristic patterns of behavior of a particular individual. The fact that groups often typecast their participants, utilizing personal roles to fill certain group functions, simply confuses the matter further.

Examined from the perspective of the whole group, roles may be thought of as serving various functions. Some roles seem to facilitate the group effort to work on problems by encouraging exploration of affect or important topics. Others serve to maintain restrictive culture and norms.[35] A host of specific titles may be assigned to the roles, but basically a group-wide function is being addressed. For instance, roles that help select or focus on group tasks might be termed the information seeker, the coordinator, the historian, and the elaborator. They function to clarify issues of importance to the members. Another set of roles that maintain or build the culture include the gatekeeper, the standard setter, and the compromiser.

Of considerable importance are roles that serve to regulate affects.[36] Some feelings need to be elaborated and explored, while others need to be diffused and modulated in order to maintain the group's functioning. In this context the encourager, the jokester, the silence breaker, and the soother function to monitor the level of affect.

It is important to understand that groups require roles both to help contain feelings and to further work. Groups might utilize a particular individual in a specific role to perform these functions or several individuals using different roles. For instance, in a situation where intense emotion is present, the group members may regulate the intensity through joking, direct soothing, or diverting. It is the function that is important, rather than the individual or perhaps even the specific mode.

Members enter a group with their own specific repertoire of roles, which they have used in other life situations. Only rarely are roles generated by group processes. One of the purposes of gaining personal historical information is for the therapist and patient to become aware of these stereotypic patterns. However, it is not unusual for an individual to take on a role with past determinants unknown to either patient or therapist. When this happens, the opportunity for therapeutic gain is great, since unconscious conflicts are observable in current behavior.

To illustrate the overlapping between group and individual behaviors, we can look at common early group behaviors. There are often one or more "hosts" or "hostesses" who will initiate the introductions and who will fill up silences. This function may become "assigned" to one person who will routinely handle affects surrounding newness, beginnings, or silences, or it may be divided among individuals. Individuals who routinely accept the host or hostess role may be demonstrating a lifelong pattern of bearing the emotional burden of their families, or exhibitionistic needs to be the center of attention no matter what the psychic cost, or perhaps a need to be the favorite child in the family. Whatever the derivation of the role, it is often quite facilitative to the group.

Often there are members who are essentially mute in the initial meetings, and this silence also is not a new behavior generated specifically for this difficult situation. Individuals bring out habitual responses of silence to cope with this new stress. It may represent a passive-aggressive position, commanding attention through the power of passivity. It may be the youngest sibling once again playing out the role of waiting until last to be fed. It may represent a chronic altruism, an assumption that the needs of others must come first. Or, of course, it could be the manifestation of terror in this interpersonal arena.

There is another subset of roles which are unique to an individual's character.[37] These roles satisfy individual needs and are fundamentally irrelevant to group development, but they may become a dominant force operating within the group. Individuals taking on these roles are viewed negatively, and there is often a strong wish to extrude them from the group. These roles include the monopolizer, the help-rejecting complainer, the naive one, the supplicant, and the playboy. The therapeutic management of some of these roles will be discussed in Chapter 11.

Of course, not every behavioral pattern or role is self-destructive or pathological. The therapist needs to discriminate between the useful and adaptive roles and the destructive and constraining roles. The same role can be both healthy and, if pushed to an extreme, pathological. Moreover, the group therapist needs to alternate continually between the group and the individual developmental perspectives (see Chapter 8). A role that may be productive for the group may be constricting for the individual, and vice versa. A balance must be struck as to which aspect to explore and in what order so as to maximize the therapeutic effectiveness of the group for all the members.

Summary

The concept of group development is valuable in orienting therapists to a number of processes common to group psychotherapy. Familiarity with the phases of development helps anchor therapists in their work and provides a road map to help them understand what is occurring within their groups.

A great deal of valuable therapeutic work can be accomplished in each phase. Indeed each phase offers unique opportunities. Further, since groups are dynamic organisms composed of living beings, the phases are not rigid and steadfast. The stages are best considered guidelines, not laws. As groups grow and are confronted with crisis and change, the phases will be revisited regularly.

As development takes place, each group forms its particular culture and norms that have a major impact upon how the group goes about fulfilling its goal of helping the members solve their problems. The therapist has considerable importance in the evolution of the culture, but the members also contribute greatly. The concept of role is linked with group requirements for building and maintaining its culture as well as the individual's past habitual methods of handling stress and anxiety. Both aspects of role require consideration and frequently can be observed as overlapping within the group.

References

1. B.W. Tuckman, "Developmental Sequence in Small Groups," *Psychol. Bull.* 63 (1965): 384–399.
2. S.R. Slavson, "Are There Group Dynamics in Therapy Groups?," *Int. J. Group Psychother.* 7 (1957):115–130.
3. A. Wolf and E.K. Schwartz, *Psychoanalysis in Groups* (New York: Grune and Stratton, 1962).
4. S. Saravay, "Group Psychology and the Structural Theory: A Revised Psychoanalytic Model of Group Therapy," *J. Am. Psychoanal. Assoc.* 23 (1975):69–89.
5. G.S. Gibbard and J.S. Hartman, "The Oedipal Paradigm in Group Development: A Clinical and Empirical Study," *Small Group Behav.* 4 (1973):305–354.
6. W. Hill and L. Gruner, "A Study of Development in Open and Closed Groups," *Small Group Behav.* 4 (1973):355–381.
7. I. Yalom, *The Theory and Practice of Group Psychotherapy* (New York: Basic Books, 1970), pp. 233–244.
8. E. Fried, "Basic Concepts in Group Psychotherapy," in *Comprehensive Group Psychotherapy*, edited by H.I. Kaplan and B.J. Sadock (Baltimore: Williams and Wilkins, 1971), pp. 47–71.
9. W.C. Schutz, *Firo* (New York: Rinehart, 1958).

10. W.G. Bennis and H.A. Shepard, "A Theory of Group Development," *Human Relations* 9 (1956):415–437.
11. Saravay, "Group Psychology and the Structural Theory."
12. M. Day, "Process in Classical Psychodynamic Groups," *Int. J. Group Psychother.* 31 (1981): 153–174.
13. P.E. Slater, *Microcosm: Structural, Psychological, and Religious Evolution in Groups* (New York: John Wiley, 1966).
14. J.P. Gustafson and L. Cooper, "Unconscious Planning in Small Groups," *Human Relations*, 32 (1979):1039–1064.
15. Slater, *Microcosm.*
16. Schutz, *Firo.*
17. Saravay, "Group Psychology and the Structural Theory."
18. Tuckman, "Developmental Sequence in Small Groups."
19. E. Fried, "Individuation Through Group Psychotherapy," *Int. J. Group Psychother.* 20 (1970):450–459.
20. W.R. Bion, *Experiences in Groups* (New York: Basic Books, 1960).
21. D.S. Whitaker and M.A. Lieberman, *Psychotherapy Through the Group Process* (New York: Atherton Press, 1964).
22. *Ibid.*, p. 166.
23. Tuckman, "Developmental Sequence in Small Groups."
24. J.E. Durkin, "Foundations of Autonomous Living Structure," in *Living Groups: Group Psychotherapy and General System Theory*, edited by J.E. Durkin (New York: Brunner/Mazel, 1981), pp. 24–59.
25. H.E. Durkin, "The Technical Implications of General System Theory for Group Psychotherapy," in *Living Groups: Group Psychotherapy and General System Theory*, edited by J.E. Durkin (New York: Brunner/Mazel, 1981), pp. 171–198.
26. H.E. Durkin, *The Group in Depth* (New York: International Universities Press, 1964).
27. Gustafson and Cooper, 1979, "Unconscious Planning in Small Groups."
28. J.P. Gustafson, L. Cooper, N.C. Lathrop, K. Ringler, F.A. Seldin, and M.K. Wright, "Cooperative and Clashing Interests in Small Groups. Part I. Theory." *Human Relations* 34 (1981):315–339.
29. M.S. Mahler, F. Pine, and A. Bergman, *The Psychological Birth of the Human Infant* (New York: Basic Books, 1975).
30. Day, "Process in Classic Psychodynamic Groups."
31. C. Garland, "Group Analysis: Taking the Non-Problem Seriously," *Group Analysis* 15 (1982):4–14.
32. B.M. Astrachan, "Towards a Social Systems Model of Therapeutic Groups," *Soc. Psychiatry* 5 (1970): 110–119.
33. E.B. Klein and B.M. Astrachan, "Learning in Groups: A Comparison of T-Groups and Study Groups," *J. Appl. Behav. Sci.* 7 (1971):659–683.
34. M. Lieberman, I.D. Yalom, and M.D. Miles, *Encounter Groups: First Facts* (New York: Basic Books, 1973).
35. K. Benne and P. Sheats, "Functional Roles of Group Members," *J. Soc. Issues* 4 (1948):41–49.
36. J. Arsenian, E.V. Semrad, and D. Shapiro, "An Analysis of Integral Functions in Small Groups," *Int. J. Group Psychother.* 12 (1962):421–434.
37. Benne and Sheats, "Functional Roles of Group Members."

Curative Mechanisms and

Processes in Group Psychotherapy

4

Each theory of psychotherapy has explicit and implicit convictions about how best to help people grow. Psychoanalytic theory belongs to the philosophical tradition which holds that "the truth shall make you free."[1] That is, people grow as they gain information and understanding. Freud recognized that a great body of information is unconscious, and that emotional knowledge (and therefore freedom) requires making the unconscious conscious. Through a variety of windows into the world of the unconscious, including transference, we may deduce a great deal about the conflicted aspects of our patients' lives and histories. Other windows are free association, slips of the tongue, body language, character styles, dreams, repetition compulsions, and resistances. In the therapeutic process, it is posited that patients will regress to a level where they have not mastered developmental tasks or have become fixated because of intrapsychic conflict.

In classic psychoanalysis patients' regression is fostered by the dependent position on the couch, the absence of visible stimuli from the analyst, and the use of free association. In group psychotherapy, regression is stimulated in part by stranger anxiety and group process (group associations). Change is effected by assisting patients in gaining emotional understanding of their reactions inside and outside the therapy situation, and examining the basic assumptions that support their characteristic perceptions and behaviors. For analytic group therapists, the opportunity to see patients actively involved in interpersonal matrixes offers unique opportunities for gaining insight into their unconscious worlds.

Neo-Freudians, notably object relations theorists, have emphasized the importance of authentic and healthy human relationships as therapeutic factors. Therapists working in this tradition stress the here-and-now relationships and "corrective emotional experience" over classical insight as the major curative force. In group therapy the presence of a network of human relationships, rather than just the single relationship to the analyst, increases the opportunities for multiple emotional experiences that can produce change.

Ego psychologists further underline the importance of relationships in rebuilding fragmented and flawed egos. Groups offer ideal settings for patients to experience and learn empathy, to recognize that life is filled with separate people, each with their own wishes, needs, and desires.

In the interpersonal tradition of Harry Stack Sullivan, Yalom[2] has developed a list of eleven "curative factors":

1. Instillation of hope
2. Universality
3. Imparting of information
4. Altruism
5. Corrective recapitulation of the primary family group
6. Development of socializing techniques
7. Imitative behavior
8. Interpersonal learning
9. Group cohesiveness
10. Catharsis
11. Existential factors

The factors are not of equal importance or strength. In group psychotherapy with neurotic and character-disordered individuals, two elements seem particularly salient: the development of a cohesive group, analogous to the holding environment and the therapeutic alliance in dyadic psychotherapy, and interpersonal learning, the correction of parataxic distortions in the here-and-now of the group. For other patient populations universality and the instillation of hope have greater importance in effecting improved functioning.

Within each of these psychodynamic frameworks important commonalities appear. All presuppose a neutral, fairly unobtrusive therapist who strives to create a safe environment. The therapist's stance, along with the anxiety created by the group setting, promotes regression in the individuals. This allows the pathologies of the members to emerge in the interpersonal transactions and the inner fantasies about the relationships within the group. Each of the theoretical variations cited emphasizes emotionally charged interchanges and the consequent development of self-understanding as vehicles for change and growth.

Consideration of the curative elements in any therapeutic enterprise must take into account both processes and mechanisms for change. Before any curative factors can take effect, a sufficiently safe therapeutic environment must be developed. Each group member brings a great many internal obstacles to the development of a trusting environment. Much of the early learning that individuals gain in their groups is the result of the examination and modification or dissolution of those obstacles; for some this may be the central element in all their therapeutic gains. But even those changes require the rudiments of basic human trust.

Ultimately it is the maladaptive habitual responses, assumptions, and interactions that are the objects of study and modification. The psychological *mechanisms* of prime importance in effecting change are imitation, identification, and internalization.[3] The *processes* of change we will consider are confrontation, clarification, interpretation, and working through.

The Mechanisms of Change

People grow and change in groups through three major psychological mechanisms: imitation, identification, and internalization.

Imitation

In therapy groups individuals have the opportunity to observe many interactions, styles of relating, and problem-solving techniques. Much of the early learning in groups is imitative. Patients who have difficulty tolerating and sharing strong emotions can first observe as other members interact intensely. As they learn that members are not harmed, but rather are typically drawn closer by such exchanges, such patients see some hope for change and, as a consequence, can begin to share feelings by imitating those who are more successful in that task. Though primarily used early in group membership, imitation remains one of the ways in which members gain new behavioral options throughout their treatment. The successes following imitative behavior make the group more attractive, enhance a wish to belong, and increase cohesiveness. This furthers identifications among the members. The use of imitation is both a result of feeling that others have been successful and a means of discovering alternative ways of thinking, expressing, or behaving. It is by no means limited to group therapy; but group therapy, by virtue of the multiple interactions and relationships, expands the opportunities for change through imitative learning.

Identification

Identification has been defined in a variety of ways. We are using it here, following the description by Loewald,[4] to mean an unconscious process in which the subject takes on parts or aspects of the object. By taking on aspects of another, the individual changes by altering perceptions or affects. Identification may be used in the service of growth or resistance, and each instance must be understood separately.

Freud initially postulated that group formation takes place as group members identify with one another via their shared affection for the leader.[5]

Without these bonds there is no group. Peer identifications also take place as the members tell about their life experiences as well as their reactions to current events, both within and outside the group. Identifications arise not only from the content of the memories, associations, and feelings, but with the process of telling about them as well. Consciously these identifications may be expressed as feelings of attraction, belonging, and attachment to the members and the group. These are the building blocks from which group cohesiveness develops. Similarly, universalization, the development of the sense that one is not alone in his or her feelings, furthers group attraction and identifications among members. A circular process begins that enhances these powerful influences members have upon one another. In turn the resultant identifications alter fundamental ways in which the members perceive and respond. The incremental building of identifications forms the base for lasting change.

Identification can be observed readily in group interactions. For example, identification can be seen in nonverbal behavior when two or more patients simultaneously shift body positions during a discussion about another member, resulting in several members unconsciously adopting the same body position. This usually reflects a similar affect or perception by these individuals regarding the individual or topic under discussion.

It is not uncommon for these identifications to be made conscious during the group. Members will point out that individuals have changed in how they respond or interact. They seem to view situations differently than they had in the past. These observations may startle the individual who had been unaware of the changes, and yet upon reflection he often easily agrees that his inner response is different, less conflicted, and more flexible.

Sometimes patients will note that they are taking positions on subjects that feel foreign to their accustomed stances. They are puzzled by their behaviors and their inner states. Such identifications usually are temporary unless the sources can be analyzed and integrated by the individual. One such source can be identification with the therapist. Sometimes this identification takes on concrete forms such as dressing in clothing and style similar to the therapist's, purchasing automobiles like the therapist's, or even male patients growing mustaches! Patients often surprise one another with the observation, "You sound just like the therapist," or, "You're playing doctor again!" Particularly important are the hoped-for patient identifications with the therapist and therapeutic attitudes: the tolerance of feelings, the introspective stance, and the effort to understand as well as react.

Imitation and identification processes are two of the major mechanisms by which change takes place. Much change can be accomplished on the basis of these mechanisms alone. They form the underpinnings for group attraction and cohesion. Through these mechanisms much of the data necessary for understanding the complex connections between the unconscious and the conscious, the past and the present, are made available. For example, imitation and identification may explain the changes that occur in those patients who grow and change although they sit rather silently in their groups.

Internalization

Internalization is the most advanced and durable mechanism of change. Internalized change is not the result of something taken in from the outside, but rather it is due to a shift in the psychic structure of the individual so that his experiences, both conscious and unconscious, are shifted to a more mature level of functioning.

Internalization produces greater flexibility in handling both internal and interactive states and is the result of working through conflicts or building new psychic structures to handle previously disruptive anxiety. The therapist can facilitate healthy internalization by detailed examination and reexamination of emotionally laden interactions. Through identification, clarification, and interpretation, individuals integrate knowledge gained in the here-and-now transactions with their sources and prior assumptions. This results in an increased integration of affects and object relationships as well as diminished inner conflict. The outcome can be observed in the therapy setting where a patient might indicate a new way of behaving to recurrent stimuli. As an example, a patient who had entered therapy suffering from paranoid ideation was eventually able to state, "This year when you announced your vacation, I again felt that you were not going to meet this group because you needed to get away from me in particular. I fantasized you were going to continue to meet all your other groups. It's the same old fantasy I've had in previous years. But this year I know it's just a fantasy, and it doesn't even have much emotional power for me. It's the price I've paid all these years for being the only child in my family to be put up for adoption."

Summary

We have separated the mechanisms of imitation, identification, and internalization for heuristic purposes. In practice shadings exist among them. Change can occur so subtly that it is often observable only after it has taken place.

The manner in which members come to value dreams might be

used as an illustration of how these mechanisms occur. When a member first reports a dream, there is usually some interest shown by the others. The therapist, too, by his verbal and nonverbal communications, indicates his interest. It is not unusual for some members to begin reporting dreams by way of *imitation* of others who have done the same. They do so to please the therapist. Furthermore, other members initially imitate the therapist's investigatory style of trying to understand the dreams. At the level of *identification,* the members may find that they have a new attitude about dreams. They may experience a sense of excitement and stimulation when a dream is being reported, and they may develop a sense of curiosity about not only the dreamer's associations to the dream but everyone's associations. These are not entirely conscious responses, but rather they arise as identifications with the therapist's *interactions* with the members. At the level of *internalization,* members may find themselves experiencing a fundamental shift in their thinking about dreams and dreaming. Dreams are now seen as useful ways of self-learning or uncovering hidden aspects of the group interactions. The use of the dream for exhibitionistic needs or as a shield diminishes, and the inner experience of the members is that dreams are valuable tools for learning. In other words, the patients internalize the therapist's value system regarding dreams.

The Curative Processes

The foregoing descriptions are made more complete by linking them to the processes by which they occur within therapy groups. Following the working model of Greenson,[6] we believe that the processes that induce and promote imitation, identification, and internalization are confrontation, clarification, interpretation, and working through. The result of these processes is increased insight and understanding, eventuating in change.

Confrontation

Foulkes[7] spoke of groups as "halls of mirrors." This phrase aptly connotes the potential effectiveness with which groups can confront individuals with aspects of themselves they previously have been unable to see. A particular advantage to this treatment modality arises from the opportunity for the multiple interactions that soon directly expose patterns of behavior. In dyadic therapy the therapist has to rely upon reports from the outside world or utilize the interactions in the two-person field.

Pines[8] has described one of the dynamics that precedes confrontation. He maintained that as an individual becomes a functioning member his neurotic inner problems become evident as a communications block. Such blocks, or blind spots, may be raised to a level of self-awareness through confrontation.

Confrontations in this context are efforts to point out to the patient his behavior, his emotional state, or his problems. They primarily address external aspects of behavior and as such are observations or responses to interactions, or comments upon the affects aroused in the confronter. Confrontations do not address inner motivations or unconscious assumptions. A comment such as "You are always interrupting others!" is a confrontation, whereas "You are always seeking attention!" is not. The latter is an attribution of meaning and as such is an interpretation. Often, particularly early in group experience when patients make comments to one another that assume or attribute meaning and motivation, they are met with denial or anger. Confrontation is an attempt to indicate to a patient that a problem exists; it is not an effort to gain or impart understanding per se. Recognition of the problem is necessary before there can be agreement about what work needs to be done.

In dyadic therapy the therapist is the confronter and therefore judges the pace at which confrontation should occur. Group therapy provides more complex and varied opportunities for confrontation because there are a great many potential confronters in a group. Indeed, to the degree that the members heed the contractual agreement to share their emotional reactions to one another honestly, there is continual confrontation and feedback. Because confrontation is considered such an integral part of group psychotherapy, a great deal of effort is spent in making the group safe for confrontation and in making sure the confrontations are useful. This is especially true because many patients enter group psychotherapy with explicit requests to have feedback about their behavior. Though consciously wishing for such information, patients discover that they also have considerable resistance to learning about themselves. Confrontations may be constructive, destructive, or a mixture. It is important to create an atmosphere that enables members to be able to give and receive important information through helpful confrontations.

Many members are quite limited in their ability to give feedback. Others can give feedback in only the most benign situations and become anxious and frozen the moment intense affects are mobilized. The therapeutic task is not only to train someone to overcome these fears, but to understand the dynamic underpinnings. The attainment of the ability to give nonjudgmental feedback or confrontation signals an advance in ego functioning. Indeed members often cite their newfound ability to confront as a major step in their therapeutic growth and one of the special advantages of group therapy.

Learning to confront successfully includes acquisition of a sense of timing, the capacity to form an alliance, and empathy. Although these elements may not be consciously integrated, their absence can be readily discerned. Timing rests in part on an appreciation of another's inner state and on a judgment as to whether the information can be productively assimilated at this time. The state of the alliance also influences the usefulness of a confrontation. It is not unusual for accurate feedback to go unheard because of conflict. In such circumstances the comment "I don't trust you, so why should I listen to you?" might be heard. Therapists have long been aware that negative transferences block learning. This is particularly so in dyadic treatment. One of the major advantages of groups is the opportunity to learn about oneself from peers, with whom less intense negative transferences may develop. Such a step may precede working on the response to authority. Finally, for a member to momentarily put himself in another's shoes and learn about his inner world is essential, not only for understanding the other's emotional state, but for being able to anticipate the effect of receiving the information.[9]

Many, if not most, confrontations carry with them an implicit request to stop doing whatever is being done. This is particularly the case when there is intense emotion in the group. For example, a member might blurt out something about another group member that has been unspoken, like "You always attack us!" or "You continually put down women!" The message is clear, though not explicit: "Stop doing that!" A hostile attack may be contained in the extreme expressions "always" and "continually," and this would evoke defensiveness in the confronted patient. This situation rarely results in increased curiosity and usually results in a struggle between the confronter and the confronted. This struggle may be productive for all concerned, but it is different from the growth-promoting confrontation. Of course, therapists are not immune to making confrontations bearing the covert message "Stop doing that!"; in these cases a struggle results between the therapist and the confronted patient.

How information is conveyed to the individual being confronted thus becomes a matter of central concern when it is done insensitively or in anger. However, most patients are capable of finding ways of confronting one another in ways that are helpful and curative.

The contract is a significant source of therapeutic leverage and provides an opportunity to confront members with their self-defeating behaviors. Patients agree to a variety of constraints in order to maximize their therapy. The contractual agreements are not adhered to at all times, nor would that be expected. Rather, patients learn to be *responsible* for their contractual commitments to the group, as distinct from always keeping the contract. The therapist should be aware that life is filled with layers of conflicting contractual agreements and that how individuals choose their priorities is very important. As patients choose to keep or break their agreements, they have many opportunities to be confronted about their characteristic styles and values. On many occasions entire groups will collude to avoid confronting a specific patient over a breach of the agreement; in this case the group-as-a-whole may be confronted, and through that strategy the members may gain new self-awareness.

Some authors have posited special confrontational techniques concerning patient's uses and abuses of the contract. Borriello,[10] for example, has elaborated a radical technique of confrontation with regard to contractual breaches, which he believes is crucial in working with patients suffering from severe acting out character disorders. Following any violation he directly tells his group that the rationale of the contract is to help patients break self-destructive patterns and that members do themselves a disservice by continuing their therapy while being unwilling to do what is required to change. Ormont[11] addressed a subtler violation of the contract. He differentiated between expressions of feelings and personal attacks, viewing the latter to be acting out and therefore antitherapeutic. Fortunately, even unsuccessful or erroneous confrontations, when properly handled, can provide an opportunity to study interpersonal modes of relating.

Most confrontations take place among members or between therapists and members. However, one form of confrontation in groups is distinct. Looking into the hall of mirrors, patients might observe others involving themselves in unproductive and pathological behavior and begin to be curious about the extent to which they too engage in identical or similar behaviors. This is a form of self-confrontation. In a therapy group no confrontation is given in isolation. Every member of the group hears and is affected, even though the confrontation may have been directed primarily at another member. Thus interventions must take into account more than an appreciation of the openness of a particular individual to hear them: they must include an awareness that the other members will have their own responses.

Clarification

Greenson stated, "Clarification refers to those activities that aim at placing the psychic phenomenon being analyzed in sharp focus. The significant details have to be dug out and carefully separated from extraneous matter."[12] The group provides special opportunities for clarification to take place. One aspect of the process is the richness of experiences in the group itself, which enables patients to see repeating patterns. Members are a well of information about one another's behavior. It is a common experience for members, after a confrontation, to remember similar pieces of interaction or behaviors that have occurred in previous meetings. Often incidents dating back months or years in the group are recalled in vivid detail; in other instances members will recall important pieces of history previously shared and will relate them to the current confrontation. Clarification serves to organize and highlight such data. Much affect-laden material, previously split off and disconnected, can now be brought to bear on a specific and related issue. It is the weight of these episodes being repeated over and over in the group that contributes to individuals questioning themselves. This increased curiosity represents an important aspect of the change process.

Clarification follows from the interactions, which include those among members as well as individuals recounting outside events and memories. The evoked response results in members recalling other, connected, emotion-laden events and memories, either within the group or outside it. In addition, more than mere recollection is taking place since in the immediacy of the recall new interactions are occurring. If maladaptive patterns are continuing, they will emerge in the interaction.

In contrast to individual psychotherapy, the main thrust of the clarification in groups takes place in a public arena. In individual therapy, while some of the clarification necessarily occurs in the examination of outside events that are reported in the therapy, most clarifications emerge from the relationship between patient and therapist. In group therapy outside events are also utilized, but predominantly the in-group relationships are sufficient to provide the necessary clarification. This provides a much larger data base for both patient and therapist to utilize in examining perceptions, feelings, and behaviors. When a patient complains about the behaviors of a spouse, for example, it is usually possible to understand that patient's contribution to the marital dilemma by an examination of interactions with group members of the opposite sex.

It has been maintained in some quarters that the intensity and extent of transference is limited in group psychotherapy since groups focus more on the here-and-now interactions. But transference *is* a here-and-now experience. It is the eruption of previously acquired distortions into the present. Groups offer an even wider set of opportunities for the exploration of such distortions. From our perspective the development of a cohesive transference response in groups is at least as intense as in individual therapy and indeed may even be amplified by the experience of multiple peer transferences.

Interpretation

An interpretation is distinct from a clarification in two important ways. First, an interpretation is aimed at the unconscious, while clarifications are directed to the conscious or preconscious of our patients. Second, clarification broadens the data base by citing similar examples and sharpening the focus on a particular behavioral constellation. Interpretation is given in order to make unconscious phenomena conscious; it attaches meaning to an event. It attempts to help the patient gain an understanding of the hidden motivations and conflicts contributing to pathological behavior.

In dyadic psychotherapy, interpretations are classically interpretations of resistances and defenses. In group therapy, just as in individual therapy, the basic tenets of psychodynamic therapy apply, namely that what produces change is the development of a transference reaction (the evidence of pathological behavior, emotional response, or attribution of meaning), with concomitant resistances to both the development and consequences of the transference.

Three major components are intertwined in a successful interpretation: the emotional, the cognitive, and the timing components. By definition, interpretations help patients become aware of something they have been unaware of previously. This is most effective if there is an optimal emotional element involved. Interpretations can be too intellectual or they can be delivered in the midst of an emotional storm. There is little likelihood that interpretations at either end of this continuum will be effective. In a properly timed interpretation, the patient is given the opportunity to truly experience the affect. The here-and-now interaction of the group enables the therapist to make interpretations at points where they have considerable emotional relevance and impact.

The timing of interpretations is critical. It is possible that the interpretations can be offered a long time after the affect was most heated because the time lag has provided enough distance for the individual to integrate what is being examined. If there is too much affect, the interpretation cannot be integrated.

Unfortunately, there are many occasions when interpretations are offered solely (though unconsciously) to protect the therapist or the group members from the intensity of affect in a situation. In such cases the therapist prematurely offers "understanding" and thereby shuts down the affect.

Interpretations, by definition, examine unconscious conflicts and wishes, as well as the subsequent defensive responses or adaptational shifts. Optimally, interpretations should go even farther and include some speculation as to causality. This does not necessarily include a genetic reconstruction, but linkages with individuals' development are not excluded.

In groups the leader is confronted with a myriad of variables in attempting to frame an interpretation that will be most useful to the patients and the group. For example, should he focus his interpretation on specific individuals, the interactions between individuals, the interaction between specific individuals and the leader, subgroups of members and the leader, fantasies about the "outside world," or the group-as-a-whole? Each focus is an apt target for interpretation, and the art of being a group therapist is to know when to use which. As Foulkes elegantly states:

> We can focus on the group-as-a-whole or on any one individual or individuals in their specific interaction. As that happens in meaningful form, any point of view and the different meanings dovetail. It is not the case that one viewpoint is right and the other wrong. It is rather as if we took photographs from various positions. One picture may be better for certain purposes and others less good, but all of them show what is true from the position from which they were taken. However, the total process must always have been defined from the total field.[13]

The following are guidelines to help group therapists decide when, how, and where to make interpretations.

Group-as-a-Whole Interpretations. The followers of Bion have demonstrated that there are always group-as-a-whole processes at work in groups. To dismiss interpretations at that level is to overlook a source of great learning for our patients. An examination of the process provides insight for the members by helping them understand their involvement in and contribution to groupwide phenomena.

There are two types of group-as-a-whole interpretation: those focused on the group's reaction to the leader and those focused on the group itself.

Leader-directed interpretations. Beginning with the formulations of Freud, emphasis on transference to the therapist has been one of the cornerstones on which psychodynamic psychotherapy is based. Therapists are very important people to their groups by virtue of the powerful position they occupy. Group-as-a-whole therapists have always made good use of leader-directed transference interpretations. Indeed any therapist who assumes the role of the relatively silent, nonintrusive psychoanalyst encourages feelings to be directed toward himself by the very nature of that role. The task of interpretation is to bring these responses into the members' awareness. As important as they are, nonetheless, there are limitations to the effectiveness of focusing exclusively on leader-related transferences. Such an exclusive focus unnecessarily diminishes the multiplicity of peer transferences and relationships that are uniquely the province of group psychotherapy.

Group-directed interpretations. In addition to transferences to therapists, it is possible for individuals to have specific transferences to the idea of the whole group. Various patients experience the group itself as engulfing, destructive, warm, protective, or secure. H. Durkin[14] and Scheidlinger,[15] for example, suggested that on occasion the transference to the therapist (irrespective of gender) is paternal, while the transference to the group is maternal. Kernberg[16] expanded that notion, suggesting that patients with preoedipal pathology are particularly prone to develop whole group transferences. He maintains that whole group interpretations are important in helping such patients gain insight and understanding.

Whole-group phenomena are most evident at fairly predictable developmental points and during crises. Whenever a boundary is breached, as when a new member enters, the entire group responds. The precise reaction for each individual varies, of course, but the group has to integrate the newcomer. After all, as soon as a new member enters, it is from that point on a different group. It may be assumed that each individual member is coping with, or avoiding, the groupwide task of assimilating or rejecting the new member.

Groupwide phenomena are operating all the time. Affect-laden interactions stir responses in each member, who in turn respond in some way. Nothing happens that does not impact on the whole field. A member's prolonged silence may have as strong an impact as the revelation of a poignant or dramatic event. Such projective mechanisms are very common in group therapy, and a whole-group interpretation aids individuals in taking back their projections and learning about themselves.

Leader-directed and group-directed interpretations are too often viewed as competing, mutually exclusive foci. In fact they are very complementary. Group-directed interpretations tend to help individuals examine issues of universality and commonality and, from that involvement in a common cause, to learn of their uniquenesses. Leader-directed interpretations tend to focus upon individual differences and from that to a deeper understanding of the fact that beneath the differences is a similar yearning for love and affiliation in all people.

Incorrect or poorly delivered interpretations in any mode may be injurious. When group-as-a-whole therapists err, it tends to be in the direction of offering interpretations in an oracular, mystical fashion, fostering regression and dependency. On occasion the interpretations are offered mechanically; the statement "The group is . . ." homogenizes the members. Such interventions almost always result in narcissistic injuries to some members. The individual feels hurt, diminished, or just plain ignored. Malan et al.[17] have documented the clinical ineffectiveness of a therapist's exclusive adherence to interpretation of group-as-a-whole, leader-directed transferences.

Such extremes are no longer typical. It is quite possible to blend a group-as-a-whole focus, which underlines the importance of group process and transference to the leader, with more interpersonally based foci, which take into account more of the humanity of individual members. One successful solution is to make individual interpretations around a common group conflict, and then, when sufficient work has been done, to make a group-as-a-whole interpretation to demonstrate certain commonalities or a primary theme.

Individual Interpretation

Interpretations in group therapy are often made to individuals. Therapists should not lose sight of the fact that groups did not come for therapy. Rather, individuals came for help and we chose to offer those persons assistance in a group setting.

One strategy available to the therapist is to make an interpretation of individual behavior preparatory to making a whole group interpretation. There may be specific advantage to this approach because it provides members with an opportunity to examine for themselves where they might fit into a particular groupwide conflict.

A second strategy for making individual interpretation does not have reference to groupwide intervention. Such interventions are primarily aimed at helping the individual member gain self-understanding. Usually such individual interpretations are most successful when they elaborate specific individual reactions to, contributions to, and resonances with the group themes going on at the time. Thus, for example, the entry of a new member sets up a number of reactions within a group. The therapist may point out the groupwide response and then indicate each member's unique contribution to it.

Not all interactions are a primary product of group transactions. Some represent a specific pathological configuration that emerges in the group. One such example arises when one member dominates and controls meetings. The therapist then has the complex task of helping the other individuals understand their reactions and contributions to the process as well as assisting the monopolizer in understanding the sources of the monopolization.

Some patterned individual behavior becomes very apparent in the group. Interpretations of these behaviors are particularly powerful when they include specific reference to the process and emotional sequencing that occurred.

> Sally, a severely borderline woman, rarely spoke in her group. When she did, she usually gave a religiously oriented "speech" about the sins of the world. After many months, the therapist noticed that Sally varied her behavior in one repetitive manner. Whenever another woman missed a meeting, and especially when a woman terminated the group, Sally became much more agitated and yet much easier to understand. When the therapist accumulated sufficient evidence of this behavior, he pointed out the behavior while also offering an interpretation. He said, "Sally, it seems that whenever a woman is not in her usual seat in this room, you feel just as you did when your mother was hospitalized." The comment was offered in a spirit of mutual curiosity, not as a dictum presented from "on high." The members immediately confirmed that they too had noticed that Sally's behavior was notably different in those specific instances. This was a beginning point in helping Sally gain increased insight into the effects on her adult personality of her psychotic mother's having been permanently psychiatrically hospitalized when Sally was three years old.

The fact that many people are present adds an important dimension to interpretations directed toward any particular individual. On the positive side, as other persons hear interpretations directed toward a specific member, they gain a deeper understanding of that person they may subsequently apply in their dealings with him. Other members may also find specific interpretations relevant for themselves, even though the interpretation was directed to another. It is not uncommon for members to have an "ah ha!" experience while sitting back and observing interactions between the therapist and other members. Finally, their observation of various resistances to hearing interpretations is often useful in members understanding the various ways they themselves resist hearing new information.

There are also some drawbacks entailed in individuals overhearing interpretations directed toward others. The most obvious and difficult problem is the fact that some patients are ready to hear an in-depth interpretation before others. The therapist is thus confronted with a dilemma: whether or not to withhold information and understanding from a member who is ready to hear and use it in order to protect another patient who might be overwhelmed by the interpretation, even though the interpretation was not directed to that member. In such instances it is better to offer the interpretation. In cases where it is clear that another patient will find such an insight painful and alarming, the therapist can offer empathic understanding that this comment will likely be difficult for him to hear even though it is directed to another. For example, as a therapist prepared to interpret erotic transference from one female patient, he first said to a newer member with a history of brutal incestuous experiences with a stepfather, "I am aware that it may be difficult for you to hear what I am about to say to Joan, but it represents an opportunity for both of you to learn more about yourselves." A rule of thumb in such matters is to side with growth and not with pathology. Thus, to withhold the interpretation from the patient who is growing in order to protect the more fragile patient usually does no good for either patient.

What to interpret. Interpretation is an art and is not conducive to learning by rote. Often the therapist "feels" rather than "knows" what is the proper target of an interpretation, since at any meeting there are probably several options for offering insight. In the early days of psychodynamic group therapy, the mechanisms for change were viewed exclusively through transference and resistance, those mechanisms used in traditional analysis. As experience in the workings of groups has been gained, therapists have learned to also understand communications as data about inner states or levels of anxiety. It is the manner in which these communications are responded to by members that can serve as a reliable guide for making interpretations. An explication of the group process or individual responses that will enable patients to more fully understand what they are unconsciously or preconsciously communicating is usually the most successful interpretation. The therapist continues to help the patients see that various dysfunctional behaviors are in fact *solutions* to earlier, often unconscious or repressed problems.

An example of the process the therapist must go through in determining when and if to offer an interpretation is the following.

> *A relatively new group of recovering alcoholics was uncertain about how they might consider the emotional components of their drinking problems. One member began the meeting with a remark about feeling upset and anxious before going to church. Another continued, remembering that she had been upset by bad dreams and wondering whether she could do anything to stop them. Yet a third wondered if the second member was speaking about dreams or delirium tremens. And all this was followed by a discussion of the physical problems associated with alcoholism, most notably blackouts.*

The therapist was confronted with a dilemma. Should he offer an interpretation that would clarify the unconscious or preconscious communications in the group? He could, for instance, point out that the members seemed to have some anxiety about coming to the group (church), and that the anxiety seemed to relate to their concern about whether psychological or emotional (e.g., bad dreams) issues might be addressed. Indeed he could point out that in response to those topics the group shifted the focus to biology (bad dreams or DT's?), which led to a physiological state of no awareness (blackouts). By documenting the path of the group's associations, the therapist could offer an interpretation of the covert communication hidden beneath the overt content and thereby could help the group gain insight into what were the "real" concerns in the room. However, such interpretations require a state of therapeutic alliance and motivation. Interpretations offered prematurely serve only to stiffen the resistance and the commitment to not knowing.

In this immature group the therapist chose not to offer an interpretation of the defenses. He understood the dilemma as a questioning of his capacity as leader, as well as the group's ability to tolerate the affective components of their problems. The choice was made to provide a model for identification rather than an interpretation. Thus the therapist quietly turned to the patient who had been disturbed by her dreams and asked that she relate them to the group.

In this instance the therapist determined that the group would be best served by *demonstrating* that he and the group could tolerate emotions, rather than by interpreting the fears about that. Had there been greater group maturity, with demonstrated capacity to tolerate powerful affect and a history of strong therapeutic alliances, the therapist would have offered the interpretation. It likely would not have been an error to offer the interpretation even at this early date. This would have allowed the therapist the opportunity to test his hypothesis regarding the capacity of members by observing the groupwide response. The modeling response, however, represented a low-risk opportunity for the group to mature and be able to risk more vulnerability at a later date.

This example not only indicates the complexities of a therapist's decision about when and if to make an intervention, it also demonstrates the variety of useful responses available to the therapist. There is rarely one correct response. The therapist could instead have offered a model for identification by turning to the woman who was anxious before going to church and asking for more details about her anxiety. This would have served just as well as the revelation of the dream material. Or a partial interpretation could have been included—something like, "Perhaps people are wondering just how much feeling can be shared in here?"

The rationale for making one choice rather than another is aided by the therapist's capacity to predict the outcome of the interpretation. Interventions that lead to an elaboration of the material being discussed, associations to new ideas, or exploration of affects, are generally effective. Closing of the topic, repetitious descriptions of similar events, or constriction of affects are indicators of an unproductive therapist intervention. In the example, the therapist predicted that interpretation of unconscious material at this time would be met with resistance and instead chose to utilize the authority of his leadership to function as a model for identification. The primary goal at this time was to help set an important group norm: "Feelings can be expressed and explored in this group."

Recent advances in technique following the concepts of psychology of the self[18-21] have given new richness to our understanding of the functioning of interpretation. In this tradition interpretations are focused on the process of narcissistic injury. Group therapy provides fertile ground for narcissistic injuries. Members are continually feeling ignored, left out, insulted, or misunderstood. When interpretations by the therapist are directed to other individuals, or even to the group-as-a-whole, some members feel injured, as if they have received major blows to their self-esteem.

In groups many sequences are activated that result from natural, everyday varieties of narcissistic injury. Interpretations may be aimed at demonstrating to the member or the group the process of their interactions, pointing out the precise sequence as it emerged in the session. This is done so that the injured members can examine the sequence to learn more about their vulnerabilities and their responses to injury. For some individuals the interpretation can provide genuine insight and increased capacity to contain their feelings of hurt. With increased ability to maintain their balance they are more able to see others as separate people with needs and wishes of their own. The result is increased reality testing. Moreover, such an interpretation might help other members by making them aware of sadistic elements of their personalities that might have contributed to the injury received by the initial patient, just as they have injured other important relationships in their lives.

Peer interpretations. Most patients enter groups not knowing how to make interpretations. In this regard we do not refer to artificial attempts to understand other members as a defensive maneuver to fend off self-exploration. The mechanisms of imitation, identification, and internalization may be instrumental in helping members gain increased interpretative skills, as they observe and are influenced by the therapist and by more interpretative members. The ability to make interpretations may represent an expansion of self-awareness or may precede it.

Peer interpretations have unique power in groups, in that patients often have less resistance to learning about themselves from their peers than they do from authorities. For certain counterdependent patients, peer interpretations seem to be the *only* interpretations that are acceptable early in treatment. The fact that peer interpretations have special influence makes it important for leaders to be willing to suffer the narcissistic assault of waiting until someone else offers an insight that the therapist had known for some weeks. The therapist will not get credit for having helped, though he actively deferred offering the insight in the hope that a peer would provide it. Of such occasions, Foulkes said, "There are times when the therapist must sit on his wisdom, must tolerate defective knowledge and wait for the group to arrive at solutions."[22]

This is not to suggest that peer interpretations are routinely superior to leaders'. In fact, peer transferences within the group can considerably complicate the interpretations given and received. From a technical standpoint peer interpretations are often ill-timed, too superficial or deep, or just plain wrong. In sum peer interpretations are vulnerable to the same dangers as those of the therapist. Such mistakes on the part of patients, of course, are not tragic, because they become grist for the therapeutic mill, setting in motion new interactions and opportunities for learning.

Working Through

Working through is the final essential element in enabling patients to change. Confrontation, clarification, and interpretation help the patient to become aware of conscious and unconscious elements that create difficulties. Through these processes patients become familiar with the many facets of the central psychological patterns and become aware of the habitual resistances to seeing or integrating those problems. However, these elements alone are insufficient to bring about deep and lasting change. In working through, the emphasis is on increasing patients' capacity to examine themselves, to understand conflicts and areas of vulnerability, to interpret their own behavior, and to help develop more varied and flexible defensive systems that protect them from undue anxieties while allowing more authentic intimacy with others and access to their own emotions. Patterns of interaction and reaction become familiar, and patients can integrate new capacities to manage conflict and develop their own personal potentials.

The working through process consumes the major portion of time in psychodynamic psychotherapy. Pathological behavior, thoughts, feelings, and reactions appear, are worked on and understood, only to reappear in slightly different form. It often seems that in the process of working through we are essentially saying to our patients, "There it is again," "There it is again," "There it is yet one more time!" The repeated opportunities for patients to examine the many facets of their problems are a major contributor to change.

It is one of the therapist's creative tasks to examine the multiple facets of a problem and find a way of presenting them to the patient or the group that will not be boring or repetitious. Sometimes obvious repetitions cannot be seen or heard until they are presented with a slight variation in meaning or phraseology. This does not mean that the initial understanding was incorrect, but individuals pick up and respond to interpretations or confrontations in their own idiosyncratic ways. The therapist must try to reach the individual on his or her own level and not ask that the therapist's words or precise manner of phrasing represent the final word. As more data are added, new material is also uncovered that adds to the richness of understanding and further helps the individual gain self-knowledge.

Therapy groups offer special advantages, along with some potential shortcomings in facilitating the working through process. In this setting, the group itself is an arena in which patients demonstrate their pathologies in great richness and subtlety. The opportunity to expose and explore many variations on a common theme results from these multiple relationships. Further, members may use the group to try out new ways of coping or managing conflict and anxiety. Groups provide instant feedback on the success or failure of such new behaviors, at least in terms of their inter-personal consequences. Though therapy groups are not the same as real life, they are more generalizable experiences than dyadic therapy.

The historic cornerstone of working through has been the analysis of resistance. In contrast, implosive or activistic therapeutic techniques concern themselves exclusively with the affect behind the resistance. They have developed powerful techniques to defeat and overwhelm the defensive structure and the resistances of the patient, and they can quickly release the latent affects. In psychodynamic therapy this is not the goal. Rather, it is the study of the resistance, the elaboration of the defenses, that is the point of the inquiry. Whatever latent conflict or emotion is hidden away will come to the surface of its own accord when the defensive structure is understood, appreciated, and made more flexible and appropriate. It is the working through process that allows the patient to become accepting of his defensive structure, to become "friends" with it.

An example of working through as an analysis of resistance is the handling of acting out. Acting out has been a topic of much concern for therapists because the situation is rife with opportunities for patients to "do" rather than to "feel." This action could take place either in or out of the treatment setting. Psychodynamic group therapists, however, understand that such action is more than acting, it is also communication. Ackerman[23] has pointed out that acting out need not be an impeding factor. Rather, patients have the opportunity to act out or demonstrate their transference reactions by their relationships with other members. Acting out has too often been used as a pejorative term. In fact, acting out is used not only to avoid feelings or understanding, but also as a covert means of communicating about and gratifying the impulse in question.

Exploration of acting out behavior can be utilized as a vital element in helping patients understand the breadth and intensity of their feelings. For instance, Ruth had experienced early losses in her life and in the group talked extensively about loneliness and emptiness whenever a member would be absent or leave. As the transferences intensified, Ruth began to cope with her distress by establishing a liaison with another member outside the group meetings, a relationship that helped her experience continuity. She also began to miss sessions herself before and following any interruptions in weekly meetings. These actions were initially unconscious, then well rationalized. Gradually, Ruth came to understand these behaviors as attempts to manage the deeper, painful feelings surrounding separations. At that point she began to experience great pain and despair and then a period of growth.

In contrast to individual therapy, where much more time might be spent in examining and understanding the patient's transferences, current life, and history, the group situation provides a breadth of experiences in the here-and-now. Working through is characterized not merely by having the same old memories reworked and reworked, or the same problem examined over and over. Rather, group patients have ample opportunity to see and live out many manifestations of their current distortions and pathologies. Working through takes place as the patient connects in-group insights with real world experiences and historical data (see example of Sarah in Chapter 7).

Summary

In this chapter we have examined the elements that are essential in the process of helping patients change through psychotherapy. Fundamental to effective group psychotherapy is the conviction on the part of the members that focusing on the intragroup events represents a major opportunity to learn about themselves. The therapist's position is that of an expert, a separately functioning individual who observes the process and the individuals and uses that vantage point to reflect to individuals that which might not otherwise be apparent to them. He is also an object for the transference fantasies of the members. Within the safety of the group, bounded by the mutual contract and protected by the presence of the leader, members are free to interact spontaneously, express strong emotions, talk about aspects of their lives felt to be shameful or terrifying, and step back and observe the effects of such sharing. Gradually they come to understand that interpersonal relating often represents consequences of intrapsychic conflict.

Individual change takes place via the mechanisms of imitation, identification, and internalization. The multiple opportunities for relating and observing that groups offer facilitate these changes.

Through the processes of confrontation, clarification, interpretation, and working through, members gain insight and self-understanding. These processes lead to shifts in the intrapsychic structures and capacities to manage stress and anxiety. Groups offer unique opportunities for each of these mechanisms and processes to work with power and effectiveness.

References

1. John 8:32.
2. I. Yalom, *The Theory and Practice of Group Psychotherapy*, 2nd ed. (New York: Basic Books, 1975), pp. 3–103.
3. H. Kelman, "The Role of the Group in the Induction of Therapeutic Change," *Int. J. Group Psychother.* 13 (1963):399–451.
4. H.W. Loewald, "On Internalization," *Int. J. Psychoanal.* 54 (1973):9–17.
5. S. Freud, *Group Psychology and the Analysis of the Ego*, translated by J. Strachey (London: Hogarth Press, 1949).
6. R.R. Greenson, *The Technique and Practice of Psychoanalysis* (New York: International Universities Press, 1967).
7. S.H. Foulkes, "Group Processes and the Individual in the Therapeutic Group," *Br. J. Med. Psychol.* 34 (1961):23–31.
8. M. Pines, "The Frame of Reference of Group Psychotherapy," *Int. J. Group Psychother.* 31 (1981):275–285.
9. W.N. Stone and R.M. Whitman, "Observations on Empathy in Group Psychotherapy," in *Group and Family Therapy 1980*, edited by L.R. Wolberg and M.L. Aronson (New York: Brunner/Mazel, 1980), pp. 102–117.
10. J.F. Borriello, "Group Psychotherapy with Acting-Out Patients: Specific Problems and Techniques," *Am. J. Psychother.* 33 (1979):521–530.
11. L.R. Ormont, "Group Resistance and the Therapeutic Contract," *Int. J. Group Psychother.* 18 (1967):147–154.
12. Greenson, *Technique and Practice of Psychoanalysis*.
13. S.H. Foulkes, "The Group as the Matrix of the Individual's Mental Health," in *Group Therapy 1973*, edited by L.R. Wolberg and E.K. Schwartz (New York: Stratton Intercontinental Medical Book, 1973), pp. 211–220.
14. H.E. Durkin, *The Group in Depth* (New York: International Universities Press, 1964).
15. S. Scheidlinger, "On the Concept of the "Mother-Group," *Int. J. Group Psychother.* 24 (1974):417–428.
16. O.F. Kernberg, "A Systems Approach to Priority Setting of Interventions in Groups," *Int. J. Group Psychother.* 25 (1975):251–275.
17. D.H. Malan, F.H.G. Balfour, V.G. Hood, and A. Shooter, "Group Psychotherapy: A Long Term Follow-up Study," *Arch. Gen. Psychiatry* 33 (1976):1303–1315.
18. W.N. Stone and R.N. Whitman, "Contributions of the Psychology of the Self to Group Process and Group Therapy," *Int. J. Group Psychother.* 27 (1977):343–359.
19. Stone and Whitman, "Observations on Empathy in Group Psychotherapy."
20. H. Kohut, *The Analysis of Self* (New York: International Universities Press, 1971).

21. H. Kohut, *The Restoration of the Self* (New York: International Universities Press, 1977).
22. S.H. Foulkes and E.J. Anthony, *Group Psychotherapy: The Psychoanalytic Approach*, 2nd ed. (Baltimore: Penguin Books, 1965), p. 153.
23. N. Ackerman, "Psychoanalysis and Group Therapy," in *Group Therapy*, vol. 8, nos. 2–3, edited by J.C. Moreno (Boston: Beacon House, 1949), pp. 204–215.

Patient Selection

5

In planning an analytical group, the therapist needs criteria to determine which patients are best suited for treatment. Clear inclusion criteria can also be helpful in communicating with other therapists who might refer patients. Unfortunately there is a dearth of data to provide specific guidelines; thus the clinician has to fall back upon accumulated experience that has focused mainly on unsuitability for group psychotherapy rather than positive indicators.

In the pioneering period the one positive indicator for group therapy was relative poverty! Cost was a primary criterion in recommending group therapy. In today's economy cost is once again a factor in making group an attractive therapeutic alternative, though ironically the relatively low cost has contributed over the years to its image as second-rate therapy.

Also in the past many patient populations were seen as poor risks. Today categorical exclusion is a waning phenomenon. Most exclusionary recommendations in the literature can be countered by other published recommendations that such patients are treatable in groups. This is particularly true in the treatment of homosexuals[1,2] and is also increasingly apparent for persons with borderline and narcissistic character disorders.[3–5]

For therapists the dispositional question is less "Should group be considered for this patient?" and more "Are there mitigating factors *against* considering group therapy for this patient?"[6]

Poor Risk Patients

Certain exclusion criteria are valid in our experience and are also supported in the literature. The most frequently stated reason for exclusion is that the patient is in an acute crisis. This can be a developmental crisis (such as marriage, divorce, retirement), situational crisis (death of a loved one, physical illness), or a crisis of pathology (eruption of a psychotic process or extraordinary anxiety). These patients require a great deal of attention, and they do not have the time or interest required to meet and develop relationships with a number of strangers in a therapy group. By the same token the group has little reason to devote great amounts of time to the crisis of a stranger.

Other populations are routinely excluded from heterogeneous psychodynamic groups. These include individuals with insufficient impulse control (so that the physical safety of other members cannot be guaranteed), chronically psychotic patients, patients with organic brain syndromes, and sociopathic patients. Taken as a whole, these patients share a common trait. None can establish the minimal object relatedness that is required for a therapy group to work effectively. They are often the patients whom individual therapists find so difficult to treat that they refer them to groups.

Patients in those categories might be effectively treated in homogeneous groups. For example, Comstock and McDermott[7] found that homogeneous groups of individuals who have recently attempted suicide held the most hope of any treatment modality for helping these patients. Similarly, groups of sexual offenders or alcoholics, who are homogeneous as to symptom but quite different in underlying psychodynamic configurations, can be very effective in diminishing pathologic symptoms. It is not uncommon for these patients to require supplemental individual therapy to assist them in integrating the data generated in their groups.

Research into selection has focused on identifying high-risk patients, who tend to drop out prematurely. If such patients can be identified, then steps might be taken to protect them and the groups. The most cited study is that of Yalom,[8] who developed a list of nine categories that characterized early departers: (1) external factors, (2) group deviancy, (3) problems of intimacy, (4) fear of emotional contagion, (5) inability to share the doctor, (6) complications of concurrent individual and group therapy, (7) early provocateurs, (8) inadequate orientation to group therapy, (9) complications arising from subgrouping.

Reexamination of Yalom's data suggests an alternative way of categorizing his information. As Yalom suggests, the categories do not clearly separate individuals, which makes it difficult to utilize the various categories. Using the tripartite perspective of (1) intrapsychic defense mechanisms, (2) interpersonal relatedness, and (3) group-related factors allows for a reassessment of the material. For instance, a patient who is fearful of intimacy might present with externalization, denial, or somatization; the same patient, depending on the perspective of the observer, could be seen as deviant, an early provocateur, having fears of emotional contagion, or having difficulty sharing the doctor. Further, the individual characterological solutions of specific patients interact with group processes. Some groups, for example, can tolerate silent, withdrawn members for long periods, while others may welcome an individual who is provocative, outspoken, and occasionally acts out.

The data on dropouts should also be considered from the perspective of the treatment process, since dropouts generally occur in response to some interaction between the patient and other group members, the therapist, or emerging group norms.

The group contract (see Chapter 7) highlights certain additional exclusionary criteria. Patients who cannot realistically be expected to abide by their contract, owing to either pathology or life circumstances (as, for example, the professional athlete who cannot commit to a regular, weekly meeting because of his team's travel schedule) should not be included in group therapy.

Thus we can see that there are four subgroups in the poor risk category: (1) patients in crisis as a result of either an adult developmental stress or an outbreak of uncontrolled psychopathology; (2) a category of diverse patients who have significant difficulties with impulse control, usually due to organicity or sociopathy, and who might best be treated in homogeneous groups; (3) patients with characterological defenses of major magnitude that severely diminish interpersonal relatedness. These defenses become problematic when a conflict develops between these character styles and group norms. (4) Patients who are unable or unwilling to agree to the contract. Our caveat regarding these criteria is a recognition that we have not reached a stage of sophistication enabling us to predict a specific individual's success or failure in therapy. In particular, we opt for an optimistic appraisal regarding the usefulness of groups to even those patients with major difficulties in interpersonal relatedness, and we are likely to put them in our groups. The interaction between character style and group composition can either enable or frustrate these individuals' participation.

Patients for Whom Group is the Treatment of Choice

Review of the Literature. Stein[9] approached the problem of selection primarily from a psychodynamic perspective. He suggested that group treatment would be appropriate for patients who exhibited intense, sticky transferences in individual treatment; those with superego problems, particularly patients with overly strict superegos; patients with obsessive-compulsive features and guilt; and those who need ego support and reality testing through identification with others. As a corollary to the problem of intense transference, Stein noted that other members served as displacement objects, enabling an individual to work on problems without the disruptive intensity of an individual transference. Examined twenty years later, Stein's criteria are suggestive of patients diagnosed as having preoedipal psychopathology. Perhaps this schema served to direct the therapist to a position of understanding rather than categorizing, thus enabling the clinician to include more comfortably these patients into group treatment.

Guttmacher and Birk[10] expanded Stein's list emphasizing the therapeutic advantages of the here-and-now axis of group therapy. This axis can be used as a selection criterion by focusing on those patients who can learn from confrontation. Patients who fulfill this criterion do not view themselves as responsible for the conflicts they experience. Their pathology is ego-syntonic. Groups offer repeated opportunity for such patients to hear from members the effect of their behaviors upon others. Further, groups allow them gradually to make their pathology ego-dystonic and thus more amenable to change. The increased interaction and the development of multiple transferences is not necessarily equivalent to the dilution and diminution of transference reactions.[11] Guttmacher and Birk, for instance, emphasize that the frustration evoked by having to share the therapist can expose intense and important envious and rivalrous conflicts.

Kadis et al.[12] proposed a slightly different schema for selecting patients, also on the basis of dynamic considerations. They suggested that patients be assessed across four dimensions: (1) ability to tolerate anxiety, including the potential for disruptive anxiety upon entering a group; (2) identification and empathy with others, including the background and similarity of experiences that would allow them to sit with others; (3) ego strength, including vulnerability to interpersonal stress and the potential to tolerate attacks, criticism, or closeness; (4) interlocking of patients' defense systems. The initial three criteria are designed to predict the kinds of responses a patient might exhibit upon entering treatment. The fourth dimension is specifically a group-related criterion that is used to predict whether the patients' characteristic defenses will meld or clash with those of other members.

Zimmerman[13] also considered group-related dimensions in the selection process. He emphasized the prospective patient's ability to maintain a sense of self in the face of group processes that might be experienced as sucking the patient into an undifferentiated mass. Patients who might be vulnerable to that pull are described as adhering inflexibly to social, professional, political, or moral positions. They might present themselves as arrogant, pedantic, and extremely prideful. These characteristics are reminiscent of the deviant whom Yalom[14] pinpointed as a possible early group dropout. In pregroup interviews, Zimmerman evaluated an applicant's ability to change role, for example to move from listener to speaker to empathizer, and so on. He raised questions about the patient's ability to maintain confidentiality and secrets, and he suggested that persons in politically or socially prominent roles, or their relatives, not be included.*

---

*Cultural differences could account for this suggestion, since Zimmerman reported on work conducted in Brazil. Grotjahn,[15] in a contrary opinion, described successful integration of famous people into his groups.

In contrast to the dynamic classifications are the behavioral/phenomenological approaches. Patients considered for groups are those having problems with intimacy or leading lonely, isolated, dreary lives. They are described as avoiding social situations or having a paucity of intimate personal relationships. Conversely, some patients might be overdependent or overdemanding and group therapy would be recommended in order to dilute these behaviors.[16] Classifications such as these tend to emphasize problems in effective interpersonal functioning at both ends of a continuum.[17] At one end are the withdrawn, socially inept, uninvolved individuals while at the other end are the demanding, self-centered, and controlling persons. Groups are expected to act as equalizers by activating the withdrawn and by socializing the more narcissistic, self-centered, or acting out individuals.

Recommendations regarding the inclusion of patients with somatic complaints seem to follow the trends we have already noted. Some believe these are precisely the patients who can learn about themselves and their inner world. Others believe somatization is a poor prognostic sign since such patients will not have the psychological mindedness necessary to utilize psychoanalytic group psychotherapy most effectively.

Group as Treatment of Choice. At this juncture of history, accumulated experience indicates that almost all patients are potential candidates for group psychotherapy. The pathologies of the modern era are primarily difficulties in gaining and tolerating authentic intimacy. The majority of our patients come with complaints about the lack of fulfillment in their lives (see Chapter 1). Rutan and Alonso[18] have stated, "Group therapy, by its very format, offers unique opportunities to experience and work on issues of intimacy and individuation. In . . . groups, the community is represented in the treatment room. It is usually impossible for individuals to view themselves as existing alone and affecting no one when in a group therapy situation over any significant period of time."

Group therapy would seem to be a natural antidote to the predominant disorder of our age. Since groups focus on individuals as relational beings and rely on relationships for growth, learning, and change, this treatment offers a response to modern mankind's fragmented ability to relate. Groups offer the hope of relatedness in the context of appropriate limits, an opportunity to gain autonomy through intimacy, not at the expense of intimacy.

Thus, if group therapy is a treatment of choice for our modern dilemmas, we will be concerned primarily with exclusionary rather than inclusionary criteria. The two major exclusionary criteria are patients who refuse to enter a group, and those for whom group is not the treatment of choice. The first instance, while seemingly obvious, requires emphasis. No patient should be forced, overtly or covertly, to join a group. If a patient does not willingly join, no matter how convinced the therapist is that group is the treatment of choice, that patient is a poor candidate. Frequently such patients will join at a later date.

The final success or failure of therapy will depend upon the complex interaction among members, therapist, and the process. There can be little doubt that different therapists have varying levels of comfort with different patients and pathologies. Therefore the therapist's affective reaction certainly affects the group's capacity to help particular patients. Some therapists, for example, are uncomfortable with homosexual or alcoholic patients. These patients ought to be excluded from the groups of *those* particular therapists. Much of the material about who can and cannot be seen probably has been influenced by personal bias and countertransference.

Special Considerations in Diagnosing and Evaluating Patients

It is our contention that group therapy should be considered as a viable option for most patients seeking treatment. Very often just raising the prospect of joining a group evokes a powerful reaction. To the degree that these reactions to the idea are relevant to their presenting problems, a group might well be a primary treatment modality. When patients see the connection between their presenting concerns and their interpersonal relations, they often willingly enter groups.

A great many patients who are potential group candidates spend a considerable amount of consultative time preoccupied with interpersonal difficulties. For instance, they may complain about their spouse, boss, children, or friends, in a seemingly endless litany. However, no change takes place and troubles persist. Before group therapy can be effective, it is often necessary to help these patients begin to accept some of their responsibility in the interpersonal difficulties that beset them. So long as they project all problems onto others in their lives, they remain uninsightful and resistant to change. When this ego-syntonic behavior is not quite so ingrained, groups can help such patients begin to see their contributions to the interpersonal impasses.

In all diagnostic evaluations, it is important to listen for and focus on a patient's interpersonal transactions. When it seems clear that this arena is central to the presenting concern of the patient, then group therapy should be actively considered as the primary treatment.

In cases where the patient becomes *too* involved with the therapist, the transference becomes unmanageably powerful. These patients used to be termed "overly dependent," but more modern formulations emphasize some patients' need for an idealizing transference in order to recommence an interrupted developmental process.[19,20,21] By virtue of the presence of the others, groups provide a helpful distance from the therapist for such patients. In many cases this allows them to examine more objectively feelings about the therapist and to compare and contrast their responses with those of others. An exception to this is the patient for whom jealousy and possessiveness are so strong that the presence of other people in the therapeutic arena is simply overwhelming.

Several examples will illustrate the process of evaluation and selection for referral for group therapy.

> *Sister Annette was a thirty-three-year-old nun who sought psychotherapy for her heightened anxiety. She felt her anxiety was rooted in her flagging dedication to the Church and to her religious beliefs. However, she could not gain any precision in describing what doubts she was having about her faith. As was the custom of the evaluating therapist, the prospect of group therapy was mentioned. Sister Annette immediately became very anxious and stated that she could "never be in a therapy group." When the therapist inquired why, she said, "There would be all those men there talking about sex. It would be no place for a nun." Using the projected data gained from her guesses about what a group would be like, Sister Annette was soon able to see that her anxiety was actually stemming from heightened sexual feelings and corresponding guilt about them. In light of this she decided to enter a therapy group to see what she could find out about her sexuality in the safety of a therapeutic setting. In the course of several years of group therapy this patient was able to own, explore, and become comfortable with her sexuality. Eventually she decided to retain her vows of chastity and to remain in the convent, and she was able to continue her career without the anxiety that had brought her to treatment.*

This case illustrates how the mere mention of a therapy group can evoke powerful and important affects that can assist in the diagnostic and dispositional questions. When the specific affect aroused is closely connected to the presenting complaint, then group could be seriously considered. Even if not, sometimes the feelings stimulated are of sufficient importance that patient and therapist agree that group could be very helpful.

> *Bill was a young man who seemed psychologically minded. He complained that he was a twenty-eight-year-old virgin in a social milieu in which dating leading to intercourse was the norm. Bill felt blocked in his understanding of why he could not date successfully. Individual therapy was fascinating and rewarding for the therapist, since Bill vividly described his inner world in a creative and captivating manner. The external focus was on Bill's continuing conflict with bosses at work. There was an absence of discussion of peer relationships and no mention of dating. When the therapist initially suggested that group therapy be added to*

> *Bill's individual treatment, Bill engagingly described that the suggestion had evoked feelings as powerful as an avalanche in his mind. The anxiety that he experienced was so intense that he declined the suggestion. Nevertheless, no change in his life was occurring, and several months later the therapist again suggested group treatment, explaining that Bill rarely spoke about troubles with dating and his social life, despite these being his initial reasons for seeking treatment. Again Bill refused, but with less anxiety and vehemence. Six months later, Bill himself raised the question of his entering a group, saying he felt his individual therapy was at an impasse. In the course of his group treatment Bill was able to examine his anxiety about sexuality, his competitiveness with men, and his seductiveness with women. After joining a group, Bill made important personal gains.*

This example indicates how group can be added to individual therapy to assist the patient. Bill shifted from interpersonal to authority problems in the individual treatment, subsequently getting stuck in a transference impasse that seemed to preclude examination of the presenting peer and social problems. The referral to a group loosened that therapy impasse. It should also be noted that the referral did not occur quickly and that the therapist's willingness to raise the issue, offer the suggestion, and accept Bill's refusal was ultimately rewarded when Bill himself was able to initiate the referral.

> *Carl was referred as a candidate for a group because of his anxiety and depression over his wife's threatening separation and divorce. Carl, though a very successful executive businessman, had almost no awareness of his inner world. Indeed his history was so bereft of any close relationships that it was remarkable that he had managed to marry. Group had been suggested to him by a previous therapist because of the barrenness of his interpersonal world. However, the evaluating therapist did not accept Carl into a therapy group. Rather, it was determined that Carl was not well suited on at least two counts. First, he was in immediate crisis. He was reeling from the prospect of losing his only viable relationship, and he was quite desperate. He would not find it easy to put that desperation aside long enough to meet, trust, and negotiate some relationship with a series of strangers in a therapy group. Second, Carl's interpersonal skills appeared so impoverished that it was likely he would be overwhelmed by a group, not assisted by it. Carl was referred again for individual psychotherapy where he began to gain insight into how disconnected from his feelings he had been, and how that meant that he was dramatically short-changing his wife in their marriage.*

This example highlights a case where the screening therapist decided group therapy was not the treatment of choice. The patient in this case quite willingly accepted the referral, but the group therapist, evaluating the patient's crisis around the divorce, recommended a period of individual therapy before exposing him to the more stimulating interactions in a therapy group.

Duane was referred for severe headaches that had forced him to take a leave of absence from work. He had consulted numerous physicians in an attempt to find a definitive diagnosis, all to no avail. Two psychiatrists were consulted, but both were unsuccessful in engaging Duane in self-exploration. The third psychiatrist he found was able to initiate a usable alliance, and Duane was able to begin looking into interpersonal stresses in his life. History revealed that just prior to the onset of his headaches, Duane had learned that his supervisor would be changing jobs and that Duane was in line for a promotion. To Duane a promotion meant giving up his old relationships and joining the ranks of management. Even more important, during that same time period, Duane's wife had taken a full-time job outside the home and was no longer devoting herself exclusively to the housework and care for their twelve-year-old son. Duane recognized that these were both important events, but he could see no connection between these events and his headaches. Despite repeated suggestions for group therapy, Duane maintained his conviction that his was a biological problem, and he was referred to a pain clinic.

This example is cited to indicate the importance of negotiation in referring a patient to group. If any modality of psychotherapy is to work, it is almost mandatory that the patient have some understanding of, and agreement with, the reasons for selecting the modality chosen. Duane could never accept the rationale for group therapy, and thus he was not referred to a group.

These four brief vignettes illustrate some of the more common problems for which patients are referred to group therapy along with some examples of initial resistances, contraindications, and steadfast refusal to accept group as a treatment modality.

Summary

In this chapter we have examined guidelines for the evaluation and selection of applicants for group psychotherapy. Historically, economic considerations had been paramount in selecting patients for groups. In more recent times a great deal of attention has been devoted to exclusion criteria but much less to inclusion criteria. Diagnostic classification systems that could assist in inclusion criteria were reviewed. These systems utilize both intrapsychic formulations and interpersonal behavioral criteria. No single current system fully accounts for the complex situation of an individual with strengths and weaknesses who is entering into a particular group with its own particular values, norms, history, and interacting individuals.

Once individuals have been selected as suitable for treatment in group therapy, three tasks remain for the therapist. One is to determine which group will be best for the patient, and which patient will be best for which group. Those issues of group composition will be explored in the next chapter. The second task is to prepare the patient for entrance into a therapy group, and the third task is to negotiate the group contract with the patient. The last two tasks will be explored in Chapter 7.

References

1. A. Stein, "Indications for Group Psychotherapy and the Selection of Patients," *J. Hillside Hosp.* 12 (1963):145–155.
2. W.N. Stone, J.S. Schengber, and F.S. Seifried, "The Treatment of a Homosexual Woman in a Mixed Group," *Int. J. Group Psychother.* 16 (1966):425–433.
3. N. Wong, "Clinical Considerations in Group Treatment of Narcissistic Disorders," *Int. J. Group Psychother.* 29 (1979):325–345.
4. B.E. Roth, "Problems of Early Maintenance and Entry into Group Psychotherapy with Persons Suffering from Borderline and Narcissistic States," *Group* 3 (1979):3–22.
5. W.N. Stone and R.M. Whitman, "Contributions of the Psychology of the Self to Group Process and Group Therapy," *Int. J. Group Psychother.* 27 (1977):343–359.
6. J.S. Rutan and A. Alonso, "Group Psychotherapy," ch. 45 in *Outpatient Psychiatry: Diagnosis and Treatment,* edited by A. Lazare (Baltimore: Williams and Wilkins, 1979), p. 612.
7. B.S. Comstock and M. McDermott, "Group Therapy for Patients Who Attempt Suicide," *Int. J. Group Psychother.* 25 (1975):44–49.
8. I.D. Yalom, "A Study of Group Therapy Dropouts," *Arch. Gen. Psychiatry* 14 (1966):393–414.
9. Stein, "Indications for Group Psychotherapy."
10. J.A. Guttmacher and L. Birk, "Group Therapy: What Specific Therapeutic Advantages," *Comprehensive Psychiatry* 12 (1971):546–556.
11. S. Ethan, "The Question of the Dilution of Transference in Group Psychotherapy," *Psychoanal. Rev.* 65 (1978):569–578.
12. A.L. Kadis, J.D. Krasner, C. Winick, and S.H. Foulkes, *A Practicum of Group Psychotherapy* (New York: Harper & Row, 1963).
13. D. Zimmerman, "Indications and Counterindications for Analytic Group Psychotherapy—A Study of Group Factors," in *Group Therapy 1976: An Overview,* edited by M.L. Aronson, A.R. Wolberg, and L.R. Wolberg (New York: Stratton Intercontinental Medical Book, 1976).
14. Yalom, "A Study of Group Therapy Dropouts."
15. M. Grotjahn, "The Treatment of the Famous and the 'Beautiful People' in Groups," in *Group Therapy 1975: An Overview,* edited by L.R. Wolberg and M.L. Aronson (New York: Stratton Intercontinental Medical Book, 1975).
16. M. Neumann and B. Geoni, "Types of Patients Especially Suitable for Analytically Oriented Group Psychotherapy: Some Clinical Examples," *Isr. Ann. Psychiatry Related Disciplines* 12 (1974):203–215.
17. H. Grunebaum and W. Kates, "Whom to Refer for Group Psychotherapy," *Am. J. Psychiatry* 132 (1977):130–133.
18. Rutan and Alonso, "Group Psychotherapy."

19. Stone and Whitman, "Contributions of the Psychology of the Self to Group Process and Group Therapy."
20. H. Kohut, *The Analysis of the Self* (New York: International Universities Press, 1971).
21. H. Kohut, *The Restoration of the Self* (New York: International Universities Press, 1977).

Issues of Group Composition

6

Successful psychotherapy groups require careful planning. The task is not simply to gather up six to ten individuals together, set a time, and commence. Rather, the enterprise requires a substantial foundation. In this chapter we will examine the issues of group composition. The first step is to ascertain whether or not there is a need in the community for a therapy group and whether it can be supported by patient referrals. When that has been determined, then the therapist can turn his attention to how to form the group most effectively.

Patient Availability

All too often new groups are formed in response to the enthusiasm of the therapist without regard to the realities of patient availability. It is a very disheartening experience to have a new group with only two or three members and no referrals in sight. Thus at the outset it is necessary to assess whether or not there is a reasonable expectation that a flow of patients will be available. To ask, "Are there sufficient patients available now to begin a group?" is not enough. The further question is "Will there be sufficient referrals in the future to guarantee successful continuation?"

Even if it is determined that a group is *needed*, that does not ensure its success. It is important to make certain that the referring community will support the enterprise. If group treatment is a new modality or is not actively supported in a particular setting, important preliminary steps have to be taken to create a favorable atmosphere.

Historically, group psychotherapy, as compared with individual psychotherapy, has been perceived as second class. Such devaluation highlights the first task of the clinician—to educate his colleagues about the efficacy of group therapy. Similarly, if the social milieu emphasizes behavioral or pharmacological treatment approaches and is not attuned to psychodynamic/analytic modalities, the possibility of obtaining referrals will be limited unless the therapist demonstrates the potential of group therapy to help patients.

Clinic Settings

In a clinic the therapist needs to understand and relate to the administrative and authority structures,[1] and the institution must be prepared to support a group program. Such preparation includes consultation with those in power positions as well as colleagues and associates who may directly influence the availability of patients. Discussions should allow for expressions of both positive and negative responses. It is important to develop sensitivity to the administrative problems posed by therapy groups, such as the need for larger interviewing and waiting rooms, and greater soundproofing and clerical support. Subtle administrative resistance may emerge if these details are not openly discussed.

Clinics in which groups do not enjoy a readymade acceptance will also benefit from an educational program for the staff. The program may be didactic presentations at staff meetings. It is preferable, however, if the therapist can have a small number of staff members actually observe a newly formed group in operation for a number of weeks. With patients' consent it is possible to have observers without adversely affecting the treatment. If there are to be observers, consent should be included in the initial patient contract. The observers could be introduced as members of the clinic staff who wish to learn more about group therapy. Such direct involvement typically engages staff in an immediate and active interest in the program. If that is not practical, the therapist should speak often with the referring therapists so that everyone continues to feel involved with the workings of the group.

It is particularly important to ensure that persons with the power of referral support the program since the flow of patients has an enormous impact upon the formation of groups.[2] The classic study by Yalom[3] on dropouts is a striking testimonial. At the outpatient clinic of Stanford University, Yalom was able to start nine new groups within a period of eight weeks simply by administratively closing off the option of individual treatment and routing all new patients to group psychotherapy. The fact that nine groups could be started in such a short time is ample evidence of the effectiveness of administrative clout.

Availability of patients also can be influenced by broad social factors. For instance, the shift in public policy sharply reducing the number of long-term patients hospitalized in state facilities has led to large numbers of patients being referred into the community for continuing care. Clinic administrators often see group psychotherapy as a solution to the increasing press of patients upon limited clinic resources. The pressures may then interfere with the therapist's ability to properly screen and select patients.

Private Practice

The private sector is not insulated from psychosocial forces nor from the need to educate and support a referral network. Group therapists quickly find that they need to develop a sizable network of referral sources. Some communities do not value group therapy as much as others, and in those communities the flow of patients is negligible unless the therapist is willing to actively promote his group. In such a situation the therapist may occasionally feel pressured to select unsuitable or inappropriate patients in order to sustain his slim referral network or even to keep his group alive.

The opposite situation is equally problematic. An established group therapist may be inundated with referrals and not have places in a group. Too frequent rejection of potential members tends to stem the flow of referrals. Keeping the spigot flowing is a problem. A therapist can often keep his network intact by locating an opening in some other group as a service to both the patients and professionals who make referrals. The therapist who provides an ombudsman function keeps his referral network flourishing.

Other Factors

Therapists considering beginning a group can obtain patients from their own or other therapists' individual case loads. The referral process involves either giving up or sharing a patient, and potent emotional issues are stimulated in both circumstances. Ironically the therapist sometimes has difficulty shifting patients within his own practice from individual to group treatment, whether or not he plans to continue the individual sessions. Exploration of this difficulty will most likely expose countertransference problems. A therapist beginning a group should review his own individual cases. If he is reluctant to refer a number of individuals for similar or identical reasons, a countertransference reaction may well underlie the decisions. Consultation or discussion with co-workers can help resolve these countertransference problems. Occasionally the result is increased patient flow, as the therapist comes to recognize and alter subtle communications to colleagues that interfered with their making referrals.

There are significant emotional considerations when a therapist refers a patient to a therapy group and stops seeing the patient individually. Hidden emotional responses on the clinician's part may become manifest in the handling of the termination of the individual therapy or in subtle undercutting of the value of the group treatment even while making the referral. Emergence of competitive themes in the termination phase suggests that the individual therapy is being pitted against group treatment. This may arise from the patient, but it may also be a countertransference of the therapist. The group therapist can be of considerable value to the referring clinician in anticipating the dynamics of the individual termination process and the transfer to a group. In most instances frank discussion of the termination and how future individual contact should be handled will aid in smoothing this sensitive phase of treatment.

For a great many patients termination of the individual sessions is not indicated, and a combination of group and individual therapy is the most useful treatment format. This combination is explored in depth in Chapter 11.

There are instances when therapists should *not* accept a patient referred from an individual therapist. Often, for example, there are overlooked countertransferential reasons for the referral. One frequent countertransference reason entails the individual therapist referring a patient to group in order to avoid unrecognized *warm* and *loving* feelings that exist in the dyadic relationship. Since many patients are referred to group principally because they have difficulty in establishing or maintaining tender relationships, a referral under these conditions represents an unconscious collusion by individual therapist and patient to avoid the intensity of their affects.

Another manifestation of countertransference is dumping unattractive patients into groups. Many times when an individual therapist finds it impossible to treat a patient, he concludes "This patient needs a group" when what he really means is, "Perhaps other patients can say directly to this patient what I, as a professional caretaker, don't feel I have a right to say!" Ironically the patient who cannot even establish a viable relationship in dyadic therapy is typically *not* a very good candidate for a group. Further, such patients sense that they are being dumped. It is an experience in life about which they have some expertise. When the referral is an attempt to avoid dealing with unpleasant sides of the individual therapy, the patient often retaliates by quitting the group prematurely.

The reason for considering some of the less complimentary reasons for group referrals is that these reasons are very often unconscious or not discussed, and knowledge of these problems will help both the individual and the group therapist in the ongoing treatment of patients.

Once patient flow has been established, the therapist next faces the problem of how to decide which patients are best seen in which group, and conversely, which patients are best for which groups.

Therapy Group Composition

The composition of a group may be viewed from two perspectives. The referring therapist wants to determine whether there is a group best suited for his patient. The group therapist has to determine which patient is best suited for a particular group. In this chapter we will look at the issues of group composition from both perspectives.

Which Group Is Best for the Patient?

A few authors (e.g., Bach[4]) suggest that it is not helpful to place patients in groups according to some notion of what groups are best for which patients. According to this point of view, groups should model life, and therefore patients should be referred solely according to who comes along next. While the pragmatics of private practice sometimes make this more the rule than the exception, such a practice is nonetheless far from optimal. One of the fundamental screening tasks is to make a determination about the best fit for patient and group. Questions such as "Should the patient be in a group with a male or a female leader or with co-leaders?" are important considerations. Often, if a patient is currently in ongoing individual psychotherapy, it is helpful if the group therapist is of the opposite sex from the individual therapist.

A more frequent consideration is the assessment of the level of functioning of the group or characteristics of specific members. Prior to adding a new member, the therapist should review the group's predominant themes. Some groups struggle with fundamental issues of trust for years, while others characteristically struggle with anger, and still others might be concerned with intimacy, individuation, or competitiveness. The presence of a patient working at a different level may even catalyze particularly painful but important sectors of pathological functioning that could otherwise go unexplored, but the therapist should not count on this happening.

The screening therapist should always judge whether potential new members for a given group are similar enough to the others so that they can connect with one another and yet different enough so that they can help one another gain perspective on the problems that they struggle with. The following are suggested ways to assess the compatibility of specific groups for specific patients.

Preliminary Formulations. By attending to the presenting problems and listening to the interpersonal history, it is usually possible to generate several viable hypotheses as to the origins of the problems. These data can be discussed with the patient as a part of the negotiation about choice of treatment modality; the formulations will be useful to the therapist in predicting the patient's probable course in the group. For example, many patients unknowingly are unable to form relationships because they suffer from insufficiently mourned losses. It can be hypothesized that in the life of the group someone important to the patient will terminate and that this will offer the patient an opportunity to relive loss experiences.

In many cases the major source of data about the interpersonal life of a patient is the dyadic relationship. If therapists will pay special heed to their affective responses, they will gain access to a veritable gold mine of information. For example, if the therapist is bored, easily distracted, feeling "alone" in the office or desirous of the clock speeding up, the chances are that he is sitting with a schizoid, obsessional, or primitive narcissistic patient (excluding the obvious alternative that the therapist is struggling with personal issues of his own that are not evoked by the patient at all). Alternatively, a borderline patient is almost never boring—frightening, stimulating, enraging, entertaining, demanding—but rarely boring. In the former instance the individual therapy can flounder on the rock-hard defenses of intellectualization or isolation of affect, and in the latter instance the therapist may be held at a distance by the aggressive, hyperactive self-presentation. For many of these patients, eventual exposure of the underlying conflicts reveals that noninvolvement is a defense against perceived terrors and dangers of intimacy. A very important component of this is the fear of nonresponse by an unempathic significant person.[5]

Hypotheses About Patient Roles and Reactions. Using the data from the pregroup evaluation, the therapist can make inferences about how the patient may respond to various stimuli in the group. By generating such hypotheses and observing the subsequent behaviors and feelings of the patient, formulations can be either validated or disproved. If major revisions are necessary, this may be the result of new information or faulty empathic connection between therapist and patient. At the same time the therapist can gain a historical vantage point that may be utilized in helping the patient understand the connections between in-group responses and those from the past.[6] For example:

> Elaine came to group to work on her terror of intimacy with men. Successful individual therapy had given her much insight into the roots of her difficulties, but she wanted to join a group in order to gain actual opportunities to meet and relate to men at an intense level. She knew from her individual therapy that the women in her family were flawed, her mother being psychotic and usually mute, and her sister being retarded. Elaine, though raised by a loving aunt, nonetheless had an image

of herself as defective and inadequate. The therapist, after having interviewed Elaine and negotiated the group therapy contract, decided to place her in a particular group because he hypothesized that a woman in that group, Francine, would stir very important, though painful, feelings for Elaine. Francine was a seriously depressed and very silent member, often not speaking for months in the group. Within two or three weeks, Elaine stated that she was leaving because she found it was not helping, and because she was getting more anxious. She stated that she was having difficulty sleeping the night before the group. In this case the therapist, having made a preliminary hypothesis, simply said, "A family with women who are silent when you need them to be helpful is a familiar problem, Elaine." Despite the fact that Elaine had never mentioned Francine, she instantly began weeping and yelling at Francine for being so "hostile." In the ensuing weeks both Francine and Elaine worked very productively on the meaning of their interactions. This represents an example of a therapist carefully selecting a group for a patient based upon hypotheses about how the specific group might be of assistance.

Assessing Individuals for Specific Groups. In assessing an individual's "fit" for a particular group, several areas should be explored.

First, the patient's ability to experience and reflect upon his or her interactions as an indicator of ego capacity must be considered. Some patients become emotionally enmeshed in the group interactions and have very limited ability to utilize their observing ego on the affect stirred in the therapy. Other patients are so intellectualized in their defensive structure that they never allow themselves to spontaneously "be" in a group. The goal for the first subgroup of patients is to help them develop the ability to move ̂   experience to observation and intellectual understanding. ̲ ̲ ̲ goal for the second group is to experience the impact of the interactions before using their intellect. The therapist should be wary of having too many patients representing either end of that continuum simultaneously in the same group.

A second consideration is the patient's ability to take on a variety of roles. Traditionally the roles of leader and follower are explored. The leader role is linked to an individual's relationship to authority and developmental experiences with parents. The follower role is linked to peer relationships in which collaboration, cooperation, and intimacy are associated and can be traced to early sibling or educational experiences. In addition, a series of other significant roles may be productively explored in the pregroup interviews. Benne and Sheats[7] distinguish among roles that will facilitate group progress and problem-solving capacity, maintain or build the way the group is working together, or satisfy individual needs. The applicant's capacity to work effectively or ineffectively within organizations and social settings will provide clues as to potential group roles.

Thus, we can find individuals who have proclivities toward being harmonizers, compromisers, standard setters, opinion givers, and moralizers.

A third consideration is the patient's capacity to acknowledge his need for others. We believe that *everyone,* irrespective of pathology, wants to love and be loved. One accurate means of diagnosing individuals may well be to assess how much they try to pretend that reality is not so.

The emphasis on experiential training groups in the 1960s highlighted an additional criterion particularly relevant to group therapy: the ability to give and receive feedback appropriately. These twin abilities are a central part of the experience in a therapy group. Ormont[8] places the task of giving feedback in a traditional psychodynamic frame. He succinctly stated that patients may express how they feel but may not attack others. His emphasis was on educating members for an appropriate interpersonal role, although he realizes that the ineffectual interpersonal behavior is part of the problem for which a patient seeks help. By highlighting this ground rule Ormont sets the stage for analyzing the difficulty of remaining in role. Equally important is the patient's ability to listen in an open fashion, without defending or justifying a feeling or position, but being able to consider what has been said. Again, such behaviors are not typically part of the repertoire of most group patients. The very nature of groups provides patients an opportunity to experience these roles. One of the very positive growth-producing experiences in group therapy is for a patient to genuinely feel helpful to others or to have the capacity to listen nondefensively to other people.

A fifth consideration in assessing a prospective patient's "fit" is the patient's empathic capacity, which is a corollary of the individual's capacity to shift roles.[9,10] The ability to empathize—that is, to temporarily put oneself emotionally in the shoes of another—implies that the individual has been able to reach a stage of development where others are experienced as separate, with needs and wishes of their own. Some prospective members only possess rudimentary empathic capacity, and their inclusion into group treatment mandates that this missing function be filled by others, a task that most frequently falls to the therapist. Empathic capacity extends beyond the interpersonal relationships and includes the group situation. Empathy with the group is translated into the requirement of maintaining confidentiality. Some individuals are either too gossipy or need to utilize group information as a base for power or to gain attention and thus cannot adequately respect the tenet of confidentiality. For such patients it is not a question of which group is best. No group is suitable, since their inclusion unduly risks harm to the other patients.

A criterion of a different sort is that the applicant have no preexisting relationships with members that would inhibit the work of the group.

It is important during the screening to learn enough about the patient's life and activities to be reasonably certain that a stranger is being introduced into the group. Exploration of work or recreational activities may expose a situation where a prospective member has continuing and significant contact with someone already in the group. Usually awareness of the patient's home address and place of work alerts the therapist to the possibility. If a reason to believe that preexisting relationships exists, then considerable tact is required to elicit sufficient data on which to base a decision to accept or not to accept such an applicant. It is clear that certain relationships are of sufficient importance as to limit the freedom to share. This is especially true in work-related situations, where, for example, one member might have administrative responsibility over another member or where a minister might find himself in a group with a parishioner. Many variations of this problem exist, especially in smaller communities, and it is part of the therapist's responsibility to take reasonable care in protecting the members' anonymity.

Despite precautions, sometimes acquaintances or friends will be placed together in a group, and then quick decisions must be made regarding the nature of the group's composition. Once a new member has walked into the room and thereby breached the confidentiality of the others, the decision regarding the continuing membership is part of the group process, though the responsibility for such a decision always rests with the therapist.

Not every preexisting relationship precludes placing people in the same group. However, in our experience putting persons with any degree of prior relationship in the same group usually results in havoc and should be avoided.

These considerations will assist the group therapist in placing individuals together in the creation of an optimal therapeutic environment.

Which Patients Are Best for the Group?

The therapist has to be concerned with both the individuals and with the group itself. Ultimately, care should be taken to ensure that the maximum effectiveness of the whole group benefits each individual. Ideally, groups are finely tuned organisms, not conglomerates of randomly selected individuals. Whereas in the previous section the concern was with which groups are best for which patients, in this section the focus is upon which patients are best for which groups.

Groups may be composed along a variety of continua. Time-limited groups are often formed on the basis of demography (women, adolescents), crisis (e.g., divorced or bereaved individuals), or symptom (e.g., alcoholics, anorexics). In such groups the emphasis is upon universality and sameness. The fact that individuals begin with the knowledge that in some fundamental ways they are similar to others serves to hasten the initial, trust-building stage.

In ongoing treatment, however, the goal is to meld together individuals sufficiently alike that they can understand and empathize with one another, but sufficiently different to offer different perspectives and different strengths to each other.

The optimal composition for an ongoing psychodynamic group is for members in the group to be similar in terms of ego development and different in terms of interpersonal style. Furthermore, it is important that each individual have at least one other person in the group with whom he or she can identify. This premise will be explicated in detail below.

It should be underscored that we are discussing issues of composition for newly forming groups. Mature groups can tolerate and benefit from greater heterogeneity among members; indeed different levels of ego development become assets. Specifically, the addition of patients with early developmental concerns allows the higher level patients direct access into primary process, while the higher level patients help the more disturbed patients translate their inner chaos into secondary process. In new groups major disparities in ego development simply frighten the members and make the development of cohesiveness very difficult.

Ego Development. The initial task of any group is to establish enough trust among the members so that the developmental process of the group may commence. Individuals approach trust building from very different perspectives, depending on their psychological health. Healthier patients approach a new group with fundamental trust in others. Less healthy patients enter with clear ambivalence about trusting others. The most disturbed patients enter with an absolute conviction that others are not to be trusted. Individuals from these three separate perspectives would have great difficulty even understanding one another, much less arriving at some acceptable level of trust that would allow the group to work.

The same could be said about the primary defenses utilized by different patients. Healthier patients rely on reality-respecting defenses (like intellectualization, rationalization, undoing), while sicker patients rely on reality-distorting defenses (such as projection or reaction formation). Our most primitive patients, on the other hand, utilize reality-denying defenses (including denial, splitting). Again, mixing these patients will make the task of forming a group quite difficult.

Patients at different developmental levels are attempting to accomplish different tasks in their groups. The healthiest patients are typically working on issues of intimacy and authenticity, while the most primitive patients are working on resolving splitting, emotionally sitting in the room with other human beings, and developing even the most minimal connectedness to others.

New groups should be composed of patients at roughly the same developmental level.

Age. Newly formed groups should also not span too wide an age range. Individuals in their fifties by and large have different life concerns than individuals in their twenties. While a wide age range can be beneficial in more mature groups, it typically makes it more difficult for members of new groups to cohere and have a sense of belonging. For example, new groups of younger adults ideally should have an age range of approximately a decade. For older adults (midthirties and older), a broader age range is workable. Further study is needed regarding the issues of adult development and life transitions in order to help us conceptualize age factors more precisely.

Gender. Though women's and men's groups offer a great deal, in ongoing psychotherapy groups it is advisable that the groups be mixed in gender. Ongoing groups are concerned with helping their members learn as much as they can about living in the real world, and as such they should include men and women. It may be a reasonable alternative for individuals particularly frightened of the opposite sex to enter a single sex group preliminary to an open-ended, ongoing mixed group.

Many clinics find that their patient populations are notably skewed with regard to gender. The most usual situation is for clinics to have many more female patients. Under such circumstances, groups may form with all women, with the stated plan that men will be added later. The goal of equal gender distribution may not be attainable. But the situation where there is only one man (or woman) in a group is to be avoided. Indeed it is preferable that the group make-up include at least three members of each gender. If one's referral network is such that this is difficult to accomplish, leave chairs open for men or women and wait until there is an appropriate patient. If the goal is eight members, then no more than five seats should be filled by one gender.

Interpersonal Style. Whatever the ego development, age, or gender, each patient also has an interpersonal style. For example, patients at any developmental level can be domineering or retiring, gregarious or shy. For the purposes of an optimally functioning group, a variety of styles is mandatory. It may well be that a good mix is the single most important aspect of group composition.

The variety of interpersonal styles has been condensed into four quadrants of a circle by Leary:[11] domineering versus submissive styles forming the vertical axis, and outgoing versus shy and withdrawing forming the horizontal axis. It is our contention that effective groups have members representing all four interpersonal styles. A group filled with shy and retiring individuals will not have the emotional electricity that one with greater variations presents. The presence of different styles gives each member the opportunity to learn from the comparisons and contrasts that will inevitably take place.

Thus, in forming a new group, care should be taken to make sure there are some outgoing, some shy, some dominant, and some submissive styles represented. If a therapist is filling a vacancy, he should take the interpersonal styles represented by the existing members into account in selecting the new member.

Summary

No two groups are identical. As the classical Gestalt psychologists noted, the whole is greater than the sum of the parts, and this is certainly the case in an effective therapy group. This effectiveness depends upon the subtle interplay between the members. Therapists have long noted how dramatically the atmosphere in a group can change when just one member is changed. Thus therapists must be very sensitive to the twin issues of "Which group is best for each individual patient?" and "Which patient is best for any particular group?"

Once applicants have been selected and assigned to a group, there remains the task of preparing the applicant to become a member. That issue will be discussed in Chapter 7.

References

1. T.F. McGee, "Comprehensive Preparation for Group Psychotherapy," *Am. J. Psychother.* 23 (1969):303–312.
2. D. Johnson and R. Howenstein, "Revitalizing an Ailing Group Psychotherapy Program," *Psychiatry* 45 (1982):138–146.
3. I.D. Yalom, "A Study of Group Therapy Dropouts," *Arch. Gen. Psychiatry* 14 (1966):393–414.
4. G.R. Bach, *Intensive Group Psychotherapy* (New York: Ronald Press, 1954).
5. M. Wogan, H. Getter, M.J. Anidur, M.F. Nichols, and G. Okman, "Influencing Interaction and Outcome in Group Psychotherapy," *Small Group Behav.* 8 (1977):26–46.

6. J.S. Rutan and A. Alonso, "Some Guidelines for Group Therapists," *Group* 2 (1978):4–13.
7. K. Benne and P. Sheats, "Functional Roles of Group Members." *J. Soc. Issues* 4 (1948):41–49.
8. L.R. Ormont, "Group Resistance and the Therapeutic Contract," *Int. J. Group Psychother.* 18 (1968):147–154.
9. W.N. Stone and R.M. Whitman, "Observations on Empathy in Group Psychotherapy," in *Group and Family Therapy 1980*, edited by L.R. Wolberg and M.L. Aronson (New York: Brunner/Mazel, 1980).
10. D.W. Abse, *Clinical Notes on Group-Analytic Psychotherapy* (Charlottesville: University of Virginia Press, 1974).
11. T.F. Leary, *Interpersonal Diagnosis of Personality* (New York: Ronald Press, 1957).

Patient Preparation and the Group Contract   7

Patient Preparation

Controversy exists about the nature and goals of preparing patients for group therapy. By the very existence of a variety of schema, it is evident that no one method has been accepted universally. We believe the process should begin with one or more individual interviews. Preparation must accomplish the following:

1. Establish a preliminary alliance between patient and clinician
2. Gain a clear consensus about the patient's therapeutic hopes
3. Offer information and instruction about group psychotherapy
4. Deal with the initial anxiety about joining a group
5. Present and gain acceptance of the contract

The time required to accomplish these tasks reflects the therapist's personal preference and experience. Experienced therapists usually can accomplish them in one visit, especially if the patient comes referred specifically for group therapy (that is, some of the working through of the idea of group therapy has already been accomplished). Stone and Rutan[1] found that the number of pregroup interviews does not correlate with patients remaining or terminating prematurely. Some patients need at least several weeks of preparation,[2] whereas others can be prepared in one meeting.

If a patient has not had prior psychotherapy, it seems wise to arrange for a series of individual interviews before the patient joins a group. This helps orient patients to what psychotherapy is about. Individuals who neither have had prior treatment nor are in concurrent individual therapy are at unusually high risk of prematurely dropping out.[3]

Frequently the response of patients to the referral process and preparatory interview(s) raises questions about their motivation for change. Motivation may be the least rigorously used word in our field since it can be presumed that any patient who seeks out therapy is motivated for change. The question is often, "What *kind* of change is desired?" Sometimes the wish is simply for symptomatic relief, sometimes to satisfy some external   **103** pressure, or sometimes for a magic solution to life's problems. Many times a patient will accept a referral to group therapy out of a wish to please the referring therapist or to avoid some difficult therapeutic impasse in the individual therapy. As therapists discuss elements involved in joining a group and negotiate the contract with the applicant, careful attention must be paid to what the patient wants and how the desired goal is to be accomplished. This is the essence of motivation.

Establishing Preliminary Alliances

The minimum task in the screening and evaluation process is for the therapist and patient to meet each other and establish a preliminary working alliance. Given the power of stranger anxiety, many patients experience groups as the most difficult form of psychotherapy to begin. Entering a group is stressful and stimulating, and it is very helpful for entering patients to have at least a minimal alliance with the therapist. For more primitive or frightened patients, this rudimentary alliance is a necessity if they are to get past the early anxiety.

Gain Consensus on Goals

Misalliance in therapy is often founded on a lack of agreement between therapist and patient as to what the patient really wants. The example of Duane in Chapter 5 is typical. In many instances a therapist would have referred Duane to a group because the *therapist* was convinced of its efficacy, despite Duane's unwillingness or inability to see its usefulness. If Duane had entered a group with his motivations, it can be presumed that he would have become a "premature terminator."

Any good recommendation for treatment is the result of a negotiation with the patient.[4,5] Group therapy, where the immediate gratification of contact with and attention of an individual therapist is diminished, is all the more dependent upon the patient's understanding and agreeing to embark upon the rigors of the treatment. The patient who feels forced or seduced into a therapy may find it very easy to forget the contractual agreements and to look for more gratifying help. If the patient is a part of the negotiation and feels a willing and active participant, the times of stress are less likely to result in revoking contractual agreements; and the patient has a better chance of remaining in treatment.

Imparting Information About Groups

While many patients have had previous experience with one or more individual therapists, not many have had group therapy experience. Moreover, since groups evoke intense affect quite rapidly, patients need to feel "grounded" by having specific concrete information about how groups work and what they can expect from being in one.

Information can be transmitted in a variety of ways. In addition to describing the general structure and rationale of group therapy[6] some authors suggest giving reading material to prospective members[7] or didactically explaining the group process.[8] Others have suggested either observing a session behind a two-way mirror or actually participating in a session followed by discussion.[9] Truax and Wargo[10] studied the effect of having applicants review excerpts of a tape recording of a "good patient" in group therapy. Those who participated in the pretraining materials showed greater improvement in the three months of study than those who had not received the training.

Although good arguments can be made for all the procedures cited, there is no evidence that any one format leads to fewer early dropouts or to greater or more rapid success during treatment. Yet the ideas embodied in the pretraining studies point the way to preparing patients for the special conditions existing in a psychotherapy group.

Typically, the information about group therapy includes the contract, specifics about how the group works, and answers to realistic questions that the patient might raise. For example, many patients ask, "How many men and how many women are in the group?" or "How long do people typically stay in your groups?" or "Will I know any of the members?" Although questions can represent metaphorical statements about deeper concerns, patients have a right to know the specifics about the venture they are about to undertake. Bader et al.[11] also note that the group therapist is more active as a screener than in the group itself. Thus applicants should be forewarned that the therapist will be less active in the group and as a consequence may seem unavailable and distant.

Physical and practical arrangements also should be explained. Patients need to know the day, time, and place of the meeting, along with the fact that these variables are not flexible. Inability to make the time commitment eliminates a patient from further consideration. The day and time of the meeting, as well as fee information, should be mentioned during the initial telephone contact in order to ensure that the applicant can conform to these basic requirements. It is best to provide the remaining orientation material during the presentation of the contract.

When members enter existing groups, the veterans quickly take on some information-giving functions, telling the newcomer by word and deed how the group works and what is expected. For example, within a few weeks a new member will likely learn that intense affect is permissible and valued, that dreams are relevant material, that honesty and self-curiosity are esteemed qualities. In a newly formed group, the treatment process and the evolving norms usually provide the data at a pace that the members can use.

Deal with Initial Anxiety About Joining a Group

Patients are typically quite anxious about joining groups. For those whose anxiety is conscious, the therapist should help them understand that anxiety about joining is universal, as well as help them explore the specifics about their anxiety. For patients whose anxiety is unconscious, the therapist should help raise their anxiety to awareness.

Exploration of dreams is one useful approach. If asked, a surprising number of patients will report having had dreams just before the initial screening session or between screening sessions. These dreams may be used to bring into focus some of the anxieties that the patient has about the forthcoming treatment. For example:

> Hedda, a nurse who was consciously very enthusiastic about entering a group, reported that after the initial screening interview she had developed a headache which she linked to her fear that the group would evoke more feelings than she could manage. This was part of the cause for her headache. She then related a dream she had the evening following the first screening session. "I was in intensive care. I said to the mother of a patient, go ahead and cry; your son has been through a lot, but don't be upset." Exploration of the dream revealed some of its meanings. The intensive care unit represented a group setting with a number of ill people. But the intensive care unit had yet another meaning. Since group therapy was being added to her individual sessions, this meant an intensification of her treatment, which further stimulated her fears. The end of the dream referred to two of her habitual defenses: support someone else ("a lot of people talk to me about their problems"), and minimize or deny anxiety. Further associations were elicited which indicated how physical complaints were used in her family to manipulate others, and during childhood her parents were particularly unavailable to the patient or her siblings because of illness. Ultimately the children had turned to one another for support, but Hedda was aware of how competitive they had been for parental attention. The dream brought all this material directly into her awareness as Hedda prepared to enter her group.

Often useful material about patients' anxieties may be gleaned by directly inquiring into their fantasies about the group or their feelings about joining. An applicant's history of entry into social groups or organizations will further elaborate and focus on typical anxieties and defenses. Therapists need to be sensitive to any subtle communication from prospective members that might inform us about the nature of their anticipatory anxiety.

Present and Gain Acceptance for the Contract

If the individual members are the bricks that make a group, the contract is the mortar that binds those parts into a therapeutic whole. As early as 1920 McDougall[12] indicated that the single most important means of harnessing the potent forces residing in groups was the establishment of an overt, agreed on set of goals and guidelines for rules of behavior.

Unfortunately, the word *contract* is often interpreted by both patients and therapists as a collection of hard and fast laws. Our position is that we are trying to establish a structure which can be most therapeutic. The patients are expected to be *responsible* for their contractual agreements, not blindly adhere to them. Patients are asked to cooperate with this arrangement; this is a conscious agreement that reflects the level of ego functioning and the therapeutic alliance. Both conscious and unconscious forces will result in patients altering or circumventing the contract.

The contract is not only between the individuals and the leader; it is also between the individuals and the entire group, although it is established by the leader. A breach of contract affects everyone. We will now present a model contract that has worked well in our experience with all psychodynamic therapy groups.

The Contract

1. Agree to be present each week, to be on time, and to remain throughout the entire meeting. We try not to make agreements that are impossible to keep or are inherently conflictual. The agreement places attendance very high on one's priority list. It also recognizes that there will be occasions when one cannot attend. Some therapists include the provision that a member who is planning to miss a meeting will tell the group in advance, and if that is not possible then the therapist will be notified. If a patient notifies the therapist that he will miss a meeting, the therapist may simply reveal that he has been notified of the absence, or he may also give the reasons cited for the cancellation. In either case the important norm is that absences should be discussed, and if possible the individual and/or groupwide meanings of the absence should be explored. When patients miss meetings without prior notification, a different dynamic ensues, and that too can be explored. Through repeated experiences in groups, members learn that absences have multiple levels of meanings.

> In one meeting both a man and a woman were absent. Both members had a conflicting commitment to attend a Cub Scout meeting with their respective sons. In the following session the therapist reflected on the

different meanings of the absences. In the man's case he considered the absence a healthy, adaptive choice. This man had come to group to deal with his distant relationship to his son, and taking time to be with him at one of his activities represented a visible sign of therapeutic growth. The woman's absence was understood very differently; it was seen as a resistance to therapy. Her presenting issue had been symbiotic overin-volvement with her son, and forfeiting commitments to the group rep-resented another reenactment of the initial problem.

Patients also should understand that the therapist will not be pres-ent each and every week. Therapists take vacations, get sick, and go to professional meetings, but they too have a responsibility to notify members appropriately when they will be away.

An interruption due to the therapist's planned brief absence gen-erally should be announced two or three weeks in advance, preferably at the beginning of a meeting. This provides the members a full session to respond and explore their reactions to the upcoming interruption. Moreover, group members soon learn to identify with the therapist and eventually discontinue the all too frequent, "Oh, by the way, I won't be here next week," announcements made at the end of a meeting. If members continue a pattern of announcing absences at the last moment, this subtle action then becomes easier to discuss when the therapist has initiated a more appropriate model.

The therapist's extended annual vacations could be announced one year in advance, and members could be reminded again three or four months in advance of the interruption.

Some therapists expect patients to schedule vacations to coincide with their own. While this is the ideal arrangement because it results in the least disruption in continuity, it is unrealistic in most circumstances. This option is viable only when the therapist takes the same vacation time each year, and the members have sufficient flexibility in their work and personal lives that they can schedule vacations accordingly.

The essence of this portion of the agreement is to encourage as much continuity as possible. Each time a single member is not present, something is lost. Nonetheless, comings and goings are an important part of life, and there is much to be learned by how individuals manage the inevitable absences.

Different kinds of groups can modify this contract for their specific needs. For example, in a time-limited group, this part of the contract can be changed to, "You agree to attend each of the meetings."

2. Agree to work actively on the problems that brought you to the group.
Ideally, people who join a therapy group do so in order to make substantial

changes in their lives. This portion of the agreement specifically asks patients to share the internal reactions that they have during the meetings, including their feelings about one another, their feelings triggered by one another and by group interactions, their memories that are awakened during a meeting, and their associations. The stimuli is presumed to be the group, and members are expected to discuss openly as much of their inner world as possible.

This stipulation serves at least three valuable purposes. First, merely talking about one's inner responses may be therapeutic. Keeping old fantasies and feelings bottled up adds to the individual's isolation. Self-revelation can appreciably alter that state of affairs. Second, once feelings are shared publicly, they are open to exploration. Members also have the chance to confirm or deny the assumptions regarding what will happen if others know what they are really experiencing. Third, they also have an opportunity for consensual validation of affective responses. If an individual becomes angry at another member and expresses it, then he can discover whether or not he is the only one experiencing anger. If others are also angry, the member can presume that in this instance his emotional gyroscope is properly aligned. It is also true that in some situations several members in a group have a similar affective response, only to learn that they share a common defensive stand. For example, individuals may at times unconsciously provoke angry responses in order to keep others at a distance or to expiate guilt.

Finally, if the member is the sole individual experiencing a particular affect, most frequently anger, he can entertain at least two hypotheses. Either he is the only one aptly responding to the situation, or he is responding to a cue from his own life and not from the reality of the situation. If it is the latter, the member has the opportunity to explore the specific and other parallel situations in order to see if he is routinely distorting.

3. Agree to put feelings into words, not actions. Patients agree that membership in a group means expressing feelings verbally, not behaviorally. Traditionally this contractual agreement proscribes violent behavior such as striking others, throwing objects, or damaging property. But violence is masked in many ways, and verbal violence, as distinguished from an expression of anger, falls within this part of the contract. Violence in the form of virulent verbal attacks by one member toward another is thus prohibited. Patients can learn to put even their angriest feelings into words without violating others.

A more problematic area for many therapists is the matter of affectionate or soothing physical contact among members. For instance, it is not unusual for one member to reach out and touch, or perhaps embrace, a weeping colleague. Since this is a socially acceptable way of expressing feelings, such actions are often unexamined or even congratulated. Some therapists may rationalize such contact as solely therapeutic, since they see no harm coming from warm touching in the group. However, ambivalence, terror, dislike, or even hate may be hidden behind the behavioral facade. There is a place in therapy groups for a gentle touch or hug as an authentic expression of communicating deeply felt emotions, but these acts always should be examined for their full meaning and impact.

Some therapists specifically prohibit eating, drinking, or smoking during groups.[13] A common rationale for this stance is that such behaviors diminish useful anxiety and tension that could more profitably be experienced. Smoking is a particularly interesting phenomenon in light of the increasing evidence of physiological as well as psychological components to smoking behavior. Smoking has important interpersonal dimensions in that it is not only irritating to many nonsmokers but is also a potential health problem for nonsmokers exposed to it. Each therapist must decide how specific to be with regard to the behavioral prohibitions, since many actions can be handled through interpretations. The therapeutic management of some of the extreme instances of acting rather than verbalizing will be discussed in Chapter 11.

4. Agree to use the relationships made in the group therapeutically and not socially. How patients may utilize the relationships made in their groups is a matter of divergent opinion among therapists. Some therapists absolutely prohibit out-of-group contact; others openly support, reinforce, and all but require it.

The fundamental use of the group is for therapeutic, not social, purposes, and in the long run the two are mutually exclusive. As patients express their feelings for one another, including their yearnings to socialize, a considerable pressure to act emerges. The wish to allow patients to use the relationships gained in their groups is understandable. For many patients the contacts with their group colleagues represent their most viable and authentic relationships. Restricting their use and enjoyment may feel unduly harsh and withholding. Nevertheless, it is more therapeutically profitable to discourage extragroup socializing, since doing so reduces the variables affecting group behavior and increases the likelihood of spontaneous revelation of affects in the group. Further, if the use of in-group relationships for social purposes is thwarted, patients tend to gain their own social networks outside the group more quickly. They feel less dependent and more autonomous when the social network utilized is really their own and not one provided by the group.

The language of this portion of the agreement contains room for creative debate. Group members are left to discuss and decide what constitutes therapeutic as opposed to social interaction. All groups do have relationships that extend beyond the actual meetings. Even the moments before and after the group session represent opportunities for important interactions. Group members can be told that any extragroup interactions may well represent important ways of managing feelings evoked in the therapy. Therefore members should discuss emotionally meaningful extragroup contacts in order to enhance learning. Within this framework of dynamic understanding, patients can be reminded that the primary use of all the interactions with group members is therapeutic.

5. Agree to remain in the group until the problems that brought you have been resolved. This part of the contract is often seen as problematic by applicants. Patients are invariably anxious about entering a group, and they often attempt to master their anxiety by envisioning their early weeks as a trial period. Some therapists deal with this by asking that entering patients agree to remain for a specified amount of time, generally three months. This practice presumably helps new patients remain through the early difficult period and long enough to develop a stronger therapeutic alliance.

The trial period is inadvisable for two reasons. First, any newcomer breaches group confidentiality, and if there is a contractually agreed upon trial period the group process will be skewed toward caution rather than openness until that trial period has expired. Second, some patients simply stay for the duration of the trial period and then leave. In this situation the therapist is left with little or no therapeutic leverage, since the patient has indeed fully adhered to the contract.

Acceptance of this contract does not prevent premature quitting, but it does remind the patients that they had agreed to remain until they had resolved their presenting problems. In addition, many patients experience this agreement as an initial source of hope and are comforted by the clear expectation that group therapy can help them resolve their problems.

This element of the contract also serves to begin the norm setting about how appropriate terminations occur. As patients consider termination, it is very useful for them to make their decisions in light of their agreement: "Have I resolved the problems I came with?" The subsequent discussion of presenting problems is one element in the review process that is essential to successful termination. Patients learn that they should not abruptly stop therapy; rather they should spend time examining the changes they have made and their feelings about ending treatment.

6. *Agree to be responsible for your bill.* In this day of third-party payment for psychotherapy, group therapy often seems to exist in a financial vacuum. That is, group therapy is sufficiently inexpensive that some patients find that nearly all of their bills are paid by insurance. This diminished fiscal responsibility may be detrimental to patients who correlate expense with emotional commitment. At the very least patients should be responsible for their bills. If possible, patients should pay the therapist directly and then receive the insurance money themselves. If there is a problem in insurance payments, the patient, not the therapist, should negotiate with the company. Finally, the therapist should fill out insurance forms only the first time. Thereafter the patient should be responsible for completing the forms, using the same repetitive data (including diagnosis) and the proper dates and amounts, with the therapist simply checking for accuracy and then signing the form.

It is wise to stipulate further that statements will be handed out during the first meeting of the month and that members are expected to pay in full before the next bill is distributed. There are certainly other ways of implementing these principles. What is important is that the fiscal elements of the agreement be spelled out in detail and patients understand that financial matters are also group business.

Patients should be charged for scheduled meetings whether or not they attend. In individual therapy, if a patient misses a meeting, the therapist can choose to fill that hour and therefore not suffer a financial loss because of the patient's absence. In groups we do not have the option of temporarily replacing an absent member. Thus no matter the reason for absenteeism, members are charged for their seats. If this agreement is used, patients need to be reminded that third-party payers do not reimburse for missed meetings.

Some therapists prefer a less rigorous approach to fees and do not charge patients for vacations or unavoidable absences such as illnesses or required business trips. In these cases the therapist is placed in the position of having to work with the patient to determine which absences are "acting out" and which are unavoidable. For the therapist choosing this option, the key variable is consistency so that patients can gain the most from analysis of how they choose to attend meetings and handle payment of fees.

The important principle is the separation of the therapist's financial interests and the patient's therapeutic responsibility. In whatever manner therapists manage fees, part of the contract relates to their expectable earnings. Further, the contract is a structure that patients might use for their own internal needs, as an opportunity to rebel or to deprive the therapist of real or imagined gratification. This principle enables the therapist to comfortably examine absences whether or not a fee is charged.

In modern America it often seems easier to discuss intimate sexual experiences than financial matters. Therapists face more than a strong social taboo when they bring up a member's overdue fee because in so doing extremely strong feelings of shame, embarrassment, narcissistic injury, and rage are mobilized. Yet to avoid dealing directly with the meaning of money and the payment of fees runs the considerable risk of colluding with patients' resistances. Financial matters are not private matters because there are invariably groupwide meanings and reverberations when a patient falls behind in paying fees.

As a part of the continuing emphasis that everything can be discussed in the group, the therapist must deal forthrightly with fees. Toward this end, we prefer that statements be distributed and payment received during sessions. This simple practice invites candid discussion of financial matters in the group.

7. Agree to protect the names and identities of your fellow group members.
This portion of the agreement is saved for last because there is usually an input overload when the contract is discussed, and members often do not recall all its elements. Mentioning the requirement to protect other members' anonymity last gives it a deserved special emphasis because confidentiality is a cornerstone upon which group therapy relationships are built.

Therapists often ask that patients agree to "keep in confidence all that is shared within the group." We believe this is a troublesome way of handling the issue for at least two reasons. First, it is an agreement not likely to be kept. As the group becomes important to people, they will talk about their experience with others. Sessions can be very stimulating, and talking about what happened is a very reasonable way to begin to integrate strong emotions. Every therapist will recognize his propensity to seek out a colleague after an affect-laden meeting in order to blow off steam and further process what happened. Obviously, such discussions go on as a matter of course between cotherapists. It would be unreasonable not to expect the members to do the same.

Second, to ask patients not to speak of their group experience is to place them in a double bind. On the one hand, by virtue of being treated in a group, they are told overtly and covertly that it is healthy and helps them to grow to share intimately with other human beings. On the other hand, they are told, "But don't tell anyone about this!"

In fact, we hope our group patients *do* talk with their significant others about their group experiences. If they are in concurrent individual therapy, it is therapeutically imperative that they discuss the meetings. It is also enriching to share some of what is learned in a group with loved ones. The end point of group therapy, after all, is not that individuals merely become intimate and honest with other group members, but rather that they gain authenticity with others in the mainstreams of their lives.

The fundamental concern with confidentiality is that the anonymity of the members be protected, and the agreement to protect names and identities serves that purpose well.

Summary

Entering a therapy group is a difficult task for anyone to accomplish. Group applicants come to us because they have *more* than the usual amount of anxiety in interpersonal situations, and thus careful preparation for their entrance into groups is a necessity if successful therapeutic work is to follow.

An important ingredient in proper preparation of a patient is imparting and gaining acceptance of the treatment goals. If there appears to be a significant discrepancy between the patient's motivation or goals for therapy, and those of the therapist, it is wise to delay the entrance into a group until those issues can be clarified. Often a therapist, anxious to have a new member, will avoid dealing with these conflicts in the hope that they can be resolved by the group. This inevitably leads to problems that are best resolved before the applicant joins the group.

The presentation of the contract, along with examining the overall response of the patient to the idea of entering a group, offers an important opportunity for gaining information about the patient whether or not the applicant ultimately chooses to join. Patients exhibit a variety of responses such as compliance, acceptance, anxiety, rebellion, rejection, and so forth. These responses should be viewed as more than just overt responses to the contract itself; they should be seen as potential windows into the inner world of the patient.

The contract is not a formal, written document; rather, it is the verbal agreement between patient, therapist, and other members regarding the ground rules of the group's operation. The contract is the foundation for a productive and safe therapeutic environment. The specific elements we have presented should be mutually agreed upon treatment guidelines.

The following elements constitute the contract for ongoing, open-ended therapy groups. The patients agree

1. To be present each week, to be on time, and to remain throughout the meeting
2. To work actively on the problems that brought them to the group
3. To put feelings into words, not actions

4. To use the relationships made in the group therapeutically, not socially
5. To remain in the group until the problems that brought them to the group have been resolved
6. To be responsible for their bills
7. To protect the names and identities of fellow group members

We are convinced that any group needs a clear contract in order to be effective. Furthermore, the contract becomes a powerful tool in the analysis of various resistances and character traits.

References

1. W.N. Stone and J.S. Rutan, "Duration of Treatment in Group Psychotherapy: A Private Practice Experience," *Int. J. Group Psychother.* 34 (1984):101–117.
2. B.R. Bader, L.J. Bader, S. Budman, and M. Clifford, "Pre-group Preparation Model for Long-term Group Psychotherapy in a Private Practice Setting," *Group* 5 (1981):43–50.
3. Stone and Rutan, "Duration of Treatment in Group Psychotherapy."
4. A. Lazare and S. Eisenthal, "A Negotiated Approach to the Clinical Encounter. I: Attending to the Patient's Perspective," in *Outpatient Psychiatry: Diagnosis and Treatment,* edited by A. Lazare (Baltimore: Williams and Wilkins, 1979), pp. 141–156.
5. A. Lazare, S. Eisenthal, and A. Frank, "A Negotiated Approach to the Clinical Encounter. II: Conflict and Negotiation," in *Outpatient Psychiatry: Diagnosis and Treatment,* edited by A. Lazare (Baltimore: Williams and Wilkins, 1979), pp. 157–171.
6. I.D. Yalom, *The Theory and Practice of Group Psychotherapy* (New York: Basic Books, 1975).
7. E.F. Gauron and E.I. Rawlings, "Procedure for Orienting New Members to Group Psychotherapy," *Small Group Behav.* 6 (1975):293–307.
8. M. Wogan, H. Getter, M.J. Anidur, M.F. Nichols, and G. Okman, "Influencing Interaction and Outcome in Group Psychotherapy," *Small Group Behav.* 8 (1977):26–46.
9. *Ibid.*
10. C.B. Truax and D.G. Wargo, "Effects of Vicarious Therapy Pretraining and Alternate Sessions on Outcome in Group Psychotherapy with Outpatients," *J. Consult. Clin. Psychol.* 33 (1969):440–447.
11. Bader et al., "Pre-Group Preparation Model."
12. W. McDougall, *The Group Mind* (New York: G.P. Putnam's Sons, 1920).
13. L.R. Ormont, "Group Resistance and the Therapeutic Contract," *Int. J. Group Psychother.* 17 (1967):147–154.

The Role of the Group Therapist *8*

One of Freud's most famous remarks was his comparison of psychotherapy to chess. He observed, "Anyone who hopes to learn the noble game of chess from books will soon discover that only the opening and end games admit of an exhaustive systematic presentation and that the infinite variety of moves that develop after the opening defy any such descriptions. The gap in instruction can only by filled by a diligent study of games fought out by masters."[1] If the comparison with regard to the role of the individual therapist holds, it is even more pointedly true for the group therapist, who shifts among the group, interpersonal, and intrapsychic perspectives. Group therapists are continually confronted with a richness of data, and great skill is required to sort through it in order to focus upon and utilize the most relevant and powerful material. This very complexity contributes to the therapeutic potency of groups.

There are only a few attempts in the literature to offer specific assistance to therapists in organizing and giving priorities to group data.[2] We will elucidate a number of principles that should provide assistance in determining when and how to intervene. For heuristic purposes, we separate leader activity into style and focus, each composed of several continua (see Table 8-1).

The three continua that represent the style dimension are considered in parallel. That is, each leader is continually and concurrently making decisions about how active, transparent, and gratifying to be. The six continua of the focus dimension may be considered a hierarchy. The therapist's attention should first be focused on the past/present continuum, then the group-as-a-whole/individuals continuum, and so on. While the complexity of group interactions does not allow for hard and fast rules about how to attend to group data, considering the focus dimension hierarchically will often help clarify material.

Where any therapist operates on the style and focus dimensions is in part related to his theoretical persuasion.[3-7] A therapist who adheres to group-as-a-whole processes generally will choose to focus on the in-group, affect, and process ends of the respective axes. A traditional psychoanalytic therapist may highlight transference aspects of interpersonal

117

Table 8-1. Leadership Dimensions of the Group Therapist

Leadership Style Dimension		
Activity ⟵――――――――――――――――→		Nonactivity
Transparency ⟵―――――――――――――→		Opaqueness
Gratification ⟵―――――――――――――→		Frustration

Leadership Focus Dimension		
Past ⟵――――――― (Here-and-now) ―――→		Future
Group-as-a-whole ⟵――― (Interpersonal) ―――→		Individuals
In-group ⟵――――――――――――――――→		Out-of-group
Affect ⟵―――――――――――――――――→		Cognition
Process ⟵――――――――――――――――→		Content
Understanding ⟵――――――――――――→		Corrective emotional experience

transactions, fantasy life (content), and the importance of the past. Of course, these same therapists may both eschew self-revelation, gratification, and activity on the style dimension.

Although on some occasions it is most therapeutic to operate from an extreme pole of any continua, it is important for therapists to understand that there are consequences of these decisions.

Leadership Style Dimension

Members are very watchful of their leaders, heeding what they say, how they say it, what they reveal about themselves, and how they relate. The warmth in the voice, the eye contact, and the feelings exhibited are elements to which patients pay attention. Further, the leader serves as a model for observing and utilizing phenomena. Therefore it is important that therapists thoughtfully assess the manner in which they relate in order to understand fully the implications of that style on the treatment.

Activity/Nonactivity

Groups, particularly in early phases of development or at times of high stress, are likely to be preoccupied with the therapist's activity. Members complain about the quantity or the quality of the therapist's participation, creating considerable pressure for him to respond. The therapist is continually balancing the issues of silence versus response. Overactivity may result in infantilization of members, and underactivity or excessive withholding may evoke a narcissistic injury followed by withdrawal or anger.

In general, the most useful activity for leaders is an internal activity—feeling, empathizing, and hypothesizing in the fundamental task of gaining understanding. Overt activity for the leader is primarily verbal. How much does one speak? How cryptic or extensive should one's interventions be? These are separable from the *content* of the activity. The therapist's role is primarily reactive rather than initiative. The therapist waits for the group process to occur and then comments upon it.

The therapist initiates discussions very infrequently. Any agenda the therapist needs to bring to the group (the announcement of a vacation, or that a member has notified the therapist that he will not attend a meeting, or an increase in fees, for example) should be announced at the beginning of a meeting. This procedure provides members the opportunity to respond with their own associations, secure in the knowledge that the leader has no additional significant agenda to be introduced.

The patients' roles on this continuum also are primarily verbal. The therapist tries to establish the norm that change occurs most effectively when members feel, express, and talk rather than *do*. Therefore expressing a yearning to physically embrace another member is usually considered more therapeutic and beneficial than actually embracing that colleague.

The place of touching and doing in therapy is strongly contested. It is imperative that members be assured that they may experience and express any feeling, secure in the knowledge that no action will follow. When groups are allowed or encouraged to act on warm and affectionate feelings, a lingering question remains about what actions might follow when members are experiencing angry, sadistic, or even homicidal feelings. On the infrequent occasions when an actual threat of physical violence in a group exists, the therapist should not interpret the content but must clearly and promptly attempt to stop any action. Physical harm must be interfered with to the extent possible. It is reassuring to note that despite the affective power of groups, actual physical violence within them is extraordinarily rare.

Transparency/Opaqueness

This variable highlights the distinction between the members and the therapist. It is expected that members will allow themselves to be as transparent as possible, expressing their associations, emotions, histories, and thoughts. Therapists, however, should be transparent only in limited ways. It is usually helpful to reveal only that which is in the service of the treatment process. Therapists need to be particularly alert to avoid responses arising from their own inner need or in response to pressures from the members. To the degree that patients are not burdened with the therapist's personal data, their task of transferring meaning and attributes is easier. To the degree that members "know," it is more difficult for them to fantasize.

After a while members come to know a great deal about any therapist. As an actively engaged participant, the therapist reveals a great deal in nonverbal ways. Patients learn to read his body movement and facial expressions. They know when the therapist is pleased or displeased by the tone in the voice or is anxious by the rate of speech. Therapists should not be blank screens or wear facial masks. It is often impossible for a therapist not to laugh at a funny moment or become tearful when the group is struggling with sadness. If therapists are empathically connected to their groups, they are not immune to the affect that engulfs everyone. It is through the therapist's steadfastness to his task, the ability to be concerned and caring, to tolerate affects and to move forward in a therapeutic manner, that the members come to know a great deal about their therapist. Almost all patients who have had an extended period of therapy know a great deal about the persona of their therapists, though sometimes patients will opt to deny how much they know.

Much therapeutic benefit can accrue if the therapist is aware of these elements of transparency and can respond if the members comment upon it. Patients will occasionally pick up and comment on the affective state of the therapist, sensing sadness or anger, for example. Moreover, a mistake or slip of the tongue can expose the therapist's unconscious just as surely and accurately as it can expose the patient's. Since one goal of psychotherapy is to help patients become more empathic, it is counterproductive for therapists to refuse to acknowledge patients' therapist-directed accurate empathy. To acknowledge that a patient has correctly sensed something is quite different than gratuitously offering personal information.

Sometimes aspects of the therapist's personal life are public information and therefore come into the group. This occurs, for example, when the therapist is getting married or divorced, a new car is in the driveway, or something about his career or life is published in the newspaper. For female therapists, pregnancy represents a particularly powerful and public piece of personal information that becomes known to the group. When patients comment about such aspects of the therapist's life, there is no reason not to indicate that such information is correct, although the precise timing of confirming the information will vary according to the situation.

Despite these exceptions patients do not come to hear about their therapist's successes and failures, or joys and sorrows. Since groups so often take on a very familial feeling, group therapists are uniquely prone to the temptation to share irrelevant personal information. Further, there may be some magical wish on the members' part to hear how the therapist solves a problem, or to know the therapist more personally in the hope that this will somehow solve problems. Requests by members for personal information about the therapist should be explored to understand their roots, not gratified under the notion that for the therapist to be human, personal information must be shared. Opaqueness should never be confused with emotional distance or lack of personal warmth.

Gratification/Frustration

An artful balance should be made between gratification and frustration in therapy. Too much gratification results in anxiety insufficient to promote change. Too much frustration results in a relationship insufficient to promote the trust, caring, and safety necessary for personal revelation. In groups the therapist is freed to adopt an empathic observer role because the members can provide gratification when the leader does not. Thus even more than in dyadic therapy, the group therapist can utilize the observational posture without unduly distressing a patient. Overgratification may take the form of too much activity, self-exposure, or even too frequent interpretations. Yet too much frustration or too austere an environment can stifle group effectiveness. For example, some therapists inappropriately avoid eye contact when speaking to a specific member or when making a group-as-a-whole interpretation. Indeed when group members avoid eye contact, the implicit interpersonal avoidance should become a topic for exploration.

Therapists face an ever-present danger of falling prey to a countertransferential need to be central at all times in their groups. Through excessive gratification they may retain their centrality and make the group leader-dependent rather than balanced between leader-focused and member-focused. The goal in working on this axis is to allow the maximum usable amount of anxiety for each patient and for the group-as-a-whole, and not to interfere with the members' abilities to work with their feelings and relationships.

Leadership Focus Dimension

Whereas the preceding dimension concerns leadership style, this dimension concerns the leader's focus of attention. Furthermore, the continua on the style dimension are to be considered in parallel with one another while those on the focus dimension are presented in a rough hierarchy that should reflect the therapist's thinking about and organization of the data. Though the elements are presented separately, there is obvious overlap, and thus this is not a rigid hierarchy but rather a conceptual perspective that encourages the therapist to utilize both affective and cognitive processes.

There is no "right" place on these continua where a therapist should remain fixed. The weight given to a particular point on each of the continua reflects a therapeutic judgment about how best to help group members change.

Past/Here-and-Now/Future

All dynamic psychotherapies include consideration of an extended time dimension, from the past, through the present, and into the future. A particular orientation may emphasize one point more than others, as exemplified by existential therapists who place particular importance on the end of life and our ultimate finitude. In psychodynamic therapy all the points on this axis are important, but the initial focus of attention and exploration is on the intragroup responses, interactions, and feelings that have been generated in a particular meeting. Transference is a here-and-now event occurring between patient and therapist, and between patient and patients.[8] The past is relevent to the extent that it informs or distorts the present.

Indeed, two important pasts develop in therapy—the treatment and the personal. In the treatment past are the events that have taken place in the therapy. Groups develop rich legacies and members often will recall historical events or issues that help clarify current events. The personal past brought by each member also becomes known to the group over time, and the exploration of each person's reactions to current events takes on new perspective when the uniqueness of each history is understood. As members relive and remember their pasts, new associations and memories are elicited in the others.

Often what is happening in the present is unclear and can be understood only with reference to the past. The precise timing of when to link the present and the past through interpretation depends upon the clarity of the associations as metaphors and the state of the therapeutic alliance.[9]

The personal past emerges in the stereotyped roles patients adopt. These roles usually are ways of managing anxiety and conflict, and if a member can become aware of patterned behavior and the meaning of that behavior, associations from the past will add to the patient's knowledge of the patterns.

As with all elements in therapy, the past may be used defensively to avoid the present. The therapist is not immune to this tendency, and a common error is to prematurely shift the focus to the past in order to contain intense affects in the present. Patients also revert to the past as an intellectual or obsessional defense, and such flight should be considered in light of its use in maintaining both group and individual equilibrium.

Therapists can utilize their own affective responses as indicators of the need to explore the past. Feelings of boredom, lack of interest, or a sense of repetitiveness may suggest that the members have mobilized defensive patterns. These defenses might represent a response to an unattended group conflict, a product of individual roles, or newly emerging transferences. The past, either near or remote, then may shed light on the present conflicts.

Finally, the future is also always present. Patients come to therapy in order to make their futures better. They plan, think, and feel about what is in store for them. Many in-group behaviors can be best understood as practicing or trying out new responses. The fantasies of what someone will do or feel or how he will react in some outside situation is commonplace and clearly future oriented. As patients near termination they become future oriented, wondering about their ability to be different than they were when they entered therapy.

Hence, any debate about where to focus—past, present, or future—has been largely resolved: all three have an important place in treatment.

Group-as-a-Whole/Interpersonal/Individuals

Leaders must move back and forth flexibly along the group-as-a-whole, interpersonal, and individual axis. A primary focus on group-as-a-whole phenomena provides an opportunity for members to understand their shared, universal concerns and to gain understanding from their participation in the powerful conscious and unconscious group processes. The focus on interpersonal interactions assists in understanding communication blocks and distortions. The focus on the individuals within the group gives members the opportunity to examine their uniqueness. To focus on one element to the exclusion of the others is to lose touch unnecessarily with powerful therapeutic forces.

Typically, one can give dominance to group-as-a-whole observations at those times when members are responding primarily to the same stimuli. This can be at times when the group is undergoing changes—a beginning group, the introduction of a new member, the termination of a member, or the vacation of a therapist. At these times when the boundary is altered, attention to the groupwide reaction, and thereby to the individual contributions to that reaction, is most useful.

Groupwide reactions occur rather silently much of the time. Within the group there may be a subtle thrust for greater intimacy or increased expression of difficult affects. In this process the members may be working to change old group norms toward greater spontaneity, or, if the stress is too high, toward restriction of feelings. From this perspective the notion of enabling or constricting solutions to group focal conflicts highlights the group-as-a-whole perspective.[10] It is generally not one individual who interferes with the expression of feelings or the discussion of a topic, but one or more individuals with covert cooperation of the others.

Kernberg[11] has suggested that the group-as-a-whole/individual perspective might parallel the members' developmental stages. He maintained that those groups composed of individuals with preoedipal personality configurations can best utilize the group-as-a-whole focus, and those with oedipal personality configurations learn more from an interpersonal focus. In his formulations Kernberg neglects the sexual attractions and rivalries that involve the whole group and that could be clarified for all members through group-as-a-whole interpretations. Such issues are certainly at an oedipal level. The most productive interventions are either to the group-as-a-whole or to individuals who are participating in a groupwide issue. For instance, an intervention to an individual working on competitive feelings at an oedipal level in a group struggling with issues of basic trust would miss the main focus of the group. The individual might gain from the intervention, but the group focus would rapidly shift away from competition back to the central focus. Thus the intervention would not lead to elaboration or working through. The same intervention to individuals in a group working on competitiveness and intimacy may be powerful and therapeutically enabling, not only to the particular individual but to the others as well since the comment would likely stimulate relevant associations in the others.

There are occasions when one or several sessions might be devoted almost exclusively to discussing a particular member's problems. This may be appropriate in times of crisis, and the other members can learn from their own inner reactions to the situation and responses to the distressed member. However, the therapist needs to maintain a broad perspective to ensure that the focus on one or two individual members does not become a pattern and thereby a detriment to free interaction.

In-Group/Out-of-Group

Members have their in-group and out-of-group lives. The theory of group therapy assumes that individuals present the salient elements of their personalities and their conflicts in the group, and thus where possible attention is focused upon the in-group action where the elements are more available to direct analysis. As with the here-and-now continuum, there may be many roadblocks in accomplishing this task. In the vast majority of situations, however, when patients can utilize their interactions with one another or with the therapist, or their perception of the group, they will gain an important affective and cognitive appreciation of their problem.

Though the therapist should scrutinize all material from out of the group for its relevance to in-group material (metaphorical communications), it is helpful to remember that not everything is a reference to group trans-actions and feelings. The birth of a child, a marriage, a relative's divorce, or a death are examples of such external events. Members gain from the opportunity to talk about such events through the feeling of being listened to respectfully. Only a naive therapist slavishly adheres to the belief that such events are primarily transferences. It is not farfetched to believe that a neophyte therapist could interpret a story about a serious automobile accident involving a member's family as solely a metaphor for a dam-aging event within the group. However, if others associate to accidents or injuries, the accumulating evidence may suggest a group trauma that needs exploration.

The same principles hold for in-group and out-of-group as for past/present. Individuals associate to out-of-group events when a particularly relevant or insightful interpretation opens up a new way of understanding. From a technical perspective, even in instances when the therapist views the discussion of out-of-group material as an avoidance of in-group tension, it is an error to offer an interpretation that implies the out-of-group material is irrelevant. In these cases it is preferable if the therapist can tactfully link the out-of-group and in-group material.

The fundamental guideline is that most productive therapeutic work in the long run arises from the affective experience in the group itself. Nonetheless, it is an oversimplification to see that as the exclusive focus since individuals learn about themselves in their own ways and at their own rate. The therapist needs to monitor and reinforce the norm that ex-amination of in-group transactions is the most productive, but not the ex-clusive way of learning.

Affect/Cognition

Psychodynamic theory began with the notion that understanding uncon-scious elements would free individuals of their neuroses. Conscious un-derstanding would be the mainstay of the curative effort. Rather quickly it became apparent that cognitive insight is an incomplete avenue to change, and therapists began including the emphasis upon freeing up affects and emotional knowing.

The exclusive attention to either extreme of this continuum is gen-erally ineffective. What transpires in effective psychodynamic psychotherapy is a combination of emotional awareness and cognitive integration. Emo-tional knowing arises from having deeply experienced a situation and having felt the affects involved. The building blocks of learning are feelings and affects, both felt and shared. To that degree the first, most important focus of therapeutic attention is affect, not cognition. Often cognitions are viewed as resistances to the bearing of strong emotions. Nonetheless, therapeutic change is not a function of pure affect or pure catharsis. Once the affective data has been made available, a cognitive integration is very important. It is not enough that our patients feel; they must then understand as well. As with most principles, there are exceptions, and some patients change after gaining cognitive understanding that then forces them to experience affects.

The therapist has to balance the wish to provide cognitive closure with the need of patients first to explore, bear, and express fully their affective experiences.

Process/Content

Communication in groups is simultaneously occurring both verbally and nonverbally, consciously and unconsciously, and as a response to immediate stimuli, or as an ongoing trend within a particular meeting, or over a series of meetings. The process is fueled by each member's personal history, which evokes wishes, needs, transferences, distortions, and affective attribution of meaning. The process is conveyed as a flow of ideas, associations or feelings within the group. At all times members are negotiating their relationships with one another and the leader.

The content of any given meeting cannot be divorced from the process because in almost every instance there is a connection between the two. The content might be a symbolic representation of a groupwide issue, or an interpersonal transaction, or it might be a direct commentary upon the process within the group.

The therapist should keep an ear finely tuned to the process. The question, "Why is this association or series of interactions emerging at this time?" provides perspective. Is the discussion due to what happened a few moments ago, or is it related to a general issue within the group, or is it idiosyncratic? The content of associations often is highly symbolic or a metaphor of the process. Through a judicious combination of both elements, the therapist can help the individual or whole group gain understanding of unconscious functioning.

The following case briefly illustrates the interplay between process and content.

> During a meeting members found themselves involved in intense rivalry. Several began bragging about various personal exploits. The therapist initiated examination of the interactions by exploring the feelings of the members and by trying to understand the meaning of each exploit, thereby sharpening the sense of showing off or competing. The members under-

stood that each story was an example of a personal triumph, and they could then recognize that they had become competitive with one another.

The therapist then suggested that the stimulus for the competitiveness and bragging was his announcement at the start of the meeting that a new member would be joining the group in two weeks. He pointed out that the initial overt response had been muted, with a general tone of, "Oh, good, the empty chair will be filled," but that the process had shifted to the relating of exploits. The linking of content and process enabled the members to become emotionally aware of the connection between the two. There followed an elaboration of the content as the members recognized that they had many more feelings about the prospect of a new member than they had been willing to acknowledge or even to know consciously. The members could then deal more directly with the competitiveness they experienced (process leading to new content) and in some cases they were able to make genetic reconstructions (understanding more fully the advent of rebellious behaviors as children during the time of mother's pregnancy).

The use of process in this manner has been particularly advocated in modern contributions by self psychology.[12] In working with patients suffering from disorders of the self, the emphasis is placed on interpretation of the specific sequences: a narcissistic injury and the subsequent response to that injury. The content is used to highlight the process, both to the precise empathic understanding of the injury and the details of how the patient (or group) tried to regain an inner equilibrium. This approach helps the patients gain more explicit understanding of their vulnerabilities to narcissistic injury, and their responses to it. For example, members may respond to a therapist's interpretation as a criticism, and the associations may suddenly turn to religious themes. The interpretations of this behavior could then highlight the process of having felt criticized and hurt and then turning to a "higher authority" for more nurturance and protection.

Understanding/Corrective Emotional Experience

The roles of understanding and corrective emotional experiences in the curative process have often been polarized and thought to be mutually exclusive. In fact both are necessary for effective psychotherapy. The notion of a corrective emotional experience is inherent in the nonjudgmental, empathic, investigative stance of the therapist. In groups the benefits of this situation have been emphasized by Yalom,[13] who stressed the curative effect of group cohesion. The experience of belonging to a cohesive, functioning group, which includes an atmosphere where wishes and needs will be acknowledged and responded to positively has a soothing, calming, and growth-producing effect. For almost everyone this is a corrective emotional experience, and for some this is sufficient treatment. These latter individuals can stabilize themselves in the group setting and continue to grow on their own after terminating. For most patients this fundamental building block needs to be supplemented by knowledge of unconscious inner conflicts or structural deficits. Kris[14] has stated what most of us have experienced, that insight, either cognitive *or* emotional, is often insufficient to bring about real change in our patients. Fried suggested, "What matters clinically is that insight into most conflicts, be they preoedipal or oedipal, does not rectify deficits and malformations. They have to be corrected through the very repetitive experiences and challenges that groups offer in abundance."[15]

Yet understanding and insight are valuable in helping patients integrate what they have experienced. A person's sense of knowing his own sensitivities and vulnerabilities helps him master everyday stresses. Insight enables the patient to spot a troublesome area or a behavioral pattern for himself. Not all conflicts disappear; rather, they can be short-circuited through self-awareness.

Groups are unique therapeutic opportunities that offer both understanding (emotional and cognitive insight) and corrective emotional experiences (the opportunity to build new psychic structures via better and more nourishing relationships and the opportunity for trying out and practicing new behavioral patterns). Group leaders need not choose between the ends of this continuum; they need to ensure that both ends are operative and that patients are receiving both information and experiences.

A Clinical Illustration

In the following illustration the leader's role will be examined across both style and focus dimensions. As usual, to best utilize these dimensions the therapist must have an awareness of the process that has been occurring in the group as well as the presenting problems and personal histories of the members.

> *A group had been proceeding very nicely for a period of months, including the successful and moving termination of a patient a month before. Suddenly in one meeting the members became moribund and depressed. After a prolonged silence, Sarah, who had experienced a long period of warm and affectionate feelings for the therapist (feelings the therapist also felt for her) exploded in a fury. She accused the therapist of not appreciating her gains, of not caring for her, and of giving all his attention to the other women members. Everyone present was confused by the sudden depressed silence at the beginning of the meeting and by Sarah's surprising outburst, which seemed unwarranted.*

The therapist, knowing the group process and Sarah's presenting problem and family history, was able to hypothesize about the seemingly strange responses. The process was initiated by the loss of the loved member, and the group was depressed because they had not sufficiently mourned that loss. Instead, with the leader colluding, they had focused on warm and loving feelings to the exclusion of their envy and rage.

Sarah's initial presenting problem was her "insane jealousy" of other women, and her outburst toward the leader was a replay of her primary symptom. The etiology of her problem, in large measure, had to do with the loss of esteem she experienced at six years of age, when a baby sister came into the family. As the group was saying its final goodbyes to the departing group member, Sarah turned her attention to the future and the expected "new baby" in the group who would come to fill the empty chair. And, just as her history had led her to expect, she anticipated rejection from the leader and acted as if it had actually happened.

The understanding of current group processes seemed sufficient for understanding the depressed response of most members. However, Sarah's response did not yet fit, and there was no overt stimulus. It was unclear what had precipitated her outburst until the therapist reviewed for himself the presenting problem and significant historical events in Sarah's life. Indeed the precipitant turned out to be a group event, but not the one that had been affectively important to the others. With this material raised to consciousness, the therapist then could make decisions about his intervention by utilizing the dimensions in Table 8-1. From the style dimension the therapist reviewed the three continua.

Activity/Nonactivity. He chose to remain quiet and allow both the group depression and Sarah's attack to reach a crescendo before offering any responses. Had he not had some sense of what was transpiring, he might have felt compelled to intervene sooner in order to calm both the group and himself. He was not inactive; he made a series of choices. He did not interfere with the attack and the full expression of the negative feelings; he did not offer a defense, or a correction of her distortions about his warmth for her; he determined that all the members of the group could profitably bear the strong affect for at least sixty minutes before any closure was considered. Then he made a clarifying interpretation.

Transparency/Opaqueness. He chose to remain opaque. The leader determined that it would not serve Sarah to "correct" her distortion about his warmth for her. Sarah would be better served by his helping her "understand" her distortion, and that required allowing her to elaborate it fully.

This was facilitated by not confusing her with contradictory data; so he kept a neutral position and accepted her attack.

Gratification/Frustration. The leader was experienced as somewhat frustrating early in the meeting when he simply accepted and encouraged the members to express their feelings and did nothing to relieve the pain. However, there was sufficient alliance with the leader that the members were able to persevere, secure in the knowledge that he would sooner or later offer his observations. That is, they were secure in their conviction that his nonresponse was not sadistic or humiliating in its intent.

Moving to the focus dimension, we can examine the leader's technique on each of the continua.

Past/Here-and-Now/Future. The full interpretation moved up and down this axis and included references to the recent past (the termination), the distant past (Sarah's history, in order to help her with her distortion), the present (the group's current reactions), and the future (the coming of the new member). To focus exclusively on any single aspect of the time line would have been to miss important material.

Group-as-a-Whole/Interpersonal/Individuals. When he did respond, the leader made both a group-as-a-whole and an individual response. He first responded to the whole group, commenting that Sarah's powerful response and the group's depressive stance had been linked; both were indications of members working through the termination of the lost member. He then helped Sarah understand how her reaction to him was a powerful distortion, linked to her worry about the loss of esteem in light of the forthcoming "baby." Sarah readily accepted the interpretation, confirming it by reporting a dream that the new member was a woman, despite her rational conviction that a man would replace the man who had terminated.

In this situation the therapist chose to focus on the individual in order to help the group-as-a-whole. This decision was predicated on the leader's observation that Sarah was filled with the most overt affect, and his conviction that not only was she experiencing a powerful replay from her own history, but also in some important way she was probably a spokesperson for affects that were relevant for the group-as-a-whole.

In-Group/Out-of-Group. In this illustration, the *members* did not bring out-of-group material into the session. Interestingly, this time it was the *therapist* who ultimately introduced out-of-group material, linking the in-group affects to the now departed group member and Sarah's family history. This process of first experiencing affects *in* the group and then placing them in relevant context outside the group is the ideal process.

Affect/Cognition. The balance between affect and cognition was weighted in favor of affect first. The leader was careful not to interpret prematurely, thereby robbing neither Sarah of the opportunity to really experience her hurt and rage, nor the group of their depression. The cognitive integration was added later.

Process/Content. As usual the axis of process and content was an important one. The leader accepted the content as content on one hand, and he interpreted the content as a coded communication about the group process on the other. That is, Sarah *was* furious and convinced that he did not care about her. The leader did not deny that overt content. But he attempted to see that content in light of recent group process as well. Giving primacy to the process allowed the leader to help the members explore very important, hidden feelings about the recent termination. Had the leader not looked to the process and linked the present content to the ongoing process, an important opportunity for learning would have been missed.

Understanding/Corrective Emotional Experience. Finally, understanding alone was considered terribly important, but insufficient, to help Sarah and the group change. Rather, over the ensuing weeks, Sarah could put aside the intense rivalry with other women and "try out" new behaviors and perceptions of herself in relation to important men. Finally, when some months later a woman entered the group, Sarah responded very differently. She commented, "For the first time I feel free to enjoy women rather than just experience them as competitors."

Summary

The focus of the group therapist's attention should be varying, not static. In each meeting there are allusions to current in-group issues, historical antecedents, emotionality and cognition, and all the other ingredients listed above. The therapist is often bewildered by the amount of data that confronts him, and in some cases he becomes paralyzed or simply focuses on the most obvious or superficial data.

The two dimensions and their component continua provide a way of ordering the plethora of data generated in every group. Then, with this structure, therapists are better prepared to make decisions about the use of self along the leadership style dimension and appropriate interventions along the leadership focus dimension. We suggest that therapists view the data in the order that the leadership focus dimension continua have been presented. The sequence begins with examination of the here-and-now, and then is followed by group-as-a-whole, in-group material, affect and process continua. One can then move across the continua as needs dictate.

References

1. S. Freud, "On Beginning the Treatment" (Standard Ed., vol. 12, 1913), pp. 121–144.
2. J.S. Rutan and A. Alonso, "Some Guidelines for Group Therapists." *Group* 1 (1978):4–13.
3. P.F. Kauff, "Diversity in Analytic Group Psychotherapy: The Relationship Between Theoretical Concepts and Technique." *Int. J. Group Psychother.* 29 (1979):51–66.
4. M. Lieberman, I. Yalom, and M. Miles, *Encounter Groups: First Facts* (New York: Basic Books, 1973).
5. I. Yalom, *The Theory and Practice of Group Psychotherapy*, 2nd ed. (New York: Basic Books, 1975).
6. A. Wolf and E.K. Schwartz, "The Role of the Leader's Values," in *The Leader in the Group*, edited by Z.A. Liff. (New York: Jason Aronson, 1975), pp. 13–30.
7. J. Christ, "Contrasting the Charismatic and Reflective Leader," in *The Leader in the Group*, edited by Z.A. Liff. (New York: Jason Aronson, 1975), pp. 104–113.
8. R. Michels, "The Present and the Past," *Bull. Assoc. Psychoanal. Med.* 20 (1981):49–56.
9. G.A. Katz, "The Non-interpretation of Metaphors in Psychiatric Hospital Groups," *Int. J. Group Psychother.* 33 (1983):56–68.
10. D.S. Whitaker and M.A. Lieberman, *Psychotherapy Through the Group Process* (New York: Atherton Press, 1964).
11. O.F. Kernberg, "A Systems Approach to Priority Setting of Interventions in Groups," *Int. J. Group Psychother.* 25 (1975):251–275.
12. P.H. Ornstein, "The Evolution of Heinz Kohut's Psychoanalytic Psychology of the Self, in *The Search for the Self*, edited by P.H. Ornstein. (New York: International Universities Press, 1978), pp. 1–106.
13. Yalom, *Theory and Practice of Group Psychotherapy*.
14. E. Kris, "The Recovery of Childhood Memories in Psychoanalysis," *Psychoanal. Study Child* 2 (1956):54–88.
15. E. Fried, "Building Psychic Structures as a Prerequisite for Change," *Int. J. Group Psychother.* 32 (1982):420.

Special Leadership Considerations *9*

A number of leadership issues arise with sufficient regularity to warrant special attention. In this chapter we attend to the issues of cotherapy, leader absences, transferring of groups, the removal of patients from groups, and countertransference.

The Use of Cotherapists in Group Psychotherapy

The use of two therapists to lead a group is common. Rabin[1] has even suggested that most therapists prefer working with a colleague.

A variety of advantages are cited favoring a cotherapy model. Dual leadership allows for a fuller and more complementary view of the group and protects against blind spots of either therapist.[2] Furthermore, each therapist has the opportunity to slide back and forth between the active and passive mode, and in so doing one cotherapist may be more actively responsive and the other more observational.[3] Parallel to this is the advantage of watching a colleague work and learning from that opportunity.[4] Cotherapy offers the pragmatic advantages of providing ongoing coverage at times of sickness or vacation, increased limit-setting capacity in working with certain patient populations (e.g., children, severely acting-out patients, geriatric patients), or dealing with larger groups. It also provides an opportunity for peer consultation and support.[5,6]

The process of the treatment may be enhanced by cotherapy. This model theoretically offers a replication of a two-parent family. Even in cases where the therapists are of the same gender, it has been reported that patients respond transferentially as if to a male/female pair.[7] Other authors stress the unique value of having male/female cotherapy teams that stimulate parental transferences,[8] as well as each patient having a same-gender therapist with whom to identify.[9] Another advantage stems from the manner in which cotherapists relate to one another, handle conflict, and communicate acceptance. Their behavior provides a model that patients may utilize for imitation or identification.[10,11]

In addition to these suggested assets, cotherapy is also considered of particular value in the training of group therapists. The presence of a cotherapist lessens anxiety,[12] provides a sense of support, and allows for a shared responsibility.

Despite these advantages, however, cotherapy is not the preferred leadership model in most situations. In fact, many of the arguments *for* cotherapy are actually arguments *against* it. For example, is it really advisable to reduce the therapist's anxieties? Should not the therapist confront similar anxieties about entering alone as the members must face? Middleman[13] agreed that dulling the anxiety that therapists face is not in the service of their training nor in the service of the group members' therapy. Likewise the argument that cotherapy allows the therapists to drift in and out of focus, relying on their counterparts to remain attentive, is a weak argument for cotherapy because at times of highest stress *both* therapists simultaneously would likely want to back away. In the treatment process therapists are stimulated by the variety of angry, sexual, competitive, and aggressive affects in the group. Optimally some of these feelings can be used to sort out the members' transferences and projections onto the therapists, but often these feelings are focused between the two therapists. Put in an oversimplified form, children can encourage parents to fight or love each other.

In addition to the task of understanding the treatment process, the therapists must be vigilant to their relationship. Two people working together under the tension of a wide range of affects, as occurs in a group, are likely to have periods of stress. In one sense cotherapy is like a marriage, and the cotherapists who may have been courting before the treatment began are placed in a marriagelike relationship once it begins. The ordinary adjustment period is stressed by the immediate task of rearing children. Sometimes cotherapists become so preoccupied with how they are working together that the group is neglected. Under any circumstance sorting out and keeping the relationship straight consumes energy and time. No cotherapy pair automatically works smoothly. It cannot. What makes it function is the maturity and willingness of the leaders to work on the difficult problems that arise between them.

MacLennon has pointed out that transferences arise between therapists, which adds to the complexity of sorting out the members' real and transferential relationships.[14] This further complicates the therapists' working together. The traditional boundaries between therapists and patients prohibit socialization, but there is no similar prohibition between cotherapists. Indeed cotherapists are encouraged to use one another to unwind and review the meetings; thus they have considerable informal, semisocial contact. The stimulation and arousal of affect inherent in therapists' roles requires that cotherapists be especially alert to the potential for acting rather than talking. We have seen significant therapeutic and social complications arising from cotherapists acting on their feelings toward each other.

Patients may experience difficulty with a cotherapy format; many individuals find it harder to confront or disagree with two therapists presenting a united front.[15] Others, rather than learning from differences between therapists, are frightened by the cotherapists' inevitable conflicts.

Rutan and Alonso[16] have suggested an intriguing alternative to the traditional model, which they term *sequential cotherapy*. In this approach two leaders are employed, but each leads separately for a prespecified number of weeks. The nonleading cotherapist becomes a silent observer. This model offers some of the advantages suggested for cotherapy (such as peer consultation, sharing of the responsibility, binocular vision) while neutralizing some of the competitive features of traditional cotherapy. This model has particular advantages as a teaching tool, since the silent therapist can more easily consult with trainees.

Conclusion

Overall, the disadvantages of cotherapy outweigh the gains that accrue from this leadership format. In training situations there may be some particular advantages to having cotherapy, but a price is paid in the therapists' time and energy as well as potential complications in the patients' therapy.

Leader Absences

Therapists take vacations, attend professional meetings, become ill, and occasionally have competing priorities that mandate their not being present to lead their groups. Absences should be rare and the decision to miss is not one to take lightly. Nonetheless, even the most conscientious group therapist cannot be present every week. The question then becomes, how is the group best served in this situation? A variety of options is available. These include

1. Canceling the group
2. Providing a make-up meeting
3. Holding a double session before or after the leader's absence
4. Inviting the group to meet without a leader
5. Providing a substitute leader

Given the paramount importance of continuity and cohesion, any breaches in the frame are matters that threaten the effectiveness of the group. Any absence of the leader is an important event, and the members' feelings concerning the event must be fully explored and used to enhance learning. No procedure should be viewed as an attempt to blur the affects connected to the leader's missing one or more meetings.

As Rutan et al.[17] have pointed out, there are theoretically valid rationales for each of the responses cited. The advantages and liabilities of each are explored below.

The Specific Options: Pro and Con

Canceling the Group. It is a fact of life that time lost is lost forever, and canceling a group reinforces that reality. The cancellation of a meeting does not dull the most important reality—the therapist's absence has an impact on the life of the group. It is an option that does not offer false restitution. The search for painless solutions to life's dilemmas is one source of pathology for many patients. Thus for most members, this option holds great promise.

There is almost invariably a spectrum of reactions to the interruption. Learning is enhanced as patients have the opportunity to see how one member may ignore or deny that the therapist's absence has any meaning, whereas another may have a tantrum in reaction to missing one week. For groups locked into a dysfunctional idealization of the leader, the cancellation of a meeting may have the salutary effect of reminding the members of the humanity of the therapist. For groups primarily dealing with issues of grief and loss, cancellation of a session may reawaken buried feelings in a very direct manner. Not only do patients experience the loss of the group for a week or more, but they also experience the leader's expectation that they can survive it.

Patients do not always learn best by actually experiencing the full deprivation that may have led to developmental arrests. Some patients need a time of idealizing their group therapist,[18] and they would be harmed by premature deidealization of the leader. The reexperiencing of painful affect may simply reactivate the repetition compulsion without any working through.

Finally, there are some occasions when groups, or specific members, may not survive the loss of continuity. Vulnerable members dropping out in anticipation of or in reaction to an extended absence is not unusual.

Providing a Make-up Meeting. If leaders provide an opportunity to make up the lost meeting or meetings, this can demonstrate a commitment to the group and can heighten awareness of the mutual responsibilities involved in relationships. This option allows the group to meet even though the regularly scheduled weekly meetings do not occur.

If a make-up meeting is to be held, the time should be negotiated with the group rather than imposed by the leader. However, this negotiation should be based upon a limited number of times offered by the leader. This is best limited to no more than three possibilities. Then the negotiation becomes a highly significant event, during which patient pathologies and motivations can come into clear view.

One major problem with this option is that it tends to suppress angry feelings. Who can bite the hand that feeds? Indeed therapists may invoke this option out of a need to please or avoid anger, rather than out of a more thoughtful consideration of the pros and cons. If a make-up meeting is utilized, the therapist needs to listen carefully for the members' negative affects linked to the original cancelation. Patients should not end up feeling grateful to the exclusion of other feelings about the lack of consistency.

A second problem is the difficulty of finding a suitable alternate time. Anyone who has tried to arrange a meeting for six to eight people knows how complex and frustrating this can be. Almost invariably someone is unable or unwilling to meet at the time agreed to by the majority. A decision to hold a meeting then stirs up feelings of exclusion or favoritism since other times might have been preferable for the offended individual.

Once the therapist raises the question of an alternate time or day to meet, he must be prepared to meet if a reasonable number of members agree. The determination about what constitutes a reasonable number is in itself a problem. To plan an alternate session only if all members can attend is an error because one or more rebellious or defiant members can undermine the proposal. A viable option is to accept a date and time that a majority of members find acceptable. When the discussion and negotiation are over, the decision to meet or not is the therapist's and should not rest upon a group vote. When the therapist, taking into account all the discussion, makes a decision, then the members can decide to attend or not and the decisions are open for examination.

Holding a Double Session. If one meeting is canceled, it is sometimes useful to meet the group for twice as long the week after the absence. Such an extended session should occur *after* the missed meeting rather than before it, since double sessions often stir up considerable affect and the members should not have to wait a prolonged time before meeting again. Furthermore, holding a double session after a missed session does not interfere as much with the experience of the missed week. Holding a double session is similar to holding an alternate session since it indicates the therapist's willingness to be responsible to the contract, even while altering it. While not meeting at the agreed upon time, at least the therapist is offering to meet the allotted amount of time.

A particular advantage to this option is the fact that the extended amount of time allows for more sharing from some members. Very often in psychodynamic groups a feeling arises that there is too little time. While we do not propose to defeat patients' defenses through sheer fatigue, as happens in marathon groups, the extension of time permits greater self-exposure. The danger of overwhelming defenses is minimized by the fact that the double session occurs in the context of an ongoing group.

The problems with this option again include the possibility that the patients may not experience or express their feelings about the leader's unavailability, the possibility that more fragile members will be endangered by the expanded time, the suggestion that twice the amount of time will somehow offer twice as much help, and the inevitable thorny question of whether there is to be a double session for every missed meeting or just for some. The latter concern applies as well to holding a make-up session.

Inviting the Group to Meet Without the Leader. Not infrequently, members wish to meet during the leader's absence. Usually such a proposal dies during subsequent discussion. The response may be different if the therapist initiates the idea. A host of dynamics related to authority and power are mobilized, and marked emotionality generally results as members vehemently support or oppose the idea. Even with all the discussion, and irrespective of who initiates the idea, there are still occasions when the members may choose to meet. Under these circumstances, the therapist needs to be especially alert to coercive pressures placed on the more reluctant members. In utilizing this option, the therapist should make the usual group room available and clearly discourage the group from meeting elsewhere. It should further be stipulated that the group should meet at the usual time and for the usual duration. This structure enhances continuity and provides symbolic safety.

The therapist's initiating a suggestion to meet without him may be a response to circumstances where an unusual number of sessions might be canceled or other meetings with the therapist could not be arranged. Countertransference guilt may also motivate such a suggestion. In general, we have been unimpressed with the therapeutic usefulness of a leaderless meeting and for that reason do not recommend it. There is one additional alternative to the therapist's absence, that of providing an alternate therapist.

Providing Substitute Leadership. An unusual and yet viable response to a therapist's absence is the provision of a substitute. Where possible, a consistent substitute leader should be available to be called upon whenever a primary therapist is absent. A substitute allows for continuity and predictability to the boundaries of therapy groups without implying that the group leader is all-giving or idealized. In the course of time, groups begin integrating the substitute leader as an important figure.

This model offers a range of unique opportunities.

1. The group can actively explore the meaning and effect of the leader's absence, with the help of another leader.
2. By meeting with another therapist, the group gains from the added perspective and potentially differing transferences such leadership can provide. Ideally the substitute therapist should be of the opposite gender from the ongoing leader.
3. A group is able to continue functioning in those rare circumstances when a leader must be absent for a prolonged period, for example, illness, injury, or pregnancy.
4. Peer consultation between the therapists is provided. As the substitute has the opportunity to meet with the group on different occasions over time, he has the overview perspective of seeing the patients periodically, and he can help the ongoing therapist assess the progress of the members and of the group itself.

Providing a substitute leader also has its disadvantages. The introduction of a second leader occasionally enhances splitting and other regressive defenses resistant to interpretative reversal. And the introduction of a second therapist means that a form of cotherapy is operating without working together during the sessions to unravel the transferences. The process becomes even more complicated if there is more than one substitute or if the usual substitute is unavailable when the primary therapist cannot meet with the group. The latter situation may create a double disappointment.

Conclusion

If there is any plan to deal with leader absence other than the usual exploration of the feelings and memories evoked, this must be made clear to the group members from the beginning, preferably as a part of the original group contract. Generally groups can tolerate leader absences very well, and unless there are extenuating or unusual circumstances, we prefer not to hold a meeting and not to make up the time, thereby allowing the members to experience and learn from the therapist's absences just as they do from the absences of their colleagues.

Transferring Leadership of a Therapy Group

Though therapists move, get ill, or retire, most commonly groups must change therapists when a particular leader (or set of coleaders) has finished a period of training. Since beginning new groups is an arduous and often lengthy process, training programs, which are dependent upon there being groups for students to run, attempt to maintain ongoing groups that change therapists.

A change of therapists is never easy. Often the transition becomes a crisis so filled with affect that the group suffers rather than learns from the experience. It is not unusual for one or more patients to drop out instead of making the transition. Occasionally a whole group is destroyed.

A number of strategies have been tried to make this crisis an opportunity for learning rather than an assault. Each clinical situation requires close examination because each model has its strengths and shortcomings.

Models of Transition of Leaders

No Overlap. In this model a departing therapist leads until the announced termination date, and the succeeding therapist does not meet with the group until after his termination. This rigorous model focuses on the loss of the old and the impact of the new; it maximizes the affective response. It is chosen when the judgment is made that members can effectively learn by facing the full impact of the loss of the therapist. In order to choose this option the members' ego strengths or the group's developmental level is judged adequate to manage the intense affect aroused. This model also promotes fantasies about the incoming therapist. Patients face that unknown collectively, but each individual has fantasies about the benevolence or destructiveness of the new therapist. Sometimes these fantasies can be terrifying. Even when this approach is well handled, some patients may be overwhelmed and quit treatment.

Observation. In this model (utilized primarily in training centers) the incoming therapists begin by silently observing the groups they are to lead.[19] The primary asset of this model is the sense of a beginning connection between therapist and members. Although there may have been only minimal or nonverbal interchanges, the group has a realization that the incoming therapist knows about them, and the neophyte therapist has the experience of seeing the members at work without the responsibility or pressure of having to intervene. The observer also would have participated, after the meeting, in discussions with the therapist and/or in the supervision, thereby increasing his knowledge of the group's functioning. An optimal observation period is from three months to one year. Among the problems with this model are the increased time commitment to training and the emotional meaning of moving from the student or observer to therapist role—in the eyes of both the members and therapist.

Stage Phasing. In this model the incoming therapist becomes visible to the group prior to actually becoming leader. The incoming therapist first appears as a silent observer and then functions as cotherapist during the final weeks of the outgoing leader's tenure. The assets of this approach are smoothing the transition, decreasing stranger anxiety, and making overt the comparisons and contrasts between the two leaders. The problems are the blurring of the goodbye issues with the outgoing therapist and the hello issues to the incoming therapist. Moreover, members generally have difficulty expressing their feelings directly because there is almost invariably a marked disparity in their alliance with the two therapists. Therefore this model may be most useful when the assessment has been made that focusing on the very intense affects will be counterproductive.

Cotherapists. If cotherapy is used, the cotherapists ought to be in different training years so that there is a bridge of one senior therapist in the group at all times.

Discussion

The central issue remains how to maximize learning while minimizing unproductive anxiety and stress during the changeover of leaders. As we will discuss in Chapter 12, terminations reactivate feelings linked to loss, death, and new beginnings. Members' responses to individual absences or group interruptions might be useful in predicting feelings aroused by the therapist's actual departure. But the changeover can awaken deeply felt and deeply experienced affects, perhaps stemming from the separation-individuation stage of development.[20] Even though patients may develop an ability to see the real aspects of the therapist, intense transferences are awakened. However, not everything is transference, and members experience a genuine loss when a therapist leaves.

Another aspect of the problem is that of maintaining a healthy working alliance.[21] Groups provide more opportunity for establishing good working alliances due to their public nature.[22] Members can examine their perceptions and experiences in light of those of their colleagues and use consensual validation as one means of discriminating valid from distorted perceptions. This is not to suggest that affects are suppressed by reality, but members are able to use their trusting relationships with their colleagues to explore and assess affects as they arise. Groups might thereby also be more able than individual therapy to retain working alliances even when therapists change because the important linkages among the members is retained.

Our experience in training centers suggests that a two-year tenure as a group therapist is preferable for both the student and the group. It is not unusual for the members to spend a considerable amount of time preparing for the departure of the old therapist and reacting to the new. At a minimum this might take two to three months on either side of the changeover. When feelings are most intense, twice that amount of time may be therapeutically desirable. The time consumed by too frequent leadership shifts diminishes the opportunity for undisturbed work on areas other than separation and loss. A two-year term of leadership provides members the opportunity to explore other areas, for example peer relationships rather than focusing so extensively on authority issues. These considerations should be placed in the context that the average length of time for a patient to finish a substantial piece of work is close to two to three years even in an ongoing, leader-constant group.[23]

Whatever strategy is chosen, utilizing the following guidelines will facilitate the therapeutic transferring of group leadership.

Guidelines

1. The departing leader needs to work thoroughly on his own feelings regarding his leaving. Most frequent are feelings of guilt about abandoning the group and the inevitable competitive feelings with the new leader. In training settings, where the new leader is almost always less experienced, the outgoing leader might gain perspective by recalling how little he knew when he took over!

2. The change of leaders may be usefully considered as akin to the reaction of protest and despair when sudden and premature loss of contact with mother occurs.[24] We must help the members avoid "detachment" by giving them the opportunity to rage and weep over this act of abandonment, and to connect it to all the similar wanton acts in their histories. This will enable patients to say an effective goodbye—owning the gains and loves as well as the rages and disappointments with the outgoing therapist. Such work allows the members to test reality and demythologize the departing therapist, and results in enabling members to reconnect to someone new. Even if this is not possible for each individual, the natural differences among members will call forth a broad spectrum of responses to the loss, and the group-as-a-whole can tentatively move forward.

3. The incoming therapist must work on his anxiety about replacing the old leader. It is important that the new therapist use supervision to work on the anxiety and uncertainty about venturing into the complex treatment modality. Transference looms large, and new therapists often lose sight of the fact that the outgoing therapist began in the same spot only a short time before, and instead they perceive their predecessor as a beloved, skilled, and irreplaceable individual. The patients' worries that their new therapist will not be capable of curing them will strike a vulnerable spot, since in all likelihood the therapist has never had previous experience in leading a group and is filled with the self-same doubt as the patients.

4. Both the outgoing and incoming therapists need to examine their narcissistic vulnerabilities and their competitive strivings so that they are able to tolerate the patients favoring one or the other. No matter how experienced or how clearly therapists understand the transferential basis of the members' angry feelings, they feel hurt and defensive under continuing attacks and criticisms. It may be useful for the outgoing therapist to realize that the anger may represent growth, members now being comfortable enough to stop being "polite." Furthermore, a common defense against the pain of goodbye is to go away mad rather than sad. Likewise, incoming therapists will have to endure the role of stepparent for some time, while the patients continue to work on their relationships with the natural parent who has left. The feelings of being ignored or belittled are never easy, and new therapists have trouble maintaining their therapeutic balance under such conditions. It may be helpful to remember that the newcomer will probably be leaving the group in one or two years and both he and the incoming therapist probably will experience a repetition of the patients' reactions.

5. It is important that the incoming therapist receive great amounts of data—not only about the lives and pathologies of the patients, but also about the history of the group itself. It is very useful if he can participate in the group supervision for some weeks prior to taking over leadership. The nuts and bolts of who sits where, how the group typically begins, where patients routinely sit, and the like must be part of the information provided. The incoming therapist is not bound by that tradition, but he needs to be aware of it.

6. In training settings supervision should bridge all changes in leadership. When leaders change, if at all possible the old supervisor should continue during the transition. In this way the group continuity can be borne by the supervisor.

7. The incoming therapist should make individual appointments with all the patients. The history provided by the outgoing therapist is not

a substitute for reviewing it directly with a patient. The patients can review their presenting problems and progress or lack of it, and their satisfaction or lack of it. The individual interview also serves to bond the members to the new therapist. Goodbyes to and reviews with the old therapist should be accomplished in the group.

8. It has been our experience that more mature groups (groups that have been in existence for several years and have experienced some change in leadership) are likely to gain from a no-overlap model. Indeed, the transition can often promote growth. In younger groups the baton of leadership must be handed over more cautiously, probably invoking one of the bridging techniques—the new leader either sits in as an observer or joins as a cotherapist toward the end of the outgoing therapist's term.

9. If several therapists are leaving groups with fewer than four active members, the blending of two groups might be considered.

Removal of Patients From Group Psychotherapy

The necessity of removing a patient from a specific session or from continuing in treatment in a group is exceedingly rare. When it does occur, it is clearly a leadership responsibility and not a matter for group vote. The crisis of actually removing a patient from a group must be distinguished from the fantasy on the part of a therapist of wishing that a patient would leave. That fantasy is not rare at all!

There are two types of removal of a patient from a group: temporary, with the expectation that the individual will return to the group, and permanent. In both instances the therapist must practice careful self-scrutiny so that the decision is based upon sound clinical judgment and not countertransference.

Temporary Removal

A patient may be asked to leave a group session because of a temporary loss of capacity for self-control. Loss of control might result from an exacerbation of a psychotic process, usually in the form of uncontrolled mania or, less frequently, a relapse into an acute schizophrenic process. In most instances the deterioration is apparent over a number of sessions, during which the decompensation can be addressed and various responses, such as individual appointments or hospitalization, can be discussed and explored. Most likely the individual would not be asked to leave during a session.

However, if the patient becomes disruptive and out of control so that removal during a meeting is necessary, the therapist is faced with the decision of whether or not to accompany the patient and make immediate arrangements for additional treatment. If a patient is so out of control that he cannot safely remain in the group, there is little reason to believe he can suitably take care of himself. The therapist is most often in the best position to accompany the patient. Taking the disruptive patient away from the stimulation of the group room may result in some calming, and the patient may be able to sit alone for a short period while the therapist returns to the group. However, the therapist must exercise careful clinical judgment in deciding between the needs of the remaining members and the patient in crisis. In these circumstances the remaining members are expected to continue until the regular ending time even if the therapist does not return.

Another situation calling for temporary removal is a sudden propensity for acting out. In the face of violent outbursts, where there is a threat of physical harm to another, the initial response of the therapist is a forceful reminder that the group contract prohibits acting on feelings and that such actions are incompatible with continuing presence in the meeting. The therapist must attempt to provide appropriate limits and ego controls before making any interpretations regarding the causes of the rage. In the great majority of cases, clearly stating the limits is sufficient to quiet the patient. In rare instances the patient, after inquiry, may still feel unable to maintain self-control and then will leave the session by mutual agreement.

A specific instance of inability to retain self-control can happen when a patient attends a session intoxicated. Intoxication per se is not a reason for removal. Stating routinely that alcoholic patients are not allowed to attend a meeting if they have been drinking is like prohibiting depressive patients from attending while depressed. Rather, it is the patient's ability to contain himself that is instrumental in making the decision.

Permanent Removal

Obviously, removing a patient should be a last resort. Three circumstances are usually the basis for asking a patient to permanently discontinue participation in a therapy group. The first is a significant and continuing inability or unwillingness to comply with the group contract; the second is an unrelieved lack of progress; and the third, which is rare, is when a patient makes such progress that he has outgrown the present group and should be moved to a higher functioning group. In all cases the situation is not acute and does not require immediate action but, rather, is the result of careful deliberation and work over time.

Inability to Comply with the Contract. Sometimes patients' life circumstances are altered and they can no longer attend regularly. Naturally, alterations in attendance should be explored for potential elements of resistance, but there are real life changes that are not resistance. The final decision in these cases rests with the therapist, and each case must be viewed separately. A temporary change (for example, an overseas assignment, schooling required by work, or having a baby) that necessitates an individual's absence for one to three months is a dilemma. The time-limited nature of such an interruption generally should not necessitate removal from the group. More problematic is the situation where a change (for example, a new job) necessitates continuing intermittent absences. When ongoing regular attendance is not possible, the patient must be asked to leave the group. The leaving should not be precipitous but should be planned with a termination date so that all the members can work with the complex feelings evoked by the patient's forced departure.

Another decision point arises when patients are continually unable to manage their feelings without putting them into action. This occurs either in or out of the group. Within the group some patients continually monopolize, interrupt, or engage in other disruptive behaviors and are unable to gain control or understanding. Still other patients are verbally abusive in malicious, hurtful ways that seem immune to interpretation and understanding. In the majority of cases even these patients eventually comply with the contract and learn from their disruptive behaviors, but removal from the group remains as the choice of last resort.

Another way patients demonstrate inability to talk rather than act is through continuing contacts with other members outside the meeting. Some patients persist in utilizing the group primarily for social purposes. Usually these are seriously character-disordered individuals who are frightened of group intimacy and who pair as a protection. Yet patients who have not been acting out may do so as the only way available to convey their response to the stress of a conflict within the group.[25] Careful scrutiny of the group process is in order before the therapist acts to remove a member.

The most serious of these problems is continuing sexual intercourse between group members. Sexual relations, whatever the specific internal meaning of the actions, evoke in the other members powerful feelings of envy, frustration, and distrust. If the involved couple is unable to discuss and explore their relationship openly in the group, one or both individuals might be asked to leave.

Nonpayment of fees is another contract violation that occasionally requires eviction. Patients who do not pay their fees might be giving messages that could include resistances or intense affects involving the entire membership. It is not easy to deal with these openly in the group, but it is imperative that it be done.

In all instances of contract violation, the therapy may reach a point following every reasonable effort at analysis when it is judicious to indicate that continuation of particular behaviors jeopardizes the patient's remaining in the group. Such a statement should include a specific period of evaluation. By using a time frame, no single action can result in immediate expulsion, and flexibility is retained by the therapist. Also, by flagging the problem, the responsibility for its continuation is clearly with the patient. This approach removes the therapist from the position of the punitive parent. A rigid rule is invariably tested and places the therapist and patient in the no-win position: the therapist is either inconsistent or authoritarian.

> *One patient consistently underpaid his bill so that his overdue bill slowly mounted. The behavior seemed immutable to discussion and exploration. When the therapist questioned the meaning of the behavior, the patient was "hurt" and said he was doing the best he could do. The other members began experiencing rage at the patient. The therapist eventually had to indicate firmly that unless the patient paid his bill in full within the next month, his remaining in the group was doubtful. He was startled and humiliated by this pronouncement, but the following week he angrily threw a check for the full amount due at the therapist. He was sullen for weeks, and he occasionally fell slightly behind in his bill after that. His sense of embarrassment and hurt over the confrontation abated only slightly over the ensuing years, but the limit setting was clearly useful in allowing him and the group to move past an impasse. Only years later was the patient able to be insightful as to the etiology of the withholding of fees.*

Too Little Progress. In some cases it gradually becomes clear to the therapist, and often to the members of the group as well, that a particular member simply cannot or will not use the group for therapeutic purposes. Sometimes this is the result of an error in diagnosis or in the choice of a particular group. In other cases the patient progresses to a certain point in the treatment and cannot move farther. The decision to stop the group treatment should be the result of a mutual dialogue and should represent a joint decision. Again in this situation very careful deliberation is required because it is often difficult to predict when a patient might move to a new plateau. There is also some temptation to ask a silent member to leave, but a number of such patients who are almost mute for months or years are making significant gains from their group membership.

Substantial Progress. A related situation occurs when a member of a group of highly disturbed patients makes substantial progress and finds himself working on issues at a dramatically higher level of development than the other members in the group. Rather than terminate, the option exists of moving the patient to a higher functioning group. Such a proposal should be discussed openly in the group.

Group Dynamics Related to Removing Patients From Groups

Seldom does anyone leave a group without a ripple. The response depends upon the level of the group development, the individual, and the groupwide contributions to the reasons for a patient's leaving. We have focused on the therapist's decision or initiation of the process of removal. In reality, therapists need to recognize their responsibility to act in situations where the group itself is endangered by an individual's action. Once a therapist has evicted a patient, he must then help the group deal with the powerful consequences. Members become very fearful when their leaders utilize such authority, and an ongoing question is, "If someone can be excommunicated from this group for behaving badly, what will happen to me when I show my worst side?" Even though members may have consciously agreed with the decision to evict, associations to primitive, destructive and uncaring authority figures are almost inevitably present. Another prominent dynamic is guilt or shame, either for what the remaining members did or did not do to "save" the lost member. A mature view of the individual and group contributions to the forcible departure of a member is difficult to attain, but the entire process can be therapeutic if it is actively explored.

Countertransference

Therapists' use of their own inner experiences opens up very important avenues to learn what is happening in a therapy group. Freud[26,27] recognized that patients, with their intense transferences, awoke unconscious responses in the therapist. Classically these inner reactions, when they interfere with the therapist's ability to respond therapeutically, have been labeled *countertransference*. More recently, the concept of countertransference has been expanded to include all the therapist's emotional reactions, both conscious and unconscious, evoked by the patient.[28] The narrow definition brought precision, but therapists felt that their affective responses represented something harmful. The broader definition freed therapists to utilize their responses in the service of understanding.

Some responses the therapist experiences are obvious and clear reactions to the individual or group dynamics. Others are more obscure, arising in the form of fantasies or behavioral responses. As a therapist listens to the group members interact, he often becomes aware of feelings or fantasies within himself. These responses may reflect feelings or conflicts arising from the members but not yet conscious to them, or they may arise from the therapist's own needs.

> *In one group there had been a continuing problem of dropouts and irregular attendance. The therapist was aware of his frustration and discouragement with the progress of the group. During a session there seemed to be some progress, and the therapist suddenly found himself wondering whether he should take a vacation three months hence. The fantasy startled him, and he wondered whether it was a reflection of the members' wish for closeness and his feeling pressure not to disrupt the continuity. Or perhaps he was feeling guilt about some of the decisions he had made regarding patient selection, and he had to be punished by not taking a vacation. Listening to the members' associations with the perspective of these hypotheses enabled the therapist to appreciate the intensity of the wish for intimacy reverberating throughout the meeting, and of course the opposite side of the coin, the wish to flee. These conflicts were made conscious and brought into focus through interpretation, and the patients then were able to reexamine their feelings about the dropouts and irregular attendance. From that point on, the group became much more cohesive, and irregular attendance and premature quitting became insignificant problems.*

Therapists often feel upset, annoyed, or sometimes even enraged during group meetings when the members are particularly needy or defensive. These affective responses, if acted upon, are countertransferential in the narrow definition. However, the insights gained from the vantage point of ego psychology have helped therapists understand that some of their affects may be a result of patients' projections or projective identifications. Therapists, through these mechanisms, end up with many of the feelings that patients experience and then disown. In a group co-led by a psychiatrist and a social worker, these processes emerged with unusual clarity.

> *During the male psychiatrist's annual vacation, the group was led singly by the female social worker. Almost immediately the members began to speak at length of a variety of physical illnesses. Eventually they asked the social worker whether she knew the side effects of some of the medications they were taking. The social worker rapidly became aware of feeling helpless, frustrated, and irritated. Indeed, the patients had successfully induced in their remaining therapist the affects they experienced as a result of their separation from their physician therapist. The recognition of these feelings by the remaining therapist allowed her to help the patients more directly face their feelings associated with loss, beginning with the cotherapist's vacation and then important separations in their pasts.*

Therapists, as they gain experience, find that their therapeutic style is generally consistent. They arrive promptly, end the meeting at the proper time, deal with absence, lateness, or delinquent fees in a particular fashion. Deviations from the usual way of handling patients' contractual breaches may be a countertransference clue. Indeed, it is the therapist's capacity to build a consistent view of himself and how he interacts that enables him to become aware that unconscious forces are impacting upon his work.

Other behaviors that often depict countertransference are therapist lateness, drowsiness, yawning, becoming too verbal (or, conversely, too quiet), or the use of a therapeutic strategy that is not typical (say, using role play, or a Gestalt technique, in a group that has not previously used such methods). Eruptions of the therapist's unconscious into the group, such as blocking on a patient's name, or forgetting to announce a vacation or to hand out bills, are further indicators of countertransference.

A number of other clues in the therapist may indicate important affects are present. The dreams that the therapist has, particularly the night before or after a meeting, are often stimulated by feelings about the group. Somatic symptoms or visual images can give leads to the potential countertransferences. Sudden coughing or a wish for a cigarette or a drink usually are good indicators of some group-stimulated feelings that are being responded to in this fashion. The experience of sudden sexual attraction to a member is a clear indicator of affects in the group transactions. Perhaps the therapist is resorting to genital sexuality as a defense against more primitive affects, or perhaps is responding directly to a member's message of warmth and sexuality. One self-observant therapist reported becoming very sleepy whenever his group began dealing with erotic topics.

An interesting active method for focusing countertransference responses is to fantasize about reforming the group. A therapist might fantasize about which patients in his current group he would like to exclude or who he would select first for a new group. Patients in either category may have stirred important previously unrecognized feelings, which the therapist acted upon in his fantasy.

Still another way of learning about countertransference is when patients, consciously or unconsciously, inform us that something has gone wrong.

> *Daniel, who had been an active member for more than two years, suddenly announced he was quitting the group in three weeks. The context of the announcement clearly indicated that this decision represented a flight from specific anxieties emerging within the group. In the preceding weeks, a great deal of treatment time had been spent helping Daniel mourn and rage about his having been dropped by his girlfriend. Concomitantly, Daniel, who was now "available," seemed to spark a host of highly competitive sexual fantasies within the group. The therapist felt Daniel's de-*

cision to leave was directly linked to the emergence of these fantasies and Daniel's wish to avoid any further heterosexual disappointments.

The group's reaction to Daniel's announcement was divided. Most members praised his decision as a sign of his having made great progress; indeed, they seemed overtly pleased by his decision. One woman, however, questioned both the timing of the decision and the manner of the announcement. The therapist was aware of feeling frustrated and angry about the decision, and after some effort to explore the process, said directly that he did not believe this was the proper time for the patient to terminate. The therapist, who had considerable experience leading groups, realized that usually he held off stating his opinion until considerable work had been done, and he could not recall having made similar remarks in a meeting in which such a decision to leave was announced. He left the session with an unusual sense of anxiety, which he thought was connected to his early expression of opinion. At the beginning of the following meeting, several members expressed outrage at the therapist's "sarcasm" the previous week. On reflection the therapist judged this to be accurate—he had forgotten, but now recalled that he had indeed been sarcastic. His sarcasm had not been toward the member who announced termination but, rather, toward the one who had most actively praised that decision. The sarcasm was clearly a countertransference action that the therapist had totally repressed until he was so strikingly confronted with it. In this instance the therapist had experienced the rage that was being passively denied by many group members and inappropriately expressed it to the patient most supportive of the member who was leaving. In retrospect his postgroup anxiety had been the signal not only about the early expression of opinion, but more directly about the repressed sarcasm.

Therapy groups evoke powerful feelings in all who sit in them, including the therapist. Classic notions of countertransference alerted therapists to the possibility that unresolved issues in their own lives might keep them from hearing and understanding their patients properly. However, that conception was too narrow and often caused therapists to worry that they were somehow doing something wrong if they experienced powerful feelings about their patients. Modern definitions of countertransference allow for the therapeutic use of the affective experiences of therapists. Attention to the affective world of the therapist is especially useful because groups are such powerful stimuli.

References

1. H.M. Rabin, "How Does Co-Therapy Compare with Regular Therapy?" *Am. J. Psychother.* 21 (1967):244–255.
2. E.W. Demarest and A. Teicher, "Transference in Group Therapy: Its Use by Co-Therapists of Opposite Sexes," *Psychiatry* 17 (1954):187–202.

3. R. Gans, "Group Co-therapists and the Therapeutic Situation: A Critical Evaluation," *Int. J. Group Psychother.* 12 (1962):86.
4. A. Solomon, F.J. Loeffler, and G.H. Frank, "An Analysis of Co-therapist Interaction in Group Psychotherapy," *Int. J. Group Psychother.* 3 (1953):174–188.
5. I.D. Yalom, *The Theory and Practice of Group Psychotherapy*, 2nd ed. (New York: Basic Books, 1975), p. 424.
6. C. Getty and A.M. Shannon, "Co-therapy as an Egalitarian Relationship," *Am. J. Nurs.* 69 (1969):769.
7. W.H. Lundin and V.M. Aronov, "The Use of Co-therapists in Group Psychotherapy," *J. Consult. Psychol.* 16 (1952):77–84.
8. Demarest and Teicher, "Transference in Group Therapy."
9. E. Mintz, "Male-Female Co-therapists: Some Values and Some Problems," *Am. J. Psychother.* 19 (1965):293–301.
10. Getty and Shannon, "Co-therapy as an Egalitarian Relationship."
11. Yalom, *Theory and Practice of Group Psychotherapy*, pp. 421–422.
12. *Ibid.*, p. 424.
13. R.R. Middleman, "Co-leadership and Solo-Leadership in Education for Social Work with Groups," *Social Work With Groups* 3 (1980):30–40.
14. B. MacLennon, "Cotherapy," *Int. J. Group Psychother.* 15 (1965):154–165.
15. Gans, "Group Co-therapists and the Therapeutic Situation."
16. J.S. Rutan, and A. Alonso, "Sequential Cotherapy of Groups for Training and Clinical Care," *Group* 4 (1980):40–50.
17. J.S. Rutan, A. Alonso, and R. Molin, "Handling the Absence of the Leader," *Int. J. Group Psychother.* 34 (1984):273–287.
18. J.S. Rutan and C.A. Rice, "The Charismatic Leader: Asset or Liability?" *Psychother. Theory Res. Pract.* 18 (1981):487–492.
19. W.N. Stone, "Dynamics of the Recorder-Observer in Group Psychotherapy," *Compr. Psychiatry* 16 (1975):49–54.
20. P.F. Kauff, "The Termination Process: Its Relationship to the Separation-Individuation Phase of Development," *Int. J. Group Psychother.* 27 (1977):5.
21. E. Zetzel, "Current Concepts of Transference," *Int. J. Psychoanal.* 37 (1956):369–376.
22. H.T. Glatzer, "The Working Alliance in Analytic Group Psychotherapy," *Int. J. Group Psychother.* 28 (1978):147–162.
23. W.N. Stone and J.S. Rutan, 1984. "Duration of Group Psychotherapy," *Int. J. Group Psychother.* 34:93–110.
24. J. Bowlby, *Separation: Anxiety and Anger* (New York: Basic Books, 1973).
25. J. Munzer, "Acting Out: Communication or Resistance?" *Int. J. Group Psychother.* 16 (1967):434–441.
26. S. Freud, *The Future Prospects of Psychoanalytic Theory.* Standard Ed., vol. 11, 1910.
27. S. Freud, *Observations on Transference Love.* Standard Ed., vol. 12, 1915.
28. B.E. Roth, "Understanding the Development of a Homogeneous Identity-Impaired Group through Countertransference Phenomena," *Int. J. Group Psychother.* 30 (1980):405–425.

Beginning the Group

Approaching the First Meeting

At some point after all the preparatory work has been completed, the therapist and patients prepare for the first meeting. Typically everyone approaches this first meeting with a great deal of apprehension and anxiety. Therapists wonder whether the patients who have been screened, selected, and prepared will actually arrive and mesh well together. Members worry about meeting strangers, and when the task includes sharing the most intimate details and secrets about one's life, their anxiety is vastly increased. All the usual concerns about trust and safety are, quite appropriately, central in the minds of the participants. This anxiety and apprehension regarding the initial meeting represents the first shared experience.

Everyone, including the therapist, approaches the unknown situation with his or her own particular fantasies, defenses, and coping mechanisms. Prior experience does not seem to matter—even senior therapists are filled with anticipatory anxiety. If the therapist minimizes the intensity of his anxiety, his capacity to utilize his own emotional life as a barometer of the group members' experience is diminished. Just as the therapist is concerned about how the group will work together and respond to him, and how he will respond to them, so too are the members. The anticipatory anxiety they experience may exaggerate coping patterns, but their very exaggeration exposes them more clearly.

Group Boundaries and Physical Setting

Prior to the first meeting, the therapist has certain gatekeeping functions. The degree to which these have been accomplished will help contain anxiety and influence the patients' confidence and trust in the enterprise.

Before the first meeting the therapist must clearly inform the patients of the time, day, duration, and location of the group. Furthermore, each member should agree to the group contract prior to meeting the other members.

If there is a prototypic psychodynamic psychotherapy group, it would probably meet once weekly for 90 minutes and have eight members, four men and four women. It is certainly within the realm of traditional practice to meet twice a week, from 75 minutes to 120 minutes, include up to ten members, and have one gender compose a significant majority of the membership. These parameters must be carefully thought out and decided upon before a new group is formed.

Frequency of Meetings

Though the usual frequency of group sessions is once a week, twice weekly is not rare. Some therapists are beginning to experiment with even more frequent meetings. Birk[1] reported that patients who failed in other extensive and intensive treatments demonstrated marked improvement when seen in a therapy group that met five times per week.

The optimal frequency of meetings depends upon the capacity of the patient population to hold a memory trace of the group from meeting to meeting. If the patients consistently "seal over" and lose contact with the affect from the previous session, the leader might consider increasing the frequency of meetings. However, for most outpatient populations, once a week is sufficient. If meetings take place less than once weekly, the process seems to get lost and the therapeutic utility is diminished.

Some therapists increase the frequency of group meetings by utilizing the technique of alternate sessions, the group meeting a second time each week without the therapist present.[2] The rationale proposed to support this practice is that by meeting without the leader, members can learn to work without his presence, begin discussions of their negative feelings about him with diminished fears of retaliation, and in essence become less dependent.

It is precisely the reasons put forward in support of alternate meetings that lead us not to recommend this approach. Members need to develop the capacity to feel secure in their affects and thoughts and develop independence in the presence of an authority figure. The therapist's task is to analyze resistances and difficulties along that path. If a patient needs to idealize a therapist, the basis for such a response is best worked through in the presence of the therapist. Testimonials by satisfied individuals indicate value to the alternate session format, but there has been no research into the processes, dynamics, or the overall efficacy.

Length of Meetings

The range of clinically productive time for psychodynamic psychotherapy groups is between 75 and 120 minutes. Sessions shorter than 75 minutes usually do not provide sufficient air time for the members. In sessions of more than two hours' duration, fatigue sets in, a condition that may harden or loosen defenses. Some therapists utilize marathon time formats specifically to invoke fatigue as a therapeutic element.[3] In psychodynamic groups, however, the object is not to defeat defensive structures, but rather to examine and understand. We find little use in extending the time frame to the point where undue fatigue, on the part of either the patients or the therapist, occurs.

The sole exception to this approach to the length of meetings is the option of using a "double-length" meeting after a week in which the group has been canceled. This alternative was discussed in Chapter 9.

Group Size and Gender Distribution

The choice of group size should be predicated upon the number of patients with which a leader feels comfortable. The usual range is from six to ten members. For some therapists the dynamics that unfold with groups of ten feel comfortable and understandable, where for others ten in a room feels unmanageable. There is often a connection between the number of members and the length of meeting, with larger groups meeting for somewhat longer periods.

Clinically, ten members seems to be the upper limit for productive work in a psychodynamic group, although Winick et al.[4] reported on groups having up to twenty-five patients. Beyond ten, less assertive members rarely have sufficient opportunity to discuss their issues. Fewer than six members creates difficulty in effectively utilizing the group process and diminishes the richness of interpersonal input. In smaller groups there is a great temptation for the therapist to focus on the four or five individuals and lose sight of groupwide processes. Further, certain members may feel overexposed or prematurely forced into a type of intimacy for which they are not prepared. Finally, there is some indication that for groups of four or less the group becomes so concerned with survival that other issues become submerged.[5]

If at all possible, groups should begin with at least seven patients. Since research indicates that most new groups will suffer from one to three dropouts within the first few months, it is important to have sufficient membership so that there is a workable cadre remaining when dropouts occur. When groups begin with insufficient numbers, this is usually a reliable indication that appropriate referrals are in short supply and that the therapist will have continuing difficulties in maintaining a satisfactory census.

Some therapists, in anticipation of members dropping out, begin their groups with more patients than they consider optimal. This strategy, though protecting against the possibility of dropouts threatening the group's survival, ultimately forces some patients to leave. We believe no therapist should ever begin a group with more than the number with which he is comfortable, since until the census reaches the therapist's original goal, he will remain uncomfortable and be less able to make optimal therapeutic interventions.

Ongoing groups should have a balance of men and women. Often women seeking treatment significantly outnumber men. In such instances it is possible to begin a group with a preponderance of women. For instance, if the therapist's goal is eight members, the group might begin with five women and whatever number of men are available. The remaining seats would be reserved for additional men.

Time of Meeting

Given the logistical problems involved in gathering eight to ten individuals together weekly, most therapy groups meet before or after usual working hours. Arranging sessions when there is less likelihood of time conflict increases the potential for referrals. Therapists must continually weigh the merits of a time convenient for their personal lives as opposed to a time that creates the best opportunity for the group to survive and flourish. In major metropolitan areas it is possible to run groups during the day. Even in such settings, however, the referral network is notably narrowed. Daytime groups typically draw from nonworking, self-employed, professional, student, or night-working populations. Early morning groups can avoid work conflicts but are a problem for parents of infants or school-age children. In the vast majority of instances, groups meet in the late afternoon or early evening.

Group Space

Groups differ markedly from dyadic therapy in space requirements. Too small or too large a room alters everyone's level of comfort and ability to work. Furthermore, the presence or lack of a waiting area will affect where and how members assemble prior to the meeting time and will have significant impact upon the range of choices they have in relating to one another. For example, in a clinic setting members may have to sit in a communal waiting area with other patients, an arrangement that diminishes pregroup exchanges.

Optimally the group room itself can be made available at least 15 minutes prior to the beginning of a meeting so that the members may convene there. Some patients may enjoy the socialization prior to group, whereas others avoid it. These are not chance choices, and the subgrouping patterns and conversations that begin prior to the meeting are often important therapeutic material.

· The seats themselves connote a great deal about how the group works and what is expected. How a therapist decides to set up the room with sofas and chairs is variable. (Sitting on pillows or on the floor is to be discouraged in adult groups.) Some therapists set a group size and leave a chair for the leader and for every potential member of the group. This arrangement emphasizes that members are absent and that there will be newcomers entering in the future. Furthermore, an empty chair looms large in a group after a significant member has terminated and is a powerful stimulus to the group's mourning process. An alternative procedure would be to set up chairs only for those expected to attend a meeting. No chair would be present for a terminated member, for someone on vacation or for someone who called and announced an absence. Patients would be expected to retain the inner image of the absent member. The general principle in either approach is consistency.

The seating arrangement should be comfortable enough so that individuals can sit easily for 75 to 120 minutes. Individuals select seating based on conscious and unconscious determinants. These choices are often connected to the patients' character styles or to dynamic processes taking place within the group. Observations about patterned choices help patients gain valuable insight. For example, who chooses the apparently more comfortable and less comfortable seats? Who sits near other people, and who sits farther away? Who sits near the leader, and who sits far away? We learn not only from the type of seat chosen, but also from where patients choose to sit. In some groups patients become rooted to particular chairs; in others the seating arrangement is a continual ebb and flow. It is best for the leader to sit in the same chair each week. This not only serves to underline consistency, it provides the opportunity to glean meaning from the members' choice of seating with regard to their position vis-à-vis the leader. (For a more complete discussion of nonverbal communication, see Chapter 11.)

A particularly important aspect of the group space is the door. The door is a boundary that must be regulated predictably. On occasion, patients and even inexperienced therapists will leave the door open after the session has begun with the expectation that a tardy member will soon enter. Obviously, an open door has considerable impact upon the sense of freedom and privacy. Further, such an open door symbolizes an open acceptance of the tardiness. It is preferable that the door be closed when the group session begins, thus demonstrating conclusively that the meeting has begun.

The First Meeting

The moments just before the start of the first meeting are a time of great excitement and anxiety, a common state of arousal shared by therapist and patients. When the door is closed and the first meeting has begun, patients look around apprehensively and almost always fix their gaze on the therapist. Later in the life of the group the therapist will enter, sit down, and begin observing what unfolds before him, but the first meeting represents an exception. In this case the therapist does have a responsibility for beginning the meeting.

The therapist starts by making it clear that he has met previously with each individual, that all have agreed to the same contract, and that all have significant personal issues they wish to resolve. At this point the therapist should repeat the group contract. In the case of homogeneous groups, the therapist also makes it clear that the members share a common variable. Typically he can then suggest that people get to know one another, leaving the exact manner of that introduction to the members themselves. The leader should then sit silently (not impassively or stoically!) and observe the developing interactions.

From the moment the group begins, we have an opportunity to observe the approaches our patients utilize to cope with stress. The initial data available for observation and analysis are the various styles used by the members to cope with the groupwide anxiety. How the members handle that common anxiety depends on their personality structure, their historic defense mechanisms, and the specific interactions that actually occur in the group. Therapists beginning groups should be thoroughly acquainted with the formative phase of group development, which is explored in depth in Chapter 3.

The Therapist's Role

When a group meets for the first time, there is an enormous pull upon the therapist to reduce the initial anxiety by becoming active. The therapist wants his group to begin comfortably, and he certainly wishes to avoid such intense anxiety that members never return. The members also want relief from the terrors of the unknown. The fantasy arises that the leader can reduce the anxiety. Nonetheless, he should resist the impulse to be overactive, because a style once established is difficult to break. In groups where the therapist is quite active in introductions and agenda-setting, patients feel disappointed in subsequent sessions when he becomes less active and they are faced with the unknown, seemingly without the leader's protection. Contrary to the intuition of the therapist, even new groups of primitive patients can survive and profit from a first session in which they are left largely to their own devices.

After the initial comments, the therapist's task is to begin to show the members how their fantasies and interactions in the here-and-now can be valuable in learning about themselves and the problems that they came to resolve. The first meeting is an ideal time to begin establishing the expectation that the group itself, not the therapist, is the primary therapeutic agent. The main issue is that members feel they *learned* something from their initial anxiety.

The Patients' Roles

Usually the group will begin with rudimentary introductions. Names, ranks, and serial numbers are given, after which the members will often fall silent. It is important that the therapist wait for the group to break the silence. (It only *seems* like it is going to last forever!) If the therapist indicates an early discomfort with silence by intervening too quickly, he will quickly teach his group that they can get him to respond by being silent.

If the therapist remains quiet, the members will begin to talk, sometimes about the problems that brought them, but mainly they will test the water by feeling out the others and sensing the safety and comfort that they might expect from the group. There are rare exceptions when the therapist has misjudged the members' capacity to interact, and rather than sit in prolonged silence he must intervene to protect them from the fears the silence evokes.

Eventually, though by no means necessarily in the first meeting, someone in the group will offer up the first group "gift," revealing information or feeling which makes that individual truly vulnerable if the response is insensitive. Perhaps a member begins to weep or tell in more detail why he is in the group. At this point the other members may either join or not join the new level of sharing. If the gift-giving member has not revealed something entirely foreign or too personal for a first meeting, others will inevitably tell more about themselves. In the first meeting, *what* is shared is much less important than the fact that something *is* shared and that the response is not threatening. The group is beginning to test out what can be said in this room, and they are very watchful and wary of the reactions of the other members and especially the therapist.

Ending the First Meeting

The ending of an initial group meeting should accomplish several objectives. First, if the contract was not restated at the beginning of the session, it should be done at this time. Second, the group leader should make some contact with each member. In this first meeting it is especially important that all the members know they were noticed and attended to by the leader, who might say, for example, "We noticed a variety of ways in which people dealt with this common anxiety about the initial meeting," and then relate the responses he observed.

Sometimes eye contact is sufficient to let a member know that there was contact. Beginning a group is difficult and, ironically, a very lonely experience for patients. It is unlike beginning individual therapy, where there is some cultural expectation that the therapist will listen attentively, will not be hurtful or vengeful, and will give undivided attention. In groups the patients must struggle for time and attention, and they have no assurances about how their fellow members will respond to personal exposures.

Despite the initial anxiety, almost all first sessions are judged a success by the therapist. There is a feeling of exhilaration and pleasure that the enterprise has gotten off the ground. Before the first session members had been so concerned with survival that the reality of the meeting was quite mild by comparison. Indeed, simply the recognition that others are just as worried is very helpful to the members and evokes a positive feeling.

There are few meetings in which the themes can be so accurately predicted as the first one. For example, the therapist will be helpful and almost always on target if he closes the meeting by saying, "The group has been testing to see how safe it is going to be to share what is most important in your lives with these people and with me. I'll see you next week." Or, "People have been saying 'hello' in a variety of ways."

The Early Weeks

Following the initial meeting, patients generally resurrect their defenses and characteristic patterns of interacting. Caution is an important dynamic, and an underlying characteristic is testing to see whether the group and others can be trusted.[6] Members are experientially trying to establish group norms in order to institutionalize safety. But conflicts inevitably arise, since not everyone has the same safety requirements. The tensions between the differing needs fuel the interactions, but the pace is generally slow, because to deal with these tensions directly strikes at the central pathological conflicts of many of the members. Often patients become disheartened and disillusioned about the group during this time.

The therapist has a number of important tasks to help group formation. He must monitor boundaries and norms. The primary boundary is between the group and the outside world. For a variety of reasons, members will come late or be absent. The therapist must draw attention to these contractual violations in order to establish the norm that boundary violations are to be explored for their deeper meanings, as well as the norm of valuing the importance of the here-and-now. What complicates matters is the extensive use of denial at this stage. Members generally ignore or minimize others' behavior. The therapist may feel like he is swimming upstream. Members will create all sorts of pressures to keep him from drawing the boundary violations to their attention, and especially to keep him from interpreting the meanings of the violations. Nevertheless the therapist, with as much tact and therapeutic creativity as possible, must point out what is happening.

Not only are external boundaries being addressed, but also boundaries within the group. Individuals erect barriers to giving and receiving information about one another. Usually, no one person blocks development of trust or openness, but a collusion exists in which members avoid difficult affects, use anger as a defense against involvement, switch topics, and so on. While the content that is discussed might be quite revealing as to the hidden conflicts or fears of the speakers, the focus for the therapist is the process—how members deal with anxieties and conflicts rather than merely the content of a particular conflict. The anxieties aroused in the early weeks tempt the therapist to close off affect prematurely with summarizing interpretations. Instead his task is to help members tolerate and face their anxieties generated by the process.

In this opening period, a number of interactive patterns emerge with regularity. In almost every group there is a period when advice giving is a common modus operandi. Members will present a problem or a conflict in their lives, and others will make direct suggestions about solutions. Analysis and understanding is not the goal; problem solving is. A number of dynamics may be functioning in such advice-giving behaviors. One may be to remove problems that make people uncomfortable; a second to utilize tried and true remedies rather than recognize a sense of helplessness; a third may be to focus on external problems so that the more difficult task of dealing with the in-group interactions can be bypassed; a fourth is to compete with the therapist for fantasied acclaim; a fifth may be to demonstrate the members' ineffectiveness with one another (only rarely is a suggestion intrinsically useful, because patients have already received lots of advice and suggestions before they enter the group). When confronted with a period of advice giving, the therapist must help the members understand its function with regard to the group's development.

A similar situation occurs when a group focuses on one member as "sick." Overtly, all are altruistically working to help solve an individual's problems. However, by focusing on one member the pathologies of others are obscured. The parallel with family interactions, in which a child may be the bearer of all the difficulties and therefore be labeled as "sick," is evident. A variation on this pattern is when members seem to be taking turns, "Last week we talked about Adam; now it's Betty's turn." Seldom is that process explicit, but it subtly becomes established. This unconsciously serves to limit intragroup transactions.

These are but a few examples of the ways members and therapists attempt to manage the problems of developing group trust and cohesion. The analysis of resistances, character traits, and emergency defenses all can be used for therapeutic gain, but sometimes in these early weeks the therapist and members become discouraged, primarily because the group is not meeting their expectations. Under such circumstances the therapist's countertransference can be mobilized to scapegoat members who seem to be obstructionistic, or the therapist can become defensive and less open to hearing his patients. These problems affect the group atmosphere and accelerate dropping out, a problem we will discuss in the next section.

The patients' discouragement often leads to depression, exacerbation of symptoms, or a futile attempt to involve optimism about the group through reaction formation. The critical consideration for patients and therapist during this time is to remember that the reawakening of primary defenses and pathologies is a sign that the group is in fact becoming effective, since as this happens the members begin experiencing their problems in the group itself.

Dropouts

Almost all new psychotherapy groups have one or more dropouts within the first few weeks. Such dropouts, while disconcerting and disappointing, should be considered an expectable part of beginning a group. A number of reports in the literature indicate that 20 to 45 percent of charter members leave within the first year. These data seem valid for both clinic and private practice settings, and for both very inexperienced and more highly seasoned group therapists.[7]

The reasons given for leaving are quite varied. Sometimes no reasons are given at all! On occasion patients will suddenly find they have a time conflict, perhaps even pleading that the group time be changed to accommodate them. However, any change in the group structure is contraindicated. Many a well-meaning therapist has changed the time of a group to help a particular patient avoid a time conflict, only to find that the very patient in question drops out of the group anyway. The sudden appearance of a time conflict is best understood dynamically—that is, as a communication about the patient's experience of his participation in the group.

The fact that the early life of groups is filled with people leaving prematurely dramatically reduces the members' optimism. It is not unusual for new groups to develop an atmosphere of hopelessness and discouragement, and as a consequence the members begin feeling like failures and begin questioning the efficacy of group therapy and the competence of the leader. The leader should encourage the open discussion of these fears and doubts, thereby reassuring the members that all feelings can be honestly shared.

Very Small Groups

For a variety of reasons there will be weeks when only one or two patients come to a meeting. Running a session when almost no one shows up is a problem. Unfortunately this is not unusual early in the life of a group, before cohesiveness has set in.

Inexperienced therapists often wonder whether they should reduce the amount of time or cancel the meeting if few members arrive. The press to cancel or shorten the meeting is a countertransferential attempt by the therapist to avoid his own intense affects (hurt, anger, disappointment, and so on) stimulated by such a small group. Implementing such a plan would end up negatively reinforcing the members who *kept* their contracts. Furthermore, one is never certain whether or not other members might come strolling in late.

The group still exists in the minds of the members who did appear, and it is not unusual for these meetings to have significant impact on those who attend. The technical key is for the therapist to remember that he is still running a *group*, and not doing individual or couple therapy. One of the major issues needing attention is that those who came to the meeting were let down by their colleagues, who had made commitments to attend. Old feelings of separation, loss, abandonment, divorce, and family dissolution all may be reawakened. How the attending members respond to this situation is potentially quite important.

New Members

In ongoing groups, the coming and going of members has great meaning. Each goodbye and hello means that the group itself changes. The therapist should encourage members to explore personal and groupwide meanings associated with the anticipation of newcomers prior to their introduction.

Considerable pressure may arise within the group to avoid change, even at the cost of maintaining a lower census. Members will talk openly about their anxieties with the intent of coercing the therapist into delaying new additions. An alternative strategy occurs when they may attack the therapist for making poor choices, hoping to influence him to reject some acceptable applicants. Finally, some may threaten to quit rather than face a newcomer, and on occasion a member actually leaves.

The various pressures may influence the therapist's decisions. It is not easy to decide when a group could benefit from more time to work on a loss or on the feelings surrounding the advent of new members. The repeated thought, "This is not a good time to add members," is often a manifestation of countertransference, and if acted upon may be an error. On the other hand, therapists can collude to cover over patient feelings by prematurely filling an empty chair.

New members should *never* simply arrive in a group. Old members need a period of preparation so that they may explore their reactions, but also so that they can come to each session without the concern that strangers might be present. The usual procedure is for the therapist, at the beginning of a meeting, to announce, "There will be a new member joining us on such and such a date." The length of time between the announcement and the actual entrance of the new member depends upon many variables. If a group has had an open chair for some time and has been awaiting a new member, two weeks can be sufficient lead time. If, on the other hand, the empty chair is the result of a particularly important or painful loss (a highly valued member who terminated, or one who suddenly died), the time required to sort through feelings about another person joining should be longer. All other factors then being equal, two weeks' notice seems optimal. This provides members the opportunity to work on their reactions immediately and the following week as well.

From a practical perspective a new person can be admitted when the appropriate preparation has been completed. There has been some sentiment suggesting that applicants not be added singly, but in pairs in order to protect them from being victimized by latent or overt hostility from the members. This practice is presumed to reduce the chances of newcomers dropping out prematurely. In a recent study[8] it was found that adding patients singly did not lead to unusual numbers prematurely stopping, and in fact the data suggest this approach diminishes the number of drop outs. By adding members individually, each new member has a time of separate introduction, and the norm becomes established that empty chairs will be filled when appropriate.

At times the therapist will be confronted by the situation of having two or more openings and an equal number of applicants. The question at this time is, should the new patients be added singly or together? There are pros and cons to either answer. If the patients are added singly, each has a brief individual introduction, providing for more individualization and allowing a clearer view of the introductory dynamics of that person. On the other hand, if multiple openings are filled at the same time, there is the real advantage of closing the group boundary more quickly. Furthermore, the new members often experience a powerful and immediate alliance with those who join with them. It is preferable when multiple openings exist to add the new patients together since that will most rapidly reform the group boundary. The exception is when the number of new patients being considered outnumbers the members in the group. In that instance the entrances should be sequential so that there are never more new than old members. Naturally, on those occasions when groups have diminished to a membership of one or two, even that rule must be broken.

It is advisable to provide only the fact that a new member will be entering. Fantasies about the age, sex, marital status, and other details about the coming member all contain useful material from which the old members can learn.

Each group develops initiation rites.[9] The therapist sets a tone by restating the contract, thereby reminding the old members of the agreements. Frequently the agreements are misremembered, and this habitual restating allows for corrections as well as explorations of the meanings of the misremembering. Repetition of the contract puts everyone on equal footing in this area.

Some groups appear warmly and enthusiastically to greet the newcomers, and only through closer scrutiny is any ambivalence exposed. Retention of the fantasy of the old group, which subtly excludes the newcomer, may be expressed by reminiscing or by cryptically referring to prior events. Another common initiation procedure is for groups to have dramatic and highly emotional meetings. In part such meetings can be understood as exhibitionistic demonstrations of how much emotion, personal revelation, and confrontation can be tolerated. These dramatic meetings often have another unconscious element as well—an attempt to frighten off the newcomer or at least to test his mettle. Questioning new members about their histories and reasons for coming to group is yet another initiation pattern. This questioning can vary widely in its form and intent, ranging from courteous inquiry of a new member, thereby offering him an opportunity to make connections with the other members, to sadistic grilling with no altruistic motivation. Impressions at the time of change are valuable data and available only briefly. Whatever initiation rites are used to greet newcomers, the therapist must help the group learn from this process.

References

1. L. Birk, "Intensive Group Therapy: An Effective Behavioral-Psychoanalytic Method." *Am. J. Psychiatry* 131 (1974):11–16.
2. A.L. Kadis, "The Alternate Meeting in Group Psychotherapy," *Am. J. Psychiatry* 10 (1956):275–291.
3. I.D. Yalom, G. Bond, S. Bloch, E. Zimmerman, and L. Friedman, "The Impact of a Weekend Group Experience on Individual Therapy," *Arch. Gen. Psychiatry* 34 (1977):399–418.
4. C. Winick, A.L. Kadis, and J.D. Krasner, "Training and Professional Practice of American Group Therapists," *Int. J. Group Psychother.* 11 (1961):419–430.
5. C.C.F. Fulkerson, D.M. Hawkins, and A.R. Alden, "Psychotherapy Groups of Insufficient Size," *Int. J. Group Psychother.* 31 (1981):73–81.
6. W.N. Stone and J.P. Gustafson, "Technique in Group Psychotherapy of Narcissistic and Borderline Patients," *Int. J. Group Psychother.* 32 (1982):29–47.
7. W.N. Stone and J.S. Rutan, "Duration of Group Psychotherapy," *Int. J. Group Psychother.* 34 (1984):93–110.
8. *Ibid.*
9. S.R. Kaplan and M. Roman, "Characteristic Responses in Adult Therapy Groups to the Introduction of New Members: A Reflection on Group Process," *Int. J. Group Psychother.* 11 (1961):372–381.

Special Technical Considerations 11

In this chapter we address a number of special clinical considerations that arise often in the practice of group therapy. These are the therapeutic management of dreams, scapegoating, nonverbal communication, combined (individual and group) therapy, and treating primitive patients, specifically borderline and narcissistic patients, in groups.

Dreams in Group Psychotherapy

Background

An old Talmudic saying states, "A dream that has not been interpreted is like a letter that has not been opened." Freud was the first to interpret dreams rigorously, scientifically, and systematically. As with much of his work on unconscious material, Freud gained a foothold in working with dreams by postulating that they are a valid, psychic communication that *can* be understood. His major contributions were developing a way of understanding the covert meaning from the manifest content and recognizing that dreams often represent wish fulfillment.

Subsequently, in individual therapy, dreams were utilized as a valuable window into the unconscious. Group therapists, following this lead, expanded the intrapsychic focus to include interpersonal and group-as-a-whole processes.

Any groupwide conflict or shared anxiety may be vividly portrayed in the manifest dream or exposed through the members' associations.[1,2] Problems of joining and trust may be themes of dreams graphically presented in the first stage of group formation, whereas rebellion, power, and autonomy may be portrayed at later stages.[3] Some conflicts may have been dimly recognized or consciously avoided only to reappear directly or thinly disguised in the manifest dream content.[4,5] Transferences or attitudes toward the therapist also may be brought to light via dreams. Conversely the dreamer could be informing the therapist about a countertransference affecting the whole group.

In the interpersonal sphere, dreams convey valuable information about the state of the relationships among members. There are often direct references to the group or to specific members (although not necessarily those with whom there is conflict). In the traditional intrapsychic sphere, dreams in groups also provide access to individual member's resistances, wishes, transferences, and conflicts.

Clinical Illustrations

The New Member.

> *A chronically depressed man, in the middle of a lengthy and painful divorce, entered an ongoing therapy group in order to learn more about himself and his troubled relationships with women. The night following his first group session, he dreamed that he was in line waiting to be seated in a restaurant. As he was waiting, a group of people pushed by him and were seated by the maître d'. He turned around and left the restaurant, reversing a sign on the front door to indicate the restaurant was closed.*

From the perspective of group development, the oral imagery of the restaurant is consistent with the dreamer's position as a new member and reflects one of the themes of initial participation in a group: "Will I get enough?" Such imagery is typical of early group participation and does not automatically indicate major personal conflicts at an oral dependent level of development.

From the group-as-a-whole perspective, the dream represented the newcomer's perception that the old members were favored by the therapist, as depicted by the maître d'. The dream indicated the newcomer's concern that he would not be able to join fully.

From the interpersonal perspective, the patient revealed a chronic defensive pattern invoked to manage rejection and pain—withdrawal and retaliation.

Finally, from the intrapsychic perspective, there are suggestions about the transference to the therapist and ego distortions represented in the maladaptive manner of handling his ambivalence about nurturance and dependency.

Sequential Dreams.

> *A woman entered a group in which continuing and vociferous conflict among several members dominated her first meeting. At her second meeting she reported a fragment from a dream she had had the night of the first meeting. "I was driving a truck. Instead of going forward, it went backward into a very tight place."*

The old members quickly recognized the group level of the dream's meaning—the new member had felt stymied by the group conflict, unable to move forward on her own issues, and backed into a corner. The therapist wondered whether the heated conflicts had been exaggerated in order to frighten off the new member, and he was concerned that perhaps he had brought in the member at an inopportune time.

> *In her third meeting the woman presented two additional dream fragments from the intervening week. "I was in a crowd of friendly people, and all of a sudden I gave birth to a baby!" She immediately associated to the group and to her new perception that the group seemed much more friendly in her second meeting. She said, "The baby is me. The group is a new beginning." She then moved to her next dream, beginning enticingly, "Now for the one in which I die." She dreamed that she was in a group of people, some of whom she recognized from work. Suddenly a man got up and shot her in the head.*
>
> *She associated to a man she had felt very angry with, and said that this dream had nothing to do with the group. Later in the session, however, she added an omitted detail. In the dream, one of the bystanders, immediately before she had been shot, had said, "It's what you deserve." This was the same phrase she herself had used earlier in the meeting. The repetition of the phrase helped her overcome an initial resistance to connecting the dreams to the feelings evoked in the treatment and recognize her fears in the here-and-now group interaction.*

This woman's dreams across the two meetings illustrate a common sequence for new members. At first she felt somewhat overwhelmed by the group. When she felt safer, she could conceive of attaining her wishes. Only then could she expose her underlying fear of being attacked and wounded by one of the veteran members.

The next sequence of dreams represents various group members' contribution to a common group stress. The dreams were all reported in the first meeting following a series of canceled sessions due to the therapist's absence.

The Unavailable Professor.

> *A woman reported a dream she had had during the interruption. "I was looking for the therapist at his university office, but he was busy with other students and did not have time for me." She reported feeling "stunned and devastated." In the associations that followed, a man reported a dream he had during the interruption. "I was taking a test in mathematics and an English professor, who was trying to help me, suddenly disappeared and was unavailable." Then he spontaneously remembered a recurrent dream from his early childhood, "I was riding in a street car and my mother was waiting for me at the end of the line. Just as I arrived she flew off and someone said she was a witch." Finally, a second woman reported a dream, which she termed a nightmare. "My daughter was*

inhabited by the devil and I was trying to exorcise it but I couldn't do it." She awoke in a highly anxious and frightened state.

This fascinating sequence of dreams illustrates the interconnectedness of dreams by different members, each portraying the dreamers' responses to the common stress of the therapist's absence and the canceled sessions.

The representation of the unavailable therapist in the first dream as the unavailable professor was echoed in the second as the disappearing professor, and then in the third as the disappearing mother/witch. The last reference reminded the second woman of her dream involving exorcism, and it was through that linkage that she could begin to identify herself with the child who needed the devil removed.

The dream content also showed the reverberating theme of the therapist's other interests taking precedence over his interest in the members. One member's dream portrayed him as too busy with others, the second as not qualified to teach the course (an English professor in a mathematics course) as well as being unavailable, and finally the malevolent persona of the witch.

A Group Resistance.

> *A woman reported a dream "about the group." "I was in some sort of bus. Every time the bus came to a dangerous area, we would skirt it or avoid it. This occurred several times in the dream. I thought the bus had passed my stop, but a man who was a cooking expert and a teacher got on the bus, and it seemed to head back to the right destination."*

The dreamer initially spoke of how she habitually avoided all conflict, often by not knowing what she felt. But she implied others had joined her, since she directly identified the dream as being about the group. Her interpretation of the dream was that the "cooking expert" was the group therapist. Analysis of the dream elements by the group highlighted and confirmed the manifest content that the bus was in fact controlled by the passengers, and the teacher was not the driver. Through this they were able to begin to acknowledge how all the members had been contributing to the avoidance of the "dangerous" sexual feelings in the room.

Despite the emphasis on group process, it should be remembered that dreams are also communications about the inner states of individuals.

The Gravedigger.

> *A long-time group member had spent most of his therapy minimizing the impact of his self-righteous intellectualizing on others. His interpersonal life was characterized by a great deal of acrimonious arguing,*

which his group interactions paralleled. During one session in which the
therapist again pointed out to this man that members were trying to tell
him how painful they felt his comments to be, he suddenly reported a
dream. "I was digging around uncovering corpses. They were all in brown
bags so that you didn't smell them or see them, but it was still pretty
disgusting. I came across one corpse, and for no apparent reason I just
cut off its head." He reported awaking both shaken and disgusted.

The patient's understanding was that the head belonged to a particularly
obnoxious, pompous, self-righteous colleague. The therapist, after eliciting
the associations of others, suggested that this dream might represent the
patient's efforts to get rid of a particularly distasteful part of himself. He
immediately agreed, saying that as he was reporting the dream he realized
that he was talking about how the group must perceive him, and how he
always anticipated criticism as he spoke.

His dream clearly conveyed this patient's dawning awareness of
something wrong within himself as well as with the interpersonal impact
he made.

Technique in Dream Interpretation in Group Therapy

Group therapists can dramatically affect the reporting and analysis of dreams
by their patients simply by showing interest. Ignoring dreams results in
extinguishing their presentations.

The classic tool in breaking the dream code is free association.
When all members associate to a dream this tool is even more effective,
since the collective associations may reflect a multidimensional report on
the state of the group as well as of the individuals within it. As illustrated
in the foregoing examples, some of the associations may be other dreams
or even interpretations. While the interpretations may be either accurate
or inaccurate, they represent data about the contributer's personal conflicts.
The therapist should try to elicit associations from the dreamer and the
other members before making an interpretation.

Since feelings are usually the least disguised elements of dreams,
the therapist helps the members learn to explore the affect of dreams. Members frequently assist one another in overcoming resistance to full exploration
of dreams by sharing openly their own feeling responses. Usually the affects
can be linked to shared feelings, and in this manner the therapeutic value
of the dream is enhanced.

We do not recommend a rote practice of asking each member to
respond to a dream. Rather, the flow of group associations helps clarify
the dream's unconscious components. Thus what may appear to be abrupt
changes in topic to avoid charged material may simply be an associative
path that further elaborates or clarifies the latent meaning.

> *As a group discussed their feelings about one another and about group interactions, one woman protested that she had not felt what others had been feeling. She angrily said she felt the therapist was pressuring the members to express feelings, and she was unable to do so. She then reported a dream, which she presented as an afterthought and which to her had no obvious connection to the conversation that had gone before. "I dreamed there was an old black lady working on a man's head. I was behind a screen and couldn't see very well. Someone asked me to move something to the other side of the screen, but I wasn't able to do it."*
>
> *The dreamer immediately associated the black lady in the dream to the group therapist (a white male), "who works on heads." Then she felt confused and said, "I can't see what this dream is about, and most of the time I can't see what this group is about."*
>
> *The associative process seemed to abruptly shift as a man began to talk to the dreamer about their accidental meeting outside the group. He said that he was frightened of her since she had been so seductive at that meeting and thereafter. A raging argument ensued regarding who was trying to seduce whom. As the discussion continued and the feelings subsided, the therapist asked about the man's initial comment that he was frightened. The woman was startled and then acknowledged that she had never heard him say he was afraid, saying "I didn't know he was afraid. I just knew I was afraid and had to protect myself by attacking him."*

This particular dream, and the ensuing process, added more data to a growing awareness on the part of the dreamer that she could not hear others' anxieties and fears. There was much more in the dream that was not analyzed in the illustration. For example, the dreamer identified the therapist as a black woman, but other data suggest that the patient herself was also represented by the black woman. She worked on the man's head with her seductiveness, and she did not know what she was doing because she could not see. Using data from prior group meetings, the following sequence was likely operating: she controlled through seductiveness, was unable to recognize others' anxious responses, and when confronted about her blindness reacted with anger and started a fight. More analysis of the dream also would produce results for the man, since he exhibited similar characteristics. In previous sessions he had demonstrated seductive behavior when he felt insecure about himself.

Dreams can serve a great many needs. Their presentation might contain important dependent, competitive, exhibitionistic, or narcissistic wishes on the part of the dreamer. In such situations other members might respond by ignoring the dreamer and the dream, or by presenting dreams in a competitive fashion. A plethora of dreams can be presented in order to avoid or resist other more powerful feelings. This is often the case when the therapist finds that the group is flooded with dream material so that great blocks of time are devoted to hearing and analyzing dreams.

Dreams are so filled with potential meaning that therapists have the difficult job of deciding how much time can profitably be spent analyzing dreams without losing sight of the ongoing, in-group process.

Scapegoating

The term *scapegoat* comes from the biblical story of Aaron confessing all the sins of the children of Israel over the head of a goat, which was then sent into the wilderness symbolically bearing those sins.[6] Allport[7] hypothesized that prejudice, at root, is societal scapegoating to provide a sense of solidarity among the majority. In group therapy scapegoating refers to the focusing of hostile, sadistic, and hurtful attention on one particular individual. Scapegoating serves a symbolic value similar to that in the biblical story—an individual is scapegoated in order to protect the group. Toker has suggested, "The scapegoat is frequently essential for the adequate functioning of a group (whatever the nature of the group) in that he provides an area into which aggressions can be channeled and focused without presenting a threat to the psychic integrity of the individual or a threat to the stability and unity of the group itself."[8] Bion[9] also noted that fight-flight groups are prepared to sacrifice individual members in order to protect the group.

Not all painful confrontations are manifestations of scapegoating. Indeed some of the most important growth experiences are forged in strong, painful, and difficult interactions between members. Groups offer unique opportunities for receiving feedback about the less desirable aspects of one's personality. Therapists must be able to distinguish between strong but ultimately helpful confrontations and hurtful scapegoating. The distinguishing keys are the affective sense that the patient being confronted is being hurt rather than helped and that the motivation of the confrontation is to inflict pain rather than to provide information. In addition, there is an affective sense that the scapegoated patient does not deserve such an intense attack.

Central to understanding scapegoating is the concept of projective identification, first elaborated by Melanie Klein[10] and later revised in the British object relations school by W.R.D. Fairbairn[11] and by Harry Guntrip.[12] It is a defensive maneuver in which individuals or groups project into others traits or aspects of self-representation that are unacceptable as one's own. The projection is not random, but rather is directed to a willing recipient, an individual who in some substantial ways demonstrates the unacceptable qualities. The projector, in attempting to "change" the other, also maintains contact with the hated and dreaded parts of himself that cyclically require continued projection. This continual involvement with the other is the essential clue to the process of projective identification.[13] Thus projective identification refers to the two-party system that involves both projection and an acceptance of the projected traits.

Pure projection should be differentiated from projective identification. In pure projection the subject takes an unacceptable quality and disowns it by attributing it to another person. Simple projection is a one-person system, where the other person is an unknowing and unwilling party to the projections. Scapegoating may feel like pure projection in that it seems that the scapegoat is an unwilling victim. However, closer examination will indicate that scapegoats indeed played a part in their fate. In fact, they may "volunteer" for the role by engaging in behaviors that draw the group's fury, thereby setting in motion familiar patterns. Scapegoats often played similar roles in their original families.

Therapists are not immune to becoming scapegoats themselves. Levine[14] suggests group therapists are particularly subject to scapegoating when they defensively refuse to understand the members' attempts to wrest power and control. More often, therapists are not scapegoats per se, but rather are containers for negative transferences. Patients usually are the target of scapegoating.

Garland and Kolodny[15] suggest four fundamental forms of scapegoating in groups: ostracism, institutionalization, encapsulation, and inclusion through introspection. Ostracism is the most immediately malevolent form of scapegoating, since it often results in the scapegoat leaving the group. In ostracism the scapegoat is placed in an accustomed role as the different one, the troublesome one, the group buffoon, and so on. The encapsulated scapegoat is allowed only limited participation in the group. The final form of scapegoating consists of involving the scapegoat in active, intrusive introspection, a hostile dedication to finding out what makes him tick.

The analysis of scapegoating entails helping the entire group understand that the scapegoat role is unconsciously considered crucial to the emotional survival of the group. It represents a defensive operation that must be analyzed and understood. In that the scapegoated individual often suffers great pain, it is advisable to proceed as quickly as possible to the task of understanding the function of the scapegoating in terms of its role in protecting the group so that the danger of unnecessarily hurting a patient is diminished.

Scapegoating is a difficult problem for therapists. If the therapist moves to protect the patient, the rest of the group may perceive this as favoritism or interference with their justified criticism, thus making the plight of the scapegoated member even worse.

It is important to help the attacking members look at their own insecurities that are triggered by the visage or behavior of the scapegoat. It is sometimes helpful to remind the attackers that it is not the behavior of the scapegoat that is so troubling; it is the feelings that are evoked within the attacker. Scapegoating ends when the members own their projections and see the scapegoat more clearly.

Nonverbal Communication

A great deal of highly significant communication in groups takes place nonverbally. Some is conscious and obvious, and some is unconscious and subtle. Every therapist is familiar with the communication of the depressed individual who enters a session walking very slowly with head down, eyes averted, and finally sits slouched in a chair and does not speak. Other common behaviors such as lighting a cigarette, crossing legs, nodding the head, or selecting a particular seat in the group circle have both conscious and unconscious determinants.

Birdwhistle[16] has suggested that body motion is a powerful cultural tool for communication. The individual through nonverbal channels finds out who he is relative to others. He makes contacts, and conveys and receives messages through these channels. Signals are given that regulate the flow of information and the intensity of affects. Berger, in discussing nonverbal communications, stated that they function in "the establishment, maintenance, and regulation of interpersonal relationships."[17] We will examine two important modes of nonverbal communication in group psychotherapy: seating arrangement and body language, and then consider the therapeutic use of these data.

Seating Arrangement

There are no stereotypical meanings to seat selection. The role of therapist's helper is often signaled by a member's selection of the seat immediately to the therapist's right (the right-hand man), but that seat may also be selected by a patient attempting to avoid eye contact with the therapist. A member in conflict with the therapist might select a seat directly opposite him, but that same seat might be selected by a patient desiring to get the best possible view of the therapist. What is important is for the members to become curious about the particular meaning that might underlie the choice of particular seats.

If a therapist sits in the same chair each session, he can be in the optimal position to observe seating patterns chosen by the members. The members choose seats for conscious and unconscious reasons. Many choices are made primarily in relation to the therapist.

Members also indicate feelings about one another in the seating choices. Sexual attraction may be communicated by "couples" sitting beside each other each week. Groups working on male-female competition may arrange themselves with the men on one side of the group and the women on the other.

The chairs themselves can be utilized in nonverbal communication. Members sometimes move their chairs back out of the circle when they are frightened, anxious, or angry. On the other hand, members will move their chairs slightly forward when they desire attention or experience closeness.

Body Language

There is no doubt that body language communicates a great deal about affective experience. A blush or knuckles whitening on a chair are clear messages of physiological responses to affect. Because our culture places considerable emphasis on eye contact, persons who do not maintain eye contact while talking are often evidencing the presence of considerable affect. Head nodding not only signals agreement but also encourages another to continue.

In some instances body language communicates something quite different from the conscious experience or feeling of the individual. A member may complain that another has taken up too much time, only to be confronted by the observation that he had been nodding his head in agreement all the while the monopolizer had been talking.

Scheflen[18] has examined nonverbal communication via careful study of videotapes. He found that body positions may be open or closed to include or exclude others. He also pointed out that body language itself can convey mixed messages, as when the upper body is open (arms at sides) and the lower body is closed (legs crossed). Scheflen further described how subtle head nods or body shifts signal a wish to end a conversation.

In another study Scheflen[19] observed unconscious communication of quasicourting behavior in psychotherapy sessions. He noted preening behaviors, such as hair stroking, rearranging clothes, or adjusting makeup as some standard courting behaviors in women. Other characteristic body motions include prolonging a gaze, exposing a thigh, placing a hand on a hip, or protruding a breast. Men may adjust their ties, pull up their socks, or smooth their hair. Scheflen states that in most cases disqualifiers, such as not completing the messages or verbally noting that others are present, accompany courting behaviors. The timing and patterns of such behaviors are valuable data in understanding the groupwide or individual conflicts. If messages are given in an ambiguous fashion, or out of the initiator's awareness, the potential for interpersonal difficulty is considerable.

Therapeutic Management of Nonverbal Communication

Upon observing emotionally important nonverbal communication, the therapist faces several conceptual tasks. First, if possible the therapist should try to link the observation to the here-and-now transactions in the group. Second, the therapist must remember that most nonverbal communications are unconscious and must be treated respectfully. If too abrupt or direct a confrontation is made, the individual confronted may react with denial, upset, anger, embarrassment, and/or hurt. This is not only related to the content of the material but is also a response to the therapist's having observed and made public that which was out of the patient's awareness and control. Such a move generates iatrogenic resistance and does little to advance the work of the group.

As patients gain some experience with the examination of nonverbal clues they will imitate and identify with the therapist, widening the scope of the group analytic process. It is not unusual in a group that has been functioning for a number of months for patients to comment to one another about facial expressions, a clenched fist, tapping of feet or fingers, or a look in someone's eye. They also learn to recognize that shifts in body position are important communications. Even when the behaviors are conscious gestures, members may not have appreciated the force of their messages and the underlying feelings until the behaviors have been pointed out.

Concurrent Therapy (Individual and Group)

There is growing interest in the advantages that may accrue when patients are seen in individual and group therapy concurrently.[20-24] Each modality offers something that the other does not. In individual therapy there is the opportunity to focus precisely and in detail on the history, transferences, and associations of a single patient. In group therapy patients are seen in their interpersonal fields, and their characteristic relational and defensive styles are available for direct observation. Therapists who have seen patients in both modalities are accustomed to finding new information in either setting. A morose, depressed patient in dyadic therapy might demonstrate a social aptitude in the group setting that the individual therapist would have been hard-pressed to have guessed was present. A quiet, seemingly uninvolved group patient might relate a panorama of vivid reactions to and feelings about the group in the safety of a dyadic therapy.

A variety of options must be entertained when considering concurrent therapy. For example, when should the patient see the same therapist in both individual and group therapy (combined therapy), and when should he see different therapists (conjoint therapy)? When should group therapy be added to individual therapy, and when should individual therapy be added to group therapy? How should these additions best be accomplished? For which patients is the use of combined or conjoint therapy indicated, and for which patients is it contraindicated?

The following criteria set forth indications for the use of concurrent therapy.[25]

Group Therapy Added to Individual Therapy

1. Patients in individual therapy sometimes experience difficulty generating enough associational material to fuel their individual therapy effectively. Groups evoke many feelings and memories for these patients, and these affects and memories can then be used productively in both settings.

2. For those patients for whom the dyadic transference is insufficient to help them resolve their interpersonal problems, groups can assist them with relating to both sexes, different ages, and multiple personality styles. This provides an opportunity to experience a much wider range of interpersonal options, and it represents a situation more easily generalized to life.

3. Groups benefit some patients who, in the course of their individual therapy, have made significant strides toward understanding the roots of interpersonal problems and now need a laboratory in which to cement gains or further explore these issues.

4. In situations where therapists become locked into a countertransference struggle with their patients, the addition of a supplemental group can often unlock the countertransference struggle and thus save the individual therapy.

Individual Therapy Added to Group Therapy

1. The patient who is unable to express himself in the group is often assisted by individual therapy. This patient needs to be distinguished from the patient who refuses to relate in the group. Both can be helped to use the group more productively by supplemental individual therapy, but

the latter patients should probably be helped to own the hostile aspects of their withholding as an element in the referral.

2. The patient who has identified a specific piece of therapeutic work that he wants to focus on in a more extensive manner can use individual therapy to intensify that exploration. This situation generally is a result of effective work in group therapy, and to the degree that it is understood as supplementing and not replacing the group, we do not view it as a resistance.

3. Some patients find the interpersonal setting of the group too frightening and need the presence of an individual therapist to help them remain in the group. Individual therapy can assist them by exploring the roots of their fears about group membership and thus allow them to continue in the group.

4. When group members undergo an external crisis, such as a death in the family, short-term individual therapy is often a useful tool to help them through the time of crisis.

There are potential disadvantages to concurrent therapy. The most notable disadvantage occurs if the two therapies are disconnected from each other. This is particularly a danger if different therapists are involved, since neither therapist is present when the other is working. Concurrent therapy provides a fertile ground for splitting, and the antidote is for the two therapists to keep in communication about the patient. It is important to gain the patient's agreement that there will be no secrets between the individual and group therapist.

For some primitive patients the dissonance raised by two different types of therapy is more than they can integrate. This is less a factor of a particular diagnostic category and more a function of the individual's particular strengths and weaknesses. Some severely disturbed borderline patients can be greatly assisted by combined therapy, while others inevitably utilize splitting and perceive one therapist or therapy as all good and the other as all bad. With the more primitive patients, careful attention must be paid to the benefits or liabilities of having the same therapist in both individual and group therapist roles. For some the consistency of the therapist makes the divergence experience tolerable, while for others the forced sharing of the individual therapist is more than they can tolerate. Again, in consultation with the patient, these decisions must be made on a case-by-case basis.

When individual and group therapy are used concurrently, it is important that neither be viewed as superior to the other. Rather, they are adjunctive to one another. There will be times during the therapy when the patient will give more weight to one or the other, and that is to be expected. In the usual course of events, patients gradually put more and more emphasis on their therapy group, and commonly the individual therapy is terminated prior to the group therapy.

Therapists should be willing to explore in either setting reactions to and feelings about the other therapy. It is important, however, that feelings be redirected so that they are dealt with in the setting where they were evoked. In an individual therapy hour in which a patient discussed intense reactions to fellow group members the therapist might suggest, "You have some important things to discuss with the group." Such a comment is usually sufficient to indicate to the patient that these feelings should not be kept separate from the group.

When individual therapy and group therapy are viewed as cooperative by therapists and patients alike, they represent a very powerful therapeutic modality for use with a wide variety of patients.

Special Patient Populations

Borderline and narcissistic patients have received extensive attention in the current psychotherapeutic literature. They warrant special attention here because of the unique ways in which groups can help them and because of the technical considerations therapists must take into account when treating them in groups. Because there is no unanimity in definition regarding these patients, some depth of description of them is needed before techniques for treating them in groups are suggested.

The Borderline Patient

Patients with borderline personality disorder have attracted considerable interest and attention and yet remain ubiquitous and puzzling. No clear diagnostic schema exists, and efforts to categorize these individuals are based on descriptive, dynamic, or combined criteria. In general, patients with borderline disorder have "instability in a variety of areas: interpersonal behavior, mood, and self-image. No single feature is invariably present."[26] Their interpersonal relations may be characterized as unstable, intense, or withdrawn. They may have outbursts of anger directed at others or the self. Their mood is equally unstable, though a chronic depressive element is frequently present. They have neither a consistent and clearly formed identity nor an ability to develop long-range goals or plans. At times these patients may develop brief psychotic episodes.

Dynamic formulations about borderline conditions have focused on early developmental deficits, in which separation-individuation tasks have not been mastered.[27] These patients have little or no capacity to establish satisfactory and consistent internal objects.[28] Their immature ego development is further reflected in an inability to tolerate or integrate ambivalent feelings, and as a result positive and negative feelings are split so that others are perceived as all good or all bad. It is no wonder that the variability of these patients' pathological configurations, differing ego capacities, and defenses creates problems in making an accurate diagnosis and formulating a satisfactory treatment plan.

The interpersonal difficulties of these patients are usually apparent from the moment they enter a group.[29] They are particularly frightened by intimacy, closeness, and feelings of contamination or annihilation by others. They resist joining the group, and this resistance is often manifested through a variety of violations of the group contract. Early in their group membership they often take on the familiar roles of monopolizer or help-rejecting complainer as defenses against the interpersonal terrors of the group. The hostility they generate is quite familiar to them, and it serves to protect them from the greater dangers of intimacy. This fact makes these patients particularly prone to being scapegoated. They are also adept at using projective identification in order to protect themselves from closeness. Similarly, they may idealize or denigrate the therapist as a way of maintaining their distance.

In the face of these difficulties, there seems to be considerable agreement about the particular advantages of group treatment for the borderline patient. Horwitz[30] has suggested three advantages: (1) transference diffusion, which especially diminishes the negative destructive feelings about the therapist; (2) social and emotional distancing, which allows the patient to withdraw and thereby regulate the intensity of affective involvement without immediate sanctions; and (3) social pressure, which helps regulate reality testing. These advantages are relative since transference can be intensified, as well as diffused, in groups.

Questions arise as to whether technical modifications are necessary in the treatment of the borderline patient. In part the answer is related to group composition. One approach is to include one or two such patients in a group where others have reached higher developmental levels.[31] Under these conditions borderline patients seem to be able to learn from exploration or interpretation and little modification in technique is necessary.[32] The other alternative is forming homogeneous groups. There are certain advantages when all the patients are struggling with issues at the same developmental level. Diversity still remains, since each individual brings his particular history and interpersonal style to bear on group interactions.

The development of a therapeutic alliance may be an appropriate intermediate, if not final, goal for some borderline patients. Attainment of that goal implies an ability for the patient to see both positive and negative aspects of other individuals and to experience them as separate, with their own wishes and needs. Because establishing a working alliance with borderline patients is the essence of the treatment, the therapist must pay attention to the communications inherent in all his behaviors with regard to these patients.[33,34] Feldberg maintains that the therapist has to be more active than with neurotic patients.[35] Interpretation may have to be supplemented by other technical measures, such as universalization, confrontation, and drawing attention to similarities among individuals.[36]

Two particular strategies aid in this process. Many borderline individuals do not recognize the impact of their behaviors on others, and when feedback is given they are surprised, hurt, and defensive. By empathizing with their surprise, the therapist can make emotionally meaningful contact with the confronted individual. This is different from the usual strategy of focusing on helping the patient hear the interpretation.

The second strategy uses interpretation aimed at having the greatest impact on the other members, not the borderline patient. For instance the therapist might point out that a member attacks another when he is anxious or frightened. If this interpretation were made to a borderline patient, it would likely be met with denial. When the relevant interpretation can be offered to healthier members, the borderline patients can observe those members begin to appreciate the sequencing of anxiety and attack, gain perspective, and become less likely to withdraw or counterattack. The result is not only a safer group environment for all the members but also a wonderful laboratory for the borderline patient, who has been able to observe with interest and safety.

In treating the borderline patient in groups with less disturbed patients, the therapist must balance the unique needs of the borderline patient against the needs of the group-as-a-whole. For example, borderline patients often barrage therapists with questions, insisting that they have a direct answer. The basis for the question can be multidetermined; it may be an enactment of the patient's entitlement, fear of being ignored, low frustration tolerance, or a wish for contact. By answering the question directly, the therapist may soothe the borderline patient temporarily but set the patient up for the ire of the other members for receiving this "special" attention. By not answering the question directly, the borderline patient is protected from intense sibling rivalry but is left unprotected from the intense reactions to not having his needs met. The therapist must quickly assess the pros and cons of providing an answer when borderline patients begin to question him, since any response includes both.

Many of the ego deficits and problems in maintaining a sense of identity are evident as borderline patients join a group.

Despite having agreed to the usual group contract, one patient announced during his first group meeting that he would commit himself to remaining only six sessions. At the end of his six-week period, he extended his commitment for another six weeks. That was followed by yet another six-week commitment. Only then could this patient feel safe enough to publicly commit himself to remaining in the group for as long as it took to work on his problems. Not only was this patient severely cautious, his style was provocative and evoked criticism and resentment from the others. This only served to reinforce his reluctance to join fully because of his conviction that others would not like him.

Another borderline patient maintained her distance by angrily insisting that others should reveal all the intimate details of their lives, all the while remaining resolutely mute about her own life. Her rationale was that she could feel safer and closer if others were willing to be vulnerable in her presence, but the actual effect was that the others had no interest in being close to her. Nonetheless, the patient was able to persist in this stance for a number of years before consistently being able to examine her in-group behaviors.

The marked emotional volatility of borderline patients often startles the therapist and the other members.

A woman had seemed quite cooperative and insightful when the therapist focused an interpretation on her behavior. However, thirty minutes later she angrily screamed at him, "You're ignoring me!" when he focused on interactions between other members. This patient's difficulty in being able to share the therapist and maintain an inner representation of him as interested and concerned contributed to her outburst.

In another session a borderline man was told by a fellow member, "You just interrupted someone again." He denied that he had done so and refused to consider it even a possibility, even though in the previous meeting he had acknowledged that both inside and outside the group people had fed back to him that observation. His defiant stance enraged his group colleagues. Nonetheless, later in the meeting he turned to his original confronter and pleaded, "Let's be friends." He was unable to hear the response that friendship must be based on give and take and could not just be willed. The fluctuation from an angry pout to a pleading request for friendship illustrates the borderline patient's emotional instability, need for contact, and lack of awareness of others' responses to the interaction.

The therapist is often the focus of attention of the borderline patient. The task of maintaining balance in the face of incessant demands or angry outbursts is difficult.

One female borderline patient had the disconcerting habit of turning her chair so that she only talked to the therapist and only made eye contact with him. The therapist felt he was riveted to her and could not disengage himself from her.

Another patient unfalteringly insisted that the therapist follow up any clarification or interpretation with direct advice about how to change his behavior or how to make him feel his feelings.

The result of these and many other behaviors is that therapists find themselves on emotional roller coasters. They may be overstimulated or upset by the defensive maneuverings of these patients. This might be reflected in their dreams or a feeling of dread before a session.[37] A consultation with a colleague, or an ongoing formal or informal opportunity for ventilation, processing, or supervision can be invaluable for the therapist trying to maintain his or her equilibrium in the face of these emotion-laden transactions.

The borderline patient's capacity to utilize group therapy most effectively is often enhanced by the concurrent use of individual therapy.[38–40] The individual therapy format offers the opportunity for these patients to gain some perspective on the overstimulation they often experience in the group, while the group offers them the protection of peers as they explore their powerful transferences to individual therapists.

Narcissistic Disorders

Throughout this book reference has been made to Kohut's contributions to the evolution of a psychoanalytic theory of the self.[41,42] This section briefly summarizes these contributions and their application to group psychotherapy.

Following nearly a decade of extensive exploration of the clinical manifestations of narcissism, Kohut and Wolf [43] proposed a preliminary classification of narcissistic disorders (self disorders). The self has not been clearly defined, but in a general sense can be conceived of as the center of independent initiative and of subjective experience.[44] The self develops into a cohesive whole with the aid of a selfobject. In this formulation the selfobject is another individual who is available to supply missing needs and functions, but who is not experienced by the narcissistic patient as having needs and wishes of his own.

With the caveat that specific inner meaning of the behavioral patterns must be sought out, self disorders may be classified into the *narcissistic behavior* disorders, in which perverse, delinquent, or addictive behaviors are efforts to prevent the disintegration or fragmentation of the distorted self, and the *narcissistic personality* disorders, in which symptoms of hypochondriasis, depression, hypersensitivity to slights, and diminished vigor are present as indicators of the injured self.

In this classification, Kohut and Wolf[45] described several personalities. (1) Mirror-hungry personalities need confirming and admiring responses to nourish the "famished self." These individuals seldom seem satisfied, and beneath these surface behaviors exists a sense of inner worthlessness. (2) Alter-ego personalities appear to require another with whom they can feel identical in appearance, opinion, or values. Like the mirror-hungry personalities, these patients exhibit an instability and chronic disappointment with the selfobject. (3) Ideal-hungry personalities feel the need to idealize others in order to feel safe and secure—that is, to be able to merge.

Two other character types involve much greater degrees of disturbance. (4) Merger-hungry personalities need the selfobject in lieu of a self structure. There is a fluidity of boundaries between self and others. They envy others' separateness and are demanding of their attention. (5) Contact-shunning personalities avoid social contact in anticipation of rejection or frustration. These individuals also fear they will be engulfed or destroyed.

Group psychotherapy provides multiple opportunities for individuals to reenact narcissistic needs. The group format itself evokes fears of uncertainty and nonresponse, and as a consequence a type of danger to the self. Almost all group members fear the potential for narcissistic injuries until some level of reliability and trust in the therapist and in the group interactions has been established. However, it is important to distinguish between narcissistic needs that are present in all individuals and the development of coherent narcissistic transferences, which would indicate a significant disturbance of the self.

Narcissistic transferences may emerge to either the group-as-a-whole or to other individuals within the group. The power of group-as-a-whole transferences was highlighted during the height of the sensitivity movement in the 1960s, when many individuals behaved as if they were weekend T-group addicts. These people reported a glowing feeling of well-being after each weekend. It is our speculation that this was a genuine emotional high derived from having merged once more with the idealized image of the group. Similarly, patients in therapy groups feel an inner sense of togetherness and cohesion when they have developed an idealizing transference to the group. Fried has provided a sensitive example of an idealization in a quotation from a patient's letter: "I'm helped when I recall how blessed I was to share the love and the kindness of my friends in the group and you (the therapist). The memories of the intimacies we shared and the openness of our feelings helps keep me together."[46] The development of a stable and reliable transference to the group-as-a-whole is extremely valuable in helping some individuals maintain a sense of inner cohesion.[47–49]

Many narcissistic patients exhibit considerable resistance to developing transferences. They anticipate that the selfobject will not be reliable and consequently resist acknowledging the importance of the soothing and satisfying merger with an idealized object or their inner need for an affirming or mirroring response. Subtle tests regarding reliability and safety often are conducted unconsciously by the narcissistic patient prior to verbal acknowledgment of the transferential needs. Often the transference is silently well established and becomes manifest only when there is a perceived failure on the part of the therapist or the group. A silent transference to the whole group is illustrated in the following example.

> *Warren, a particularly articulate and gregarious member, spoke extensively of his difficulty in forming intimate relationships with women. He presented himself as a Don Juan, with many conquests and no loves. The narcissistic transference to the group emerged when he began to complain about any absences, which he felt ruined group cohesion. He could not verbalize precisely the inner upset he experienced, but he was vociferous in his declarations of discomfort. The transference reaction was particularly focused on one member who often arrived late and who seldom spoke. It did not matter to Warren whether the member spoke, but his mere presence seemed very important indeed. The feelings of hurt and disorganization experienced by Warren was a consequence of his viewing the group as no longer being complete and therefore no longer being available as an idealized selfobject with which to merge. As Warren was gradually able to maintain his sense of inner stability, he could discuss his fears and wishes in more detail.*

The group-as-a-whole also may be experienced as a mirroring selfobject. Nonresponse from members may be followed by withdrawal or rage. Narcissistic patients often have some degree of awareness that these responses are out of proportion to the stimulus, but only after overcoming an initial resistance will they display or talk about their inner turmoil. An illustration of narcissistic transference occurred with Sylvia, who, like Warren, was struggling to form a satisfying heterosexual relationship.

> *From time to time, Sylvia would report to the group how her relationship with her boyfriend was progressing. This was reported in a dispassionate manner, with no sense of urgency. One evening she began a meeting by announcing that her relationship had abruptly ended. As the discussion of that relationship continued, it became clear to Sylvia and the group that for months she had ignored the signals that serious troubles existed between her boyfriend and herself. Sylvia stated that she needed him in order to feel an inner hope that she was acceptable. As a consequence, she said she had lived a fantasy of who her boyfriend was, refusing to recognize his particular realistic strengths and shortcomings. The group criticized Sylvia extensively for her failure to "face reality" with her boyfriend and for not discussing the relationship in more depth in the group.*

The therapist, however, suggested that Sylvia's needs to ignore the obvious flaws in the relationship were even more important. He went on to state that it was understandable that Sylvia might have feared discussing her boyfriend in the group because it would have made her more aware of what she was avoiding. Viewed from the perspective of self psychology, the therapist had to determine whether or not the group was functioning as a satisfactory selfobject, and if not, whether prior narcissistic injuries had significantly contributed to Sylvia's reticence. It is possible that the group represented a selfobject similar to her boyfriend—needed but feared, and consequently the deficits of each were denied or avoided.

Self psychology has placed the vicissitudes of the empathic connection between the individual and the selfobject in a central position. Failures in empathy are expectable and provide for growth, since the individual under optimal conditions will develop many of the functions formerly provided by the selfobject. If the failures are too severe or too traumatic, deficits in the self develop. The therapist must maintain particular awareness of the vulnerability of the narcissistic individual to empathic failures and a host of subsequent responses.[50] For instance, rage reactions are a result of narcissistic injury, and interpretations of the empathic failure and the resultant hurt and rage will enable the injured individual to gain perspective and potentially to increase mastery over the vulnerability of the self. The therapist in this fashion reestablishes empathic connection and creates an environment for renewed growth.

Several difficult problems encountered in group psychotherapy can be reassessed in light of self psychology. The so-called help-rejecting complainer[51] probably does not exist! That is, patients who have been given that pejorative label are probably demonstrating a fundamental inability to communicate what help they desire, resulting in an empathic failure rather than a primary need to reject all help. These patients often gain a great amount of negative attention in groups, which may be preferable to being ignored or feeling isolated. They may also fear being understood (a variant of the contact-shunning personality), and these patients' behaviors may contain elements of rage and revenge, so that multiple functions are conveyed in this behavioral configuration.

Another common problem patient in therapy groups is the monopolizer, who both wishes and fears the effect of recognition and admiration. Therefore the monopolizer deals with that problem by remaining the center of attention and simultaneously fending off any real intimacy through verbal outpourings. This one-way dialogue also offers protection against hearing what others feel. Conversely the monopolizer can maintain an idealized fantasy of the group and the therapist. The nonstop talking protects him from hearing the members or leader speak and risk shattering the fantasy. The empathic task is to recognize the manifestations of this patient's marked ambivalence.

Through focusing on empathic connectedness, the therapist can gain insight into those situations where members seem to erupt in rage or hurt for no apparent reason. In most instances these reactions follow a narcissistic injury that has gone unrecognized. One source of injury is a group-as-a-whole interpretation. The generalization inevitably inherent in such interpretations cannot include detailed attention and understanding of each individual. This sets the stage for narcissistically vulnerable members to feel hurt and enraged. Another source is the inevitable intragroup conflict. Two individuals may demand attention and response at the same time, and a small slight or failure to fulfill the need of either may be experienced as a narcissistic injury.

Therapists should strive to create an atmosphere that enables the narcissistic transference to become manifest. This includes the difficult task of accepting the patient's idealizing transference rather than prematurely pushing him to correct his distortions. The time will come soon enough when the therapist will be viewed as unempathic or uncaring, and this will result in sufficient hurt in the patient for us to observe the characteristic response to narcissistic injury. When this happens, the patient's response to the group or specific members' failure to respond in accordance with his inner needs may be interpreted through empathic understanding of the patient's inner world and explication of the interactional process.

In sum, working successfully with narcissistic patients means gaining an empathic understanding of how these individuals' behavioral styles are attempts to shore up and protect their fragile sense of self.

Conclusion

In this chapter we have examined some special situations that face group therapists on a regular basis. In the next chapter, we will turn our attention to a situation that confronts every group therapist on a continuing basis: termination.

References

1. R.M. Whitman, "Dreams About the Group: An Approach to the Problems of Group Psychology," *Int. J. Group Psychother.* 23 (1973):408–420.
2. E. Klein-Lipschutz, "Comparison of Dreams in Individual and Group Psychotherapy," *Int. J. Group Psychother.* 3 (1953):143–149.

3. R. Battegay, "The Group Dream," in *Group Therapy 1977: An Overview,* edited by L.R. Wolberg and M.L. Aronson (New York: Stratton Intercontinental Medical Book, 1977).

4. N. Edwards, "Dreams, Ego Psychology and Group Interaction in Analytic Group Psychotherapy," *Group* 1 (1977):32–47.

5. A. Wolf and E. Schwartz, *Psychoanalysis in Groups* (New York: Grune and Stratton, 1962).

6. Leviticus 16.

7. G. Allport, *The Nature of Prejudice* (Cambridge, Mass.: Addison-Wesley, 1954).

8. E. Toker, "The Scapegoat as an Essential Group Phenomenon," *Int. J. Group Psychother.* 22 (1972):320–332.

9. W.R. Bion, *Experiences in Groups* (New York: Basic Books, 1960).

10. M. Klein, "Notes On Some Schizoid Mechanisms," *Int. J. Psychoanal.* 27 (1946):99.

11. W.R.D. Fairbairn, *An Object-Relations Theory of the Personality* (New York: Basic Books, 1952).

12. H. Guntrip, *Schizoid Phenomena, Object-Relations, and the Self* (New York: International Universities Press, 1969).

13. T.H. Ogden, "On Projective Identification," *Int. J. Psychoanal.* 60 (1979):357–373.

14. B. Levine, *Group Psychotherapy: Practice and Development* (Englewood Cliffs, N.J.: Prentice-Hall, 1979), pp. 120–121.

15. J.A. Garland and R.L. Kolodny, "Characteristics and Resolution of Scapegoating," in *Further Explorations in Group Work,* edited by S. Bernstein (Boston: Milford House, 1973), pp. 67–68.

16. R.L. Birdwhistle, *Kinesics and Context* (Philadelphia: University of Pennsylvania Press, 1970), p. 10.

17. M.M. Berger, "Notes on the Communication Process in Group Psychotherapy," *J. Group Process Psychoanal.* 2, no. 1 (1969):29–36.

18. A.E. Scheflen, "The Significance of Posture in Communication Systems," *Psychiatry* 27 (1964):316–331.

19. A.E. Scheflen, "Quasi-Courtship Behaviors in Psychotherapy," *Psychiatry* 28 (1965):245–256.

20. R. Battegay, "Individual Psychotherapy and Group Psychotherapy in Combination," *Acta Psychiatr. Scand.* 48 (1972):43–46.

21. J.S. Rutan and A. Alonso, "Group Therapy, Individual Therapy, or Both?" *Int. J. Group Psychother.* 32(1982):267–282.

22. N. Wong, "Combined Group and Individual Treatment of Borderline and Narcissistic Patients: Heterogeneous versus Homogeneous Groups," *Int. J. Group Psychother.* 30 (1980):389–404.

23. E. Fried, "The Effect of Combined Therapy on the Productivity of Patients," *Int. J. Group Psychother.* 4(1954):42–58.

24. A. Stein, "The Nature of Transference in Combined Therapy," *Int. J. Group Psychother.* 14 (1964):413.

25. Rutan and Alonso, "Group Therapy, Individual Therapy, or Both?"

26. *Diagnostic and Statistical Manual of Mental Disorders.* 3rd ed. (Washington, D.C.: American Psychiatric Association, 1980).

27. J.F. Masterson, *Psychotherapy of the Borderline Adult: A Developmental Approach* (New York: Brunner/Mazel, 1976), p. 3.

28. G. Adler and D.H. Buie, "Aloneness and Borderline Pathology: The Possible Relevance of Child Development Issues," *Int. J. Psychoanal.* 60 (1979):83–96.

29. B.E. Roth, "Problems of Early Maintenance and Entry into Group Psychotherapy with Persons Suffering from Borderline and Narcissistic States," *Group* 3 (1979):3–22.

30. L. Horwitz, "Group Psychotherapy for Borderline and Narcissistic Patients," *Bull. Menninger Clinic* 44 (1980):181–200.

31. L. Horwitz, "Group Psychotherapy of the Borderline Patient," in *Borderline Personality Disorders,* edited by P. Hartocollis (New York: International Universities Press, 1977), pp. 399–422.

32. W. Hulse, "Psychotherapy with Ambulatory Schizophrenic Patients in Mixed Groups," *Arch. Neurol. Psychiatry* 79 (1958):681–687.

33. H.T. Glatzer, "The Working Alliance in Analytic Group Psychotherapy," *Int. J. Group Psychother.* 28 (1978):147–161.

34. W.N. Stone and J.P. Gustafson, "Technique in Group Psychotherapy of Narcissistic and Borderline Patients," *Int. J. Group Psychother.* 32 (1982):29–48.

35. T.M. Feldberg, "Treatment of Borderline Psychotics in Groups of Neurotic Patients," *Int. J. Group Psychother.* 8 (1958):76–84.

36. Roth, "Problems of Early Maintenance and Entry into Group Psychotherapy with Persons Suffering from Borderline and Narcissistic States."

37. B.E. Roth, "Understanding the Development of a Homogeneous Identity-Impaired Group through Countertransference Phenomena," *Int. J. Group Psychother.* 30 (1980):405–426.

38. Wong, "Combined Group and Individual Treatment."

39. N. Slavinska-Holy, "Combining Individual and Homogeneous Group Psychotherapies for Borderline Conditions," *Int. J. Group Psychother.* 33 (1983):297–312.

40. Rutan and Alonso, "Group Therapy, Individual Therapy, or Both?"

41. H. Kohut, *The Analysis of the Self* (New York: International Universities Press, 1971).

42. H. Kohut, *The Restoration of the Self* (New York: International Universities Press, 1977).

43. H. Kohut and E.S. Wolf, "The Disorders of the Self and Their Treatment: An Outline," *Int. J. Psychoanal.* 59 (1978):413–425.

44. M.A. Wright, "Assumptions and Concepts Fundamental to Kohut's Psychology of the Self," unpublished manuscript, Smith College, 1981.

45. Kohut and Wolf, "The Disorders of the Self and Their Treatment."

46. E. Fried, "Group Bonds," in *Group Therapy 1973: An Overview,* edited by L.R. Wolberg and E.K. Schwartz (New York: Stratton Intercontinental Medical Book, 1973), pp. 161–168.

47. S.J. Meyers, "The Disorders of the Self: Developmental and Clinical Considerations," *Group* 2 (1978):131–140.

48. W.N. Stone and R.M. Whitman, "Contributions of the Psychology of Self to Group Process and Group Therapy," *Int. J. Group Psychother.* 27 (1977):343–359.

49. J.S. Rutan and C.A. Rice, "The Charismatic Leader: Asset or Liability?" *Psychother. Theory Res. Pract.* 18 (1981):487–492.

50. W.N. Stone and R.M. Whitman, "Observations on Empathy in Group Psychotherapy," in *Group and Family Therapy 1980,* edited by L.R. Wolberg and M.L. Aronson (New York: Brunner/Mazel, 1980), pp. 102–117.

51. W.N. Stone and J.P. Gustafson, "Technique in Group Psychotherapy of Narcissistic and Borderline Patients," *Int. J. Group Psychother.* 32 (1982):29–47.

Termination in Group Psychotherapy

12

Termination of psychotherapy is an extremely complex process. It is further complicated in therapy groups. In dyadic therapy, the leavetaking is between two individuals, and it can be modified to suit the situation. In terminating individual therapy there is usually the recognition, barring unusual circumstances, that the patient has the option of returning to the therapist in the future if needed, and it is occasionally useful to terminate the therapeutic relationship gradually by meeting less and less often and giving the patient the opportunity to "try it out" before a final termination occurs. In groups, however, the leavetaking is more public and more complicated because the member is leaving many individuals, not just one. Furthermore, terminations from groups tend to be final. That is, when a patient terminates group therapy, it is unlikely that the group would have remained unchanged should the patient need or desire further treatment. Finally, it is more difficult in groups to modify terminations to suit the needs of individual patients because this flexibility would adversely affect the therapeutic effectiveness of the group, whose members need continuity and consistency of format in order to accomplish their work.

Historical Review of the Concept of Termination

The criteria by which to judge the time to terminate therapy have varied. In the earliest days of psychoanalysis, when Freud and Breuer were involved in hypnosis, termination was based on the topographic theory of mental functioning. According to this theory, therapy was finished when the unconscious was made conscious. This goal implied the lifting of repression but not evaluating changes in psychic structure.

The theoretical picture was altered by Freud's discovery of transference neurosis. Transference, as one element of repetition compulsion, implied the existence of a stable, organized mental agency with characteristic defenses. As a result of this perspective, the transferential attachment to the analyst had to be resolved for treatment to be considered complete. Such resolution was seen as a concomitant of change in mental structures.

However, Firestein,[1] in a study of successful training analyses, found that the interview situation reawakened the old transferences, though in mild and manageable form. This study suggests that even in a healthy population, transference neurosis is by no means "obliterated" or eliminated.

Further modifications in termination criteria followed the development of ego psychology. Successful psychotherapy was correlated with the emergence of higher level defenses, greater appropriateness in the use of defenses, greater flexibility in defensive style, and the ego's capacity for autonomous functioning. The outgrowth of this shift in perspective to the level of ego functioning led directly to questions of internalization and structuralization—that is, how new or regained ego capacities are taken in and made integral.

Another important contribution to the conceptualization of termination came from the object relations school, which postulated that the primary human drive is to find objects (relationships). Criteria for termination were associated with the individual's capacity to develop object constancy—the ability to hold a reliable internal image and memory of others. This capacity was operationalized through examination of the patient's ability to find and form meaningful relationships with appropriate persons and to tolerate ambivalent feelings directed at single individuals.

More recently, the work of Kohut[2,3] has suggested another set of criteria for termination. Viewed from the perspective of self psychology, the individual develops a reliable capacity to experience others as separate individuals who have their own needs and wishes and are not present solely to fulfill a missing function of the self. The attainment of appropriate goals, ambitions, pride, and self-esteem is the result of maturation of infantile grandiosity, and the acquisition of appropriate values and ideals results from maturation of infantile idealization. Closely linked to these steps is the increased empathic capacity. We will now look at some current criteria that describe appropriate terminations from psychotherapy.

Criteria for Appropriate Termination

Advances in theory are largely reflected in the understanding of preoedipal, borderline, and narcissistic character formation. There is some degree of discontinuity among those writers who emphasize termination criteria for patients with preoedipal pathologies in contrast to patients with classical oedipal conflicts. The classical criteria for termination have included the following.

• The transference neurosis and resistances have been analyzed, with the resulting development of a more mature superego and ego ideal.

• Defenses become freer.

• Drives are discharged in a more socially acceptable manner.

• The patient has internalized the therapist's analyzing capacity.

Blanck and Blanck[4] have summarized termination criteria that seem most applicable to those patients with earlier developmental deficits and arrests.

• Attainment of identity, differentiation between self and object representations, and the capacity to retain the representation of the object independent of the state of mind.

• Indication that structuralization has proceeded because higher levels of integration have been reached.

• Object relations approach object constancy.

• Acquisition of a more competent defensive capacity.

• The ego exercises more and more of its own functions.

Kohut[5] suggested that in disorders of the self, the development of a stable, cohesive self may be sufficient for the individual to restart the thwarted growth and spontaneously move through oedipal developmental stages. In a more controversial formulation, Kohut also emphasized the development of structures in either the grandiose or idealizing axis to compensate for major disorganizational deficits in the opposite axis.[6]

Termination in Groups

All of the criteria listed above are adequate means of judging the therapeutic process. More often than not, therapists will utilize a variety of those criteria, chosen according to the theoretical orientation of the therapist.

In addition, we tie judgments about the suitability of termination to the original group contract, where patients agreed to remain in the group until they had "resolved the problems" that they brought to the group. This is a complicated judgment because many original problems have not been "cured" or eradicated, but they may have been "resolved" to the satisfaction of the patient. One example would be the patient who came to treatment in order to counter a terror of success. The patient may have discovered the roots of that terror, overcome the perpetual self-sabotaging of success, and still not have gained success. Yet it may be goal appropriate for the patient to terminate before some ideal success is achieved. Another example would be the patient who came with the specific goal of gaining the interpersonal attributes necessary to form a loving relationship, marry, and become a parent. Such a patient might terminate when he has been able to form a stable and successful loving relationship even though that is only the first step in his original design.

Almost universally, patients discover *more* problems in the course of their therapy. Thus, is termination appropriate if the patient resolves the problems that brought him but not other problems that became apparent during the treatment?

Some patients enter treatment with a curative fantasy[7] that is an organized wish for what the patient hopes to gain in therapy. It cannot be expressed via a contract because the curative fantasy contains both conscious and unconscious elements. Instead it is expressed in the process of the treatment. These patients utilize the intragroup relationships to strengthen a sector of their personalities. When this has been accomplished some of these patients terminate, leaving the therapist bewildered.[8] Although they seemingly have not fulfilled the contract, they depart quite satisfied.

The most important single criterion for determining the appropriateness of termination has to do with the judgment, "Has this patient gained the most that can be gained from continuing to meet with the group at this time?" This means that for different patients the answer will be quite different. Thus the contract functions as a rough guideline for termination. Patients may use it in a positive fashion, but they may also defensively invoke it as a rationale for leaving. Under the latter circumstance the therapist must work with the resistance to further therapy.

When an individual decides to stop treatment, he terminates from the real and the fantasied relationships with his colleagues, therapist, and the group-as-a-whole. This is an active process, and the form it takes depends upon the group norms, which define the way terminations are managed, and his prior experiences with separations.

Typically three major affective components are evoked by terminations: feelings regarding finitude (death and mortality), separation and/or abandonment, and hope (a new beginning). The degree to which each or all of these components are emphasized in particular terminations is a function of the individual and the prior group process. Though these dynamics and affects interact during the process of termination, we have attempted to separate out some of the important elements of each for heuristic purposes.

Group Dynamics in the Termination of Individuals

Because life is filled with goodbyes, the capacity to bear the affect surrounding loss is necessary if one is to be able to have intimacy in relationships. Each and every termination from a group offers all the members another opportunity to learn more about the experience of saying goodbye.

Many different kinds of terminations occur in groups. Some members quit prematurely, others leave for external reasons or with significant but incomplete gains, and most terminate successfully. Some people quit with advance notice; others just disappear.

Since loss and death are such painful experiences, members often resist experiencing the emotions surrounding terminations. They avoid their affects, and instead the responses are either totally hidden or are expressed metaphorically.

The therapist, functioning in the role of norm setter, must help draw the members' attention to the feelings surrounding loss. The therapist's attitude and willingness to confront these feelings increase the members' capacity to study their inner world. He also tries to establish norms regarding proper termination procedures, including appropriate notification of the group and setting a termination date far enough in advance to allow for sufficient exploration of the feelings evoked by the leaving.

Not all patients terminate in the same way, and not all terminations have the same impact on groups. We will now turn our attention to some common forms of termination.

Early Terminators

When termination occurs within the first few weeks of a group, the response usually reflects the level of group development. There is little sense of belonging in new groups, and members have had little time to learn about the internal state of the early terminator. What the members do know is that someone is missing, but the dynamics mobilized around that event usually remain unspoken or receive only cursory attention. Often the response is to ignore or condemn the dropout. When several members leave, there emerges a concern about the continued existence of the group. Members will become preoccupied with the future, asking about newcomers and future plans of the therapist. The therapist has the task of balancing the discussion of the group's future with the more immediate discouragement and despair.

Some Group Dynamics in Premature Quitting. Exclusive attention to an individual member is often insufficient for understanding a threatened or actual premature termination. Powerful regressive forces are activated in group formation, and the interplay between these forces and the individual is generally what prompts a dropout. For instance, people do not suffer with problems of intimacy in isolation. Instead an entire system is involved.

Pressures for intimacy and closeness may be frightening forces that prematurely propel some individuals out of groups. Group norms for instant intimacy are most likely to produce such results. Furthermore, when a group does not recognize the frail but courageous efforts of such members to become more engaged, the resulting painful narcissistic injury is covered in a raging, stormy departure or a perplexing sudden, unannounced disappearance.[9] Other group processes that contribute to early departure are scapegoating, avoidance of in-group conflict, and insistence on immediate and intense expression of feelings.

Some Group and Individual Responses to Premature Quitting. Individuals who drop out quickly present a particular therapeutic problem in new groups because there is insufficient group development to allow the generally unacceptable affects in the remaining members to emerge and be examined in an accepting atmosphere. These affects include both guilt and envy. Guilt is almost universal. It may arise from feelings that not enough was done to prevent the dropout, or from feeling responsible for the leaving because of hostile feelings or behaviors toward the departed member. In the forming phase members maintain their distance, attempt to gain control, or actively push others away. Many of these behaviors evoke fear or counterhostility that is unmodified through understanding. Thus, when such an individual leaves, the remaining members may feel guilty because of their rage, whether or not it was expressed, and from their relief and pleasure that the member is gone.

Envy is also a powerful and frequently expressed feeling. Since it can be assumed that there is a part of every member that wishes to avoid belonging to a group and experiencing the difficult task of growing, there may be envy of the departed member. This feeling is often covered by a reaction formation as those remaining avow their increased dedication to and optimism about the group.

Contributing to the difficulty in exploring feelings about the early dropout is the remaining members' competitiveness. The leaving represents a victory: There is one less person with whom to vie for attention, or with whom to compete for the therapist's favor. Because these feelings are usually personally shameful, they are likely to remain hidden.

The lack of overt affect about an early dropout should not be mistaken as signifying a genuine disinterest in the event. Sometimes no mention is made of an early dropout until someone else leaves, and then a flood of previously unexpressed sentiments emerge. It is not at all unusual for a significant discussion of an early departure to occur months later, evoked by something in the current process of the group. The therapist must attempt to tactfully help the forming group explore the reactions to an early dropout, even in the face of considerable resistance.

Premature Leaving in More Mature Groups. In more mature groups the departure of a recently added member stimulates many of the same feelings and dynamics. In addition, the therapist may be the object of anger for having selected such an individual, since the old members are acutely aware of the disruptive effect of having someone enter and depart so quickly. In the process of group development, members have acquired the capacity to explore their affects in the here-and-now of meetings. They are in a position to retrospectively examine some of their own fears of joining and their wishes to flee. They may be more empathic with the departed member and more introspective about the processes that may have contributed to the quitting. This, of course, does not mean that all new members will remain, but members of more mature groups will have more access to the feelings evoked by the departure and more capacity to utilize those feelings for learning. The groups are in fact not damaged or slowed down nearly as much as are the less mature groups.

Incomplete Treatments

Individuals who stop further along in the treatment may stop for reality reasons, or they may have achieved symptomatic relief and wish to settle for that. Despite gains, these patients demonstrate continuing deficits in interpersonal or intrapsychic maturity. Since the groups have usually reached a more advanced level of development, the remaining members are more ready to explore their feelings of hurt, disappointment, and rage at the one who left without finishing his work. Angry reactions to the loss of members are much in evidence at this stage, and considerable therapeutic gain is possible as a result of freeing up angry affects.

Beneath the anger is often a deep-seated feeling of personal or groupwide failure to help or more deeply engage the departing member. These painful affects, along with the associated depressive feelings, also can be examined in a therapeutically productive fashion. They are more readily available when the termination is forced by external factors because such terminations carry with them the added dimension of the lost opportunity. In a truncated way, forced terminations reawaken old experiences of death and separation that occurred without overt volition.

Incomplete treatments provide an opportunity to examine motivations and actions as the members try to discriminate terminations that are the result of fate or external factors from those that *seem* to be the result of external factors but that come to be seen, upon closer examination, as the final product of resistance to or acting out against the therapy. If there is sufficient time, and if the individual has not burned all his bridges, this examination may even prevent his leaving.

The therapist, in attempting to help departing patients examine the unconscious aspects of leaving, might review their initial complaints and symptoms, with the idea of seeing how the present wish to stop treatment might be a continuation of a behavioral pattern. On the other hand, the leavetaking may be the result of newly exposed conflicts or of interpersonal clashes within the group fueled by historic conflicts. The therapist might state quite directly that the work of therapy is incomplete and that this is not the most propitious time to terminate. Of course, this should always be done with tact and empathy and in full recognition of the fact that patients are free agents. On occasion, however, a forthright statement about the incomplete therapeutic work will encourage a redecision. In some instances the entire process is an unconscious test of the therapist or group, a test designed to discover whether or not the therapist or group care enough to fight to have the patient stay.

As always, the focus on the individual in question is usually insufficient to understand fully what is occurring. It is useful to help the patient be curious about why the decision to leave occurs at a particular point in time. By understanding the decision to leave in the context of the group process, the tendency to focus solely on the departing member is diminished. This provides a more complete understanding of the impetus for wishing to leave, and it also makes it easier for the member to decide to remain in the group in a face-saving manner.

One additional very important groupwide component is part of every premature termination. Some members, focusing only on the gains and overlooking the continuing difficulties of the departing patient, initially are in complete agreement with the decision to leave. Thus the resistance to continuing treatment or to exploring the conflict may be a groupwide resistance. In these circumstances exploration of the resistance in the members who sided with the announced departure should take place so that the potentially departing member may have sufficient distance to assess his own resistances.

Finally, such premature terminations highlight the very real limitations of control and power one person has over another. The opportunity for the remaining members to discover and deal with that reality can be a very maturing experience and can be distinguished from a neurotic feeling of helplessness or giving up. To believe genuinely that a member would be in error to terminate at a particular point in time, and to make every effort to communicate that conviction and still have the termination occur, is to face both the real and existential limitations of life.

The Completed Treatment

Successful terminations from groups are usually moving and powerful experiences for all concerned. Unlike terminations from dyadic therapy, terminations from groups are witnessed, felt, and shared by a number of people.

The optimal process for termination is set forth in the original group contract (Chapter 7). The contractual agreement to "remain in the group until the problems that brought you have been resolved" implies a great deal about what constitutes appropriate termination. That is, patients are expected to stay until a particular goal or set of goals has been achieved. Furthermore, at the time of discussing the contract, the procedure for termination should be explained. That is, prospective members are told that they should terminate when they have finished their work and that they should accomplish the termination by announcing their decision in a group meeting, after which they should continue to attend the group for as long as it takes to discuss the idea and to deal with the important process of saying goodbye. The therapist should help the terminating patient set a date far enough in advance for the group to deal with and learn from the related feelings. Generally, the process will be facilitated by the members' opportunities to observe a spectrum of terminations before saying their own goodbyes.

In most successful terminations, the therapist and many of the members will sense that a termination is coming. The quality of the interactions, along with reports of improved functioning outside the group, are ample data upon which to build an awareness that the work is approaching conclusion. One hallmark of a successful termination is the agreement of almost everyone in the room that the time is right (though many may be bitterly disappointed or angry about it).

When a member announces plans to terminate, major emotional responses are inevitable. Each patient has the right to determine when termination is in order, and termination is not the result of a group vote. Nonetheless, successfully terminating patients will allow and encourage input from their colleagues about the advisability of termination, and they will examine this decision as they have learned to examine all important decisions. Some terminating members will announce steadfastly, "I have decided to terminate; my last meeting will be on such and such a date." Others invite more groupwide participation in the decision. The approach can be appropriate or inappropriate, depending upon the individual and the situation. Sometimes an individual will make a hard and fast decision, including the date of the final meeting, as a way of avoiding the power of the feelings regarding separation and loss. On the other hand, an individual who desires to forestall the inevitable leaving will appear to invoke group-wide assistance, thereby delaying the implementation of a decision that has inwardly already been made. The important point is to make every possible effort to allow sufficient time and opportunity to explore the relevant affects that lead to and result from the decision of a member to terminate.

No stereotypical rule governs the length of time the termination process should take, but the most common error is allowing too little time to experience and learn from the feelings. Therapists and patients alike are hesitant about fully facing the feelings evoked by important goodbyes. Time is needed for the group to come to grips with the idea of the termination. We prefer that discussion of the idea of termination precedes setting an actual departure date. When this has been accomplished, a departure date should be set far enough in the future to allow for full exploration and elaboration of the event. As a rough guideline, this entire process might take one month for each year that the patient has been in the group.

Following an announcement of the intention to terminate, members generally respond with important derivative material, frequently by associating to other important losses. This should not be viewed as a resistance to dealing with the leavetaking, but rather as an integral part of mourning. By associating to powerful previous goodbyes, the other patients are communicating how deeply this loss will be felt. The current loss also provides an opportunity for more complete grieving of earlier, insufficiently mourned losses. As the actual departure date approaches, the group will deal more and more directly with the here-and-now feelings about saying goodbye to the departing individual.

In the termination process, an appraisal of the departing member's growth, changes, and unresolved conflicts is commonly undertaken. Previous intragroup conflicts, incompletely resolved, will often resurface. Regression takes place, often affecting many in the group, and the emotional responses may include intense efforts to dissuade the member from leaving. Sometimes the terminating member succumbs to the pressure, or to his ambivalence, and considers not stopping therapy. Again, envy of the success of a colleague may be in evidence, but often reaction formation clouds the feelings by overidealizing the terminating member. Usually these regressions are short-lived, with all members realizing the archaic nature of their responses. Indeed, the members gain satisfaction from appreciating that they can experience old feelings and conflicts and rapidly regain their balance.

It is important to appreciate that not all the pressures to prevent or delay a departure are transferential. In the place of a senior, mature, and contributing member, the group will gain a neophyte who will initially take much more than he gives. Furthermore, there are also real relationships between human beings that will be missed.

Once a definite date for leaving is set, the departure becomes a reality. The termination date should not coincide with another disruption such as the group therapist's vacation or the addition of a new member. Each major disruption requires careful attention, and to confuse the successful termination of a member with another disruption diminishes the poignancy of the loss for the group members. Maintaining continuity in the face of loss furthers appropriate grieving.

Setting the final date underlines the group's awareness that the individual in question will soon be leaving and will ultimately be replaced by someone else. The focus on the future also concerns the departing member, and members will often ask, "What will you be doing on this night in the future?" and "What will it be like in group without you?" Members also turn their attention to their own futures, often wondering how many more months or years will be required before they, too, can successfully leave the group. In this process they may review their progress, and under the influence of the positive atmosphere work on their problems with new resolve.

As the final session approaches, it is usually increasingly difficult for the members to tolerate the feelings; thus there is frequently a proposal made for action, a social gathering or a group gift to commemorate the termination. These discussions can generate considerable enthusiasm, and much energy and effort can go into the planning of a "last supper." It is difficult under these circumstances for any single member to refuse to join in. Great therapeutic skill is required to handle these situations because in addition to the genuine wish to send the successful patient off with good cheer, there is always the opposite envious or angry side. Furthermore, such proposals attempt to set a norm that homogenizes all terminations, thereby diminishing the often painful reality that people are missed and mourned differently. When confronted with such plans for action, therapists should tactfully remind the members that the agreement is to share feelings verbally rather than to act on them.

An Example.

> *The therapist entered the office for the final group meeting with Zelda, a patient terminating quite successfully after many years. To his surprise and dismay, the therapist found the room resembled a New York deli, with cold cuts, potato chips, wine, and all the utensils spread around*

in a decorative fashion. The group was in a festive mood, each member sitting with a plate brimming with food. The therapist was instantly greeted by Mildred, who offered to pour him some wine and make him a sandwich.

The therapist was confronted with a delicate therapeutic task. Clearly, great effort had gone into this lavish display, and obviously the members felt they were honoring the termination of Zelda. They had no conscious awareness of the denial implied in their party atmosphere. For the therapist to focus only on the resistant elements of the "celebration" would have been to miss part of the point. On the other hand, to have participated in the party would have been an even more serious error since doing so would have meant altering the fundamental contract.

In this instance the therapist simply noted, "The group certainly seems to be celebrating Zelda's departure," and while placing the glass of wine that he had been handed on an end table beside his chair, "but I think there are a wide range of feelings to be expressed and explored on such an important evening." As the members realized that the therapist was not going to eat or drink, the plates and glasses slowly were placed on the floor or on tables. Mildred was the last to give up the hope that this last meeting with Zelda could be given over to eating and drinking and laughing. She angrily accused the therapist of being a "spoil sport" and wondered, "What shall I do with all this food I brought?"

A prolonged and painful silence followed, punctuated by tears as various members began to experience Zelda's loss. Suddenly Mildred burst into tears, "My God! I'm doing what I did at my mother's funeral. I catered that affair; I fed everyone. I never left myself time to cry."

Endings evoke very important feelings, and therapists should resist the temptation to alter the fundamental operations of the group when terminations occur. On the other hand they must be able to respond creatively and not stereotypically. When a terminating member brings a gift, for example, there is no simple rule about whether to accept it. For some patients, the gift represents a continuing worry that without a physical reminder, the group and the therapist will not remember them. In this instance the gift usually should be tactfully interpreted and not accepted. In other cases such a gift simply represents a wish to give something to commemorate the experience, feelings amply expressed verbally as well. In this case to *not* accept the gift might well result in a final, farewell narcissistic injury.

It is a rather common occurrence at termination that members will exchange addresses and telephone numbers, with the plan of remaining in touch with the departing member. Sometimes members will inquire, "Is this a breach of contract?" We believe that the contract holds only for members who are in the group, and that what transpires between members and ex-members is not included in that agreement. That is not to imply, however, that the wish to continue a relationship should not be explored like any other wish. Sometimes that plan represents an unwillingness to acknowledge a loss and avoidance of the termination.

No separation or loss is complete. We all carry the images and memories of the individual and his interactions with us, and the hope to say a complete and final goodbye is a fantasy. Successful terminations are painful and joyous occasions mixed together, and the therapist should make every effort to help the members explore all aspects of this very important experience.

The Individual in the Termination Process

Individuals terminate from groups in a wide variety of ways. Some simply never return, disappearing without even a goodbye. But if individuals remain in groups for any protracted period of time, it becomes more likely they will engage in at least some formal leavetaking.

Terminations from groups are somewhat different than terminations from individual, dyadic therapy. In groups, because of the presence of the other members, there is less time for the detailed discussion of all the associations and memories that are stirred by the leaving. Although, as in all human endeavors, there is a wide range of individual response, individuals terminating from groups seem to experience less frequent or prolonged regression than in dyadic therapy.

In successful terminations there is a useful tendency to reminisce aloud about the treatment. Indeed therapists can facilitate reminiscing if this does not occur spontaneously. The rich and varied interactions that occurred between members and leader are remembered and discussed. Typically, members review incidents that illustrate their developing ego capacities and their abilities to manage conflict and tolerate affects. They also may discuss areas that require further attention and conflicts that remain unresolved. Yet, they convey an ability to master rather than be dominated by these incompletely resolved problems. As one departing member said, "I still get extra angry, but now I can stop it and try to work it out rather than just blame the other person." Another said, "I still tend to take care of people too much, but I don't let myself be used all the time anymore." The goal is not perfection but the capacity to recognize and accept one's weaknesses and vulnerabilities as well as strengths.

A departing member can give credit to others who were able to see things well before he could see them for himself. Moreover, he can comment upon the unique opportunities to genuinely understand someone else. There is a growing feeling of mastery as members learn about one another and appreciate what is going on beneath the surface appearances. In other words members who terminate groups successfully no longer take the position of an external observer of the other members, but have developed or expanded the capacity to empathize. For many patients this is a highly significant step.

Finally, almost all those who terminate indicate that they will miss the camaraderie, affection, and work of the group. They often wonder aloud if they will be missed or remembered. The group has become an important part of their lives, and it would be natural to speculate if the remaining members and therapist will think of them, recall their contributions, and in some fashion indicate that they have made enduring impact upon some-one.

Whole Group Terminations

In certain circumstances an entire group stops at the same time. The usual reason is that the group was formed on a time-limited basis. For example, many groups in university settings are set up according to the academic year. Homogeneous groups, organized around a particular symptom, crisis, demographic group, or diagnosis are often closed membership and time-limited. On occasion, entire groups terminate due to life events for the therapist (Chapter 9).

Though many patients in time-limited groups achieve their goals and are ready to stop at the specified time, this is not the universal situation. The dynamics that ensue are the reverse of those in effect when individuals prematurely drop out of groups. This time the group is quitting too soon. The entire termination process is complicated because the overt and covert resentments about the loss are difficult to elicit when the group's ending had been originally agreed upon. Kauff[10] described the group fantasy of the destructive witch mother in forced whole-group terminations or trans-fers. This reawakening of primitive fantasies surrounding the termination is consistent with the patients' deep-seated feelings that their basic needs will remain unmet.

As time-limited groups reach the midpoint of their life expectancy, themes of goodbye, separation, and loss become more and more dominant. The therapist has the important and difficult task of keeping the group's attention on the impending termination. There is a great temptation, aided and abetted by the patients, to discount the importance of the approaching ending. The process is complicated by members having more therapeutic work to do, in addition to exploring the forthcoming separation and loss. Thus, a balance needs to be struck between these two elements. Usually, through clarification of the metaphors of death, divorce, graduation, the therapist can help the patients understand how they are managing their feelings about the group stopping. As the ending comes closer, certain patients may demonstrate a high rate of absenteeism. For the last four or five weeks, the therapist may as a reminder count down at the end of each meeting, saying "We have five (four, three, etc.) more meetings left."

As in other effective terminations, initially the members will typically resonate to the theme of goodbye and deal with issues from their own personal histories. This is often a time when some excellent work is done on unresolved grief. As the endpoint gets closer and closer, the group begins dealing with the here-and-now goodbyes to the various members, to the leader, and to the group itself.

It is almost never in the best interests of the members of time-limited groups to alter the agreed-upon ending date. Inexperienced therapists occasionally take a vote of the members about whether or not to continue. In the usual scenario a substantial portion, if not all, of the members vote to continue the group. Those who felt coerced may quit immediately or soon after the original deadline. In the diminished group, morale is undermined and effective therapy ceases. If a group was formed on the contract that it would terminate on a specific date, it should do so. In time-limited groups, the therapist should help members evaluate the need for continued therapy. Members wishing to continue therapy may opt to join a *new* group, perhaps even an open-ended group. Ideally, that group should begin a month or so after the ending of the time-limited group. Individual members should understand that they fulfilled their contractual obligations and have no responsibility for joining another group.

It would not be surprising to see more time-limited groups in the future as a result of the shifting patterns of insurance coverage or the restrictions on treatment inherent in many health maintenance organizations.

Termination and the Group Therapist

The therapist is by no means immune to the effects of departures. Just as there are reverberations among the members of themes of separation and loss, so too are memories and affects stirred in the therapist, potentially producing powerful countertransferences. The therapist may find numerous reasons to interfere with a patient's departure, paralleling his own separation problems. Similarly, he may be uncomfortable with the wide range of intense affects evoked by terminations and therefore not interpret the resistance and acting out that is part of every termination.

In the case of premature terminations, the therapist may suffer the narcissistic hurt of not having been successful or loved. This is much more likely when a therapist is conducting just one group. Just as it would be exceedingly difficult to gain therapeutic distance and perspective if a dyadic therapist had only one patient, the feelings of hurt, failure, or discouragement when someone leaves the therapist's only group can be intense. Such situations are always powerful, but if the therapist has other groups that are going well he is somewhat protected from severe narcissistic injury. Whenever a therapist's personal issues with loss keep him from fully exploring the issues of termination, patients lose opportunities to grow.

In especially difficult groups the therapist may be filled with fantasies that if one member quits then so will the others, and thereafter he will not be burdened with the problem group. Unfortunately, this occasionally comes to pass, particularly for neophyte therapists and those who have not had the experience of successful terminations. As with learning long-term individual psychotherapy, only a few trainees have the good fortune to be in a training placement long enough to experience the successful conclusion of an intensive therapy in a group.

When there is a successful termination, the therapist has the narcissistic gratification of a job well done. In the conclusion of successful dyadic psychotherapy, the therapist often has the opportunity to state quite openly some of what the treatment experience has been like from his point of view. In a group, the emotional connection from therapist to patient is no less powerful; yet other patients are privy to and are participating in the goodbye. For some, the overt statement of caring from therapist to departing patient would be overstimulating. On the other hand most patients are significantly helped by observing the genuine relationship that has developed between the therapist and the terminating patient.

In sum, therapists should feel free to state the same things to terminating group patients that they would state to terminating individual patients. However, they should be acutely aware of the impact of such statements on the remaining patients.

References

1. S. Firestein, "Termination in Psychoanalysis," *J. Am. Psychoanal. Assoc.* 24 (1976):3–10.
2. H. Kohut, *The Analysis of the Self* (New York: International Universities Press, 1971).
3. H. Kohut, *The Restoration of the Self* (New York: International Universities Press, 1977).
4. G. Blanck and R. Blanck, *Ego Psychology: Theory and Practice* (New York: Columbia University Press, 1974).
5. Kohut, *The Restoration of the Self.*
6. *Ibid.*

7. P.H. Ornstein and A. Ornstein, "On the Continuing Evolution of Psychoanalytic Psychotherapy: Reflections upon Recent Trends and Some Predictions for the Future," *Annu. Psychoanal.* 5 (1977):329–370.

8. W.N. Stone, "The Curative Fantasy in Group Psychotherapy," in *Group Therapy Monograph No. 10* (New York: The Washington Square Institute, 1983).

9. W.N. Stone, M. Blase, and J. Bozzuto, "Late Dropouts from Group Psychotherapy," *Am. J. Psychother.* 34 (1980):401–413.

10. P. Kauff, "The Termination Phase: Its Relationship to the Separation-Individuation Phase of Development," *Int. J. Group Psychother.* 27 (1977):17.

Bibliography

Abse, D.W. 1974. *Clinical Notes on Group-Analytic Psychotherapy*. Charlottesville: University of Virginia Press.

Ackerman, N. 1949. Psychoanalysis and Group Therapy. In *Group Therapy Vol. 8*, nos. 2–3, edited by J.C. Moreno. Boston: Beacon House, pp. 204–215.

Adler, G., and Buie, D.H. 1979. Aloneness and Borderline Pathology: The Possible Relevance of Child Development Issues. *Int. J. Psychoanal.* 60: 83–96.

Allport, G. 1954. *The Nature of Prejudice*. Cambridge, Mass.: Addison-Wesley.

Arsenian, J., Semrad, E.V., and Shapiro, D. 1962. An Analysis of Integral Functions in Small Groups. *Int. J. Group Psychother.* 12: 421–434.

Astrachan, B.M. 1970. Towards a Social Systems Model of Therapeutic Change. *Soc. Psychiatry* 5: 110–119.

Bach, G.R. 1954. *Intensive Group Psychotherapy*. New York: Ronald Press.

Bader, B.R., Bader, L.J., Budman, S., and Clifford, M. 1981. Pre-group Preparation Model for Long-term Group Psychotherapy in a Private Practice Setting. *Group* 5: 43–50.

Battegay, R. 1972. Individual Psychotherapy and Group Psychotherapy in Combination. *Acta Psychiatr. Scand.* 48: 43–48.

Battegay, R. 1977. The Group Dream. In *Group Therapy 1977: An Overview*, edited by L.R. Wolberg and M.L. Aronson. New York: Stratton Intercontinental Medical Book.

Benne, K., and Sheats, P. 1948. Functional Roles of Group Members. *J. Soc. Issues*, 4: 41–49.

Bennis, W.G., and Shepard, H.A. 1956. A Theory of Group Development. *Human Relations* 9: 415–437.

Berger, M.M. 1969. Notes on the Communication Process in Group Psychotherapy. *J. Group Process Psychoanal.* 2, no. 1: 29–36.

Bertalanffy, L. von. 1966. General System Theory and Psychiatry. In *American Handbook of Psychiatry*, edited by S. Arieti. New York: Basic Books, pp. 705–721.

Binstock, W. 1979. The Psychodynamic Approach. In *Outpatient Psychiatry: Diagnosis and Treatment*, edited by A. Lazare. Baltimore: Williams and Wilkins, pp. 19–70.

Bion, W.R. 1960. *Experiences in Groups*. New York: Basic Books.

Birdwhistle, R.L. 1970. *Kinesics and Context*. Philadelphia: University of Pennsylvania Press.

Birk, L. 1974. Intensive Group Therapy: An Effective Behavioral-Psychoanalytic Method. *Am. J. Psychiatry* 131: 11–16.

Blanck, G., and Blanck, R. 1977. *Ego Psychology: Theory and Practice*. New York: Columbia University Press.

Borriello, J.F. 1976. Leadership in the Therapist Centered Group-as-a-Whole Approach. *Int. J. Group Psychother.* 26: 149–162.

Bowlby, J. 1973. *Separation: Anxiety and Anger*. New York: Basic Books.

Cartwright, D., and Zander, A., eds. 1960. *Group Dynamics*. Evanston, Ill.: Row, Peterson.

Christ, J. 1975. Contrasting the Charismatic and Reflective Leader. In *The Leader in the Group*, edited by Z.A. Liff. New York: Jason Aronson, pp. 104–113.

Cohen, Y.A. 1961. *Social Structures and Personality*. New York: Holt, Rinehart and Winston.

Comstock, B.S., and McDermott, M. 1975. Group Therapy for Patients Who Attempt Suicide. *Int. J. Group Psychother.* 25:44–49.

Day, M. 1981. Process in Classical Psychodynamic Groups. *Int. J. Group Psychother.* 31: 153–174.

Demarest, E.W., and Teicher, A. 1954. Transference in Group Therapy: Its Use by Co-Therapists of Opposite Sexes. *Psychiatry* 17: 187–202.

Diagnostic and Statistical Manual of Mental Disorders, 3rd ed. 1980. Washington, D.C.: American Psychiatric Association.

Dohrenwend, B.P., and Dohrenwend, B.S. 1974. Social and Cultural Influences on Psychopathology. *Annu. Rev. Psychol.* 25: 417–452.

Durkheim, E. 1951. *Suicide: A Study in Sociology*, translated by J. Spaulding and G. Simpson, edited by J. Simpson. Glencoe, Ill.: Free Press. (Initial publication in 1897.)

Durkin, H.E. 1964. *The Group in Depth*. New York: International Universities Press.

Durkin, H.E. 1981. The Technical Implications of General System Theory for Group Psychotherapy. In *Living Groups: Group Psychotherapy and General System Theory*, edited by J.E. Durkin. New York: Brunner/Mazel, pp. 171–198.

Durkin, J.E. 1981. Foundations of Autonomous Living Structure. In *Living Groups: Group Psychotherapy and General System Theory*, edited by J.E. Durkin. New York: Brunner/Mazel, pp. 24–59.

Edwards, N. 1977. Dreams, Ego Psychology and Group Interaction in Analytic Group Psychotherapy. *Group* 1: 32–47.

Eisenthal, S. 1979. The Sociological Approach. In *Outpatient Psychiatry: Diagnosis and Treatment*, edited by A. Lazare. Baltimore: Williams and Wilkins, pp. 73–115.

Ethan, S. 1978. The Question of the Dilution of Transference in Group Psychotherapy. *Psychoanal. Rev.* 65: 569–578.

Ezriel, H. 1973. Psychoanalytic Group Therapy. In *Group Therapy: 1973*, edited by L.R. Wolberg and E.K. Schwartz. New York: Stratton Intercontinental Medical Book, pp. 183–210.

Fairbairn, W.R.D. 1952. *An Object-Relations Theory of Personality*. New York: Basic Books.

Faris, R.E.L., and Dunham, H.W. 1939. *Mental Disorders in Urban Areas: An Ecological Study of Schizophrenia and Other Psychoses*. Chicago: University of Chicago Press.

Feldberg, T.M. 1958. Treatment of Borderline Psychotics in Groups of Neurotic Patients. *Int. J. Group Psychother.* 8: 76–84.

Firestein, S. 1976. Termination in Psychoanalysis. *J. Am. Psychoanal. Assoc.* 24: 3–10.

Foulkes, S.H. 1948. *Introduction to Group-Analytic Psychotherapy*. London: Heinemann.

Foulkes, S.H. 1961. Group Processes and the Individual in the Therapeutic Group. *Br. J. Med. Psychol.* 34: 23–31.

Foulkes, S.H. 1973. The Group as the Matrix of the Individual's Mental Health. In *Group Therapy: 1973,* edited by L.R. Wolberg and E.K. Schwartz. New York: Stratton Intercontinental Medical Book, pp. 211–220.

Foulkes, S.H., and Anthony, E.J. 1965. *Group Psychotherapy: The Psychoanalytic Approach,* 2nd ed. Baltimore: Penguin Books.

French, T.M. 1952. *The Integration of Behavior,* vols. 1, 2. Chicago: University of Chicago Press.

Freud, S. 1910. *The Future Prospects of Psychoanalytic Theory.* Standard Ed., vol. 11.

Freud, S. 1913. On Beginning the Treatment. Standard Ed., vol. 12, pp. 121–144.

Freud, S. 1915. *Observations on Transference Love.* Standard Ed., vol. 12.

Freud, S. 1921. *Group Psychology and the Analysis of the Ego.* Standard Ed., vol. 18.

Freud, S. 1937. Analysis Terminable and Interminable. Standard Ed., vol. 23, pp. 316–357.

Fried, E. 1954. The Effect of Combined Therapy on the Productivity of Patients. *Int. J. Group Psychother.* 4: 42–55.

Fried, E. 1970. Individuation Through Group Therapy. *Int. J. Group Psychother.* 20: 450–459.

Fried, E. 1971. Basic Concepts in Group Psychotherapy. In *Comprehensive Group Psychotherapy,* edited by H.I. Kaplan and B.J. Sadock. Baltimore: Williams and Wilkins, pp. 47–71.

Fried, E. 1973. Group Bonds. In *Group Therapy 1973: An Overview,* edited by L.R. Wolberg and E.K. Schwartz. New York: Stratton Intercontinental Medical Book, pp. 161–168.

Fried, E. 1982. Building Psychic Structures as a Prerequisite for Change. *Int. J. Group Psychother.* 32: 417–430.

Fulkerson, C.C.F., Hawkins, D.M., and Alden, A.R. 1981. Psychotherapy Groups of Insufficient Size. *Int. J. Group Psychother.* 31: 73–81.

Gans, R. 1962. Group Co-therapists and the Therapeutic Situation: A Critical Evaluation. *Int. J. Group Psychother.* 12: 82–88.

Garland, C. 1982. Group Analysis: Taking the Non-Problem Seriously. *Group Analysis* 15: 4–14.

Garland, J.A., and Kolodny, R.L. 1973. Characteristics and Resolution of Scapegoating. In *Further Explorations in Group Work,* edited by S. Bernstein. Boston: Milford House, pp. 67–68.

Gauron, E.F., and Rawlings, E.I. 1975. Procedure for Orienting New Members to Group Psychotherapy. *Small Group Behav.* 6: 293–307.

Getty, C., and Shannon, A.M. 1969. Co-therapy as an Egalitarian Relationship. *Am. J. Nurs.* 69: 767–771.

Gibbard, G.S., and Hartman, J.S. 1973. The Oedipal Paradigm in Group Development: A Clinical and Empirical Study. *Small Group Behav.* 4: 305–354.

Giovacchini, P. 1979. *Treatment of Primitive Mental States.* New York: Jason Aronson.

Glatzer, H.T. 1953. Handling Transference Resistance in Group Therapy. *Psychoanal. Rev.* 40: 36–43.

Glatzer, H.T. 1978. The Working Alliance in Analytic Group Psychotherapy. *Int. J. Group Psychother.* 28: 147–161.

Greenson, R.R. 1967. *The Technique and Practice of Psychoanalysis*. New York: International Universities Press.

Grotjahn, M. 1975. The Treatment of the Famous and the "Beautiful People" in Groups. In *Group Therapy 1975: An Overview*, edited by L.R. Wolberg and M.L. Aronson. New York: Stratton Intercontinental Medical Book.

Grunebaum, H., and Kates, W. 1977. Whom to Refer for Group Psychotherapy. *Am. J. Psychiatry* 132: 130–133.

Guntrip, H. 1969. *Schizoid Phenomena, Object-Relations, and the Self*. New York: International Universities Press.

Gustafson, J.P., and Cooper, L. 1979. Unconscious Planning in Small Groups. *Human Relations* 32: 1039–1064.

Gustafson, J.P., Cooper, L., Lathrop, N.C., Ringler, K., Seldin, F.A., and Wright, M.K. 1981. Cooperative and Clashing Interests in Small Groups. Part I. Theory. *Human Relations* 34: 315–339.

Guttmacher, J.A., and Birk, L. 1971. Group Therapy: What Specific Therapeutic Advantages. *Compr. Psychiatry* 12: 546–556.

Hill, W., and Gruner, L. 1972. A Study of Development in Open and Closed Groups. *Small Group Behav.* 4: 355–381.

Horwitz, L. 1977. A Group Centered Approach to Group Psychotherapy. *Int. J. Group Psychother.* 27: 423–440.

Horwitz, L. 1977. Group Psychotherapy of the Borderline Patient. In *Borderline Personality Disorders*, edited by P. Hartocollis. New York: International Universities Press, pp. 399–422.

Horwitz, L. 1980. Group Psychotherapy for Borderline and Narcissistic Patients. *Bull. Menninger Clin.* 44: 181–200.

Hulse, W. 1958. Psychotherapy with Ambulatory Schizophrenic Patients in Mixed Groups. *Arch. Neurol. Psychiatry* 79: 681–687.

Jackson, J., and Grotjahn, M. 1958. The Treatment of Oral Defenses by Combined Individual and Group Therapy. *Int. J. Group Psychother.* 8: 373–382.

Johnson, D., and Howenstein, R. 1982. Revitalizing an Ailing Group Psychotherapy Program. *Psychiatry* 45: 138–146.

Kadis, A.L. 1956. The Alternate Meeting in Group Psychotherapy. *Am. J. Psychiatry* 10: 275–291.

Kadis, A.L., Krasner, J.D., Winick, C., and Foulkes, S.H. 1963. *A Practicum of Group Psychotherapy*. New York: Harper & Row.

Kaplan, S.R., and Roman, M. 1961. Characteristic Responses in Adult Therapy Groups to the Introduction of New Members: A Reflection on Group Process. *Int. J. Group Psychother.* 11: 372–381.

Katz, G.A. 1983. The Non-interpretation of Metaphors in Psychiatric Hospital Groups. *Int. J. Group Psychother.* 33: 56–68.

Kauff, P.F. 1977. The Termination Process: Its Relationship to the Separation-Individuation Phase of Development. *Int. J. Group Psychother.* 27: 3–18.

Kauff, P.F. 1979. Diversity in Analytic Group Psychotherapy: The Relationship between Theoretical Concepts and Technique. *Int. J. Group Psychother.* 29: 51–66.

Kelman, H. 1963. The Role of the Group in the Induction of Therapeutic Change. *Int. J. Group Psychother.* 13: 399–432.

Kernberg, O.F. 1975. A Systems Approach to Priority Setting of Interventions in Groups. *Int. J. Group Psychother.* 25: 251–275.

Klein, E.B., and Astrachan, B.M. 1971. Learning in Groups: A Comparison of T-Groups and Study Groups. *J. Appl. Behav. Sci.* 7: 659–683.

Klein, M. 1946. Notes on Some Schizoid Mechanisms. *Int. J. Psychoanal.* 27: 99–110.

Klein-Lipschutz, E. 1953. Comparison of Dreams in Individual and Group Psychotherapy. *Int. J. Group Psychother.* 3: 143–149.

Kohut, H. 1971. *The Analysis of the Self.* New York: International Universities Press.

Kohut, H. 1977. *The Restoration of the Self.* New York: International Universities Press.

Kohut, H., and Wolf, E.S. 1978. The Disorders of the Self and Their Treatment: An Outline. *Int. J. Psychoanal.* 59: 413–425.

Kris, E. 1956. The Recovery of Childhood Memories in Psychoanalysis. *Psychoanal. Study Child* 2: 54–88.

Lasch, C. 1979. *The Culture of Narcissism.* New York: W.W. Norton.

Lazare, A., and Eisenthal, S. 1979. A Negotiated Approach to the Clinical Encounter. I: Attending to the Patient's Perspective. In *Outpatient Psychiatry: Diagnosis and Treatment*, edited by A. Lazare. Baltimore: Williams and Wilkins, pp. 141–156.

Lazare, A., Eisenthal, S., and Frank, A. 1979. A Negotiated Approach to the Clinical Encounter. II: Conflict and Negotiation. In *Outpatient Psychiatry: Diagnosis and Treatment*, edited by A. Lazare. Baltimore: Williams and Wilkins, pp. 157–171.

Leary, T.F. 1957. *Interpersonal Diagnosis of Personality.* New York: Ronald Press.

LeBon, G. 1920. *The Crowd: A Study of the Popular Mind.* New York: Fisher, Unwin.

Leighton, A.H. 1959. *The Stirling County Study of Psychiatric Disorder and Sociocultural Environment: My Name Is Legion*, vol. 1: *People of Cove and Woodlot*, vol. 2; and *The Character of Danger*, vol. 3. New York: Basic Books.

Levine, B. 1979. *Group Psychotherapy: Practice and Development.* Englewood Cliffs, N.J.: Prentice-Hall.

Lieberman, M., Yalom, I.D., and Miles, M.D. 1973. *Encounter Groups: First Facts.* New York: Basic Books.

Loewald, H.W. 1973. On Internalization. *Int. J. Psychoanal.* 54: 9–17.

Lundin, W.H., and Aronov, V.M. 1952. The Use of Co-therapists in Group Psychotherapy. *J. Consult. Psychol.* 16: 77–84.

MacLennon, B. 1965. Cotherapy, *Int. J. Group Psychother.* 15: 154–165.

Mahler, M.S., Pine, F., and Bergman, A. 1975. *The Psychological Birth of the Human Infant.* New York: Basic Books.

Malan, D.H., Balfour, F.H.G., Hood, V.G., and Shooter, A. 1976. Group Psychotherapy: A Long Term Follow-up Study. *Arch. Gen. Psychiatry* 33: 1303–1315.

Marin, P. 1976. The New Narcissism. *Harpers*, October 1975, pp. 44–56.

Masterson, J.F. 1976. *Psychotherapy of the Borderline Adult: A Developmental Approach.* New York: Brunner/Mazel.

McDougall, W. 1920. *The Group Mind.* New York: G.P. Putnam's Sons.

McDougall, W. 1921. *Social Psychology.* Boston: J.W. Luce.

McGee, T.F. 1969. Comprehensive Preparation for Group Psychotherapy. *Am. J. Psychother.* 23: 303–312.

Menninger, R.J. 1959. Observations on Absences of Member Patients in Group Psychotherapy. *Int. J. Group Psychother.* 9: 195–203.

Meyers, S.J. 1978. The Disorders of the Self: Developmental and Clinical Considerations. *Group* 2: 131–140.

Michels, R. 1981. The Present and the Past. *Bull. Assoc. Psychoanal. Med.* 20: 49–56.

Middleman, R.R. 1980. Co-Leadership and Solo-Leadership in Education for Social Work with Groups. *Social Work With Groups* 3: 30–40.

Mintz, E. 1965. Male-Female Co-therapists: Some Values and Some Problems. *Am. J. Psychother.* 19: 293–301.

Munzer, J. 1967. Acting Out: Communication or Resistance. *Int. J. Group Psychother.* 16: 434–441.

Neumann, M., and Geoni, B. 1974. Types of Patients Especially Suitable for Analytically Oriented Group Psychotherapy: Some Clinical Examples. *Isr. Ann. Psychiatry Related Disciplines* 12: 203–215.

Ogden, T.H. 1979. On Projective Identification. *Int. J. Psychoanal.* 60: 357–373.

Ormont, L.R. 1968. Group Resistance and the Therapeutic Contract. *Int. J. Group Psychother.* 18: 147–154.

Ormont, L.R., and Strean, H. 1978. *The Practice of Conjoint Therapy*. New York: Human Sciences Press.

Ornstein, P.H. 1978. The Evolution of Heinz Kohut's Psychoanalytic Psychology of the Self. In *The Search for the Self*, edited by P.H. Ornstein. New York: International Universities Press, pp. 1–106.

Ornstein, P.H., and Ornstein, A. 1977. On the Continuing Evolution of Psychoanalytic Psychotherapy: Reflections upon Recent Trends and Some Predictions for the Future. *Annu. Psychoanal.* 5: 329–370.

Pines, M. 1981. The Frame of Reference of Group Psychotherapy. *Int. J. Group Psychother.* 31: 275–285.

Pratt, J.H. 1969. The Home Sanatorium Treatment of Consumption (a speech delivered before the Johns Hopkins Hospital Medical Society on January 22, 1906), quoted in *Group Therapy Today*, by H.M. Ruitenbeek. New York: Atherton Press, pp. 9–17.

Rabin, H.M. 1967. How Does Co-Therapy Compare with Regular Therapy? *Am. J. Psychother.* 21: 244–255.

Rice, A.K. 1969. Individual, Group, and Intragroup Processes. *Human Relations* 22: 565–584.

Rioch, M.D. 1970. The Work of Wilfred Bion on Groups. *Psychiatry* 33: 55–66.

Rogers, C. 1970. *Carl Rogers on Encounter Groups*. New York: Harper & Row.

Roth, B.E. 1979. Problems of Early Maintenance and Entry into Group Psychotherapy with Persons Suffering from Borderline and Narcissistic States. *Group* 3: 3–22.

Roth, B.E. 1980. Understanding the Development of a Homogeneous Identity-Impaired Group Through Countertransference Phenomena. *Int. J. Group Psychother.* 30: 405–426.

Rutan, J.S., and Alonso, A. 1978. Some Guidelines for Group Therapists. *Group* 1: 4–13.

Rutan, J.S., and Alonso, A. 1979. Group Psychotherapy. In *Outpatient Psychiatry: Diagnosis and Treatment*, edited by A. Lazare. Baltimore: Williams and Wilkins, pp. 612–620.

Rutan, J. S., and Alonso, A. 1980. Sequential Cotherapy of Groups for Training and Clinical Care. *Group* 4: 40–50.

Rutan, J.S., and Alonso, A. 1982. Group Therapy, Individual Therapy, or Both? *Int. J. Group Psychother.* 32: 267–282.

Rutan, J.S., Alonso, A., and Molin, R. 1984. Handling the Absence of the Leader. *Int. J. Group Psychother.* 34: 273–287.

Rutan, J.S., and Rice, C.A. 1981. The Charismatic Leader: Asset or Liability? *Psychother. Theory Res. Practice* 18: 487–492.

Saravay, S. 1978. A Psychoanalytic Theory of Group Development. *Int. J. Group Psychother.* 28: 481–507.

Scheflen, A.E. 1964. The Significance of Posture in Communication Systems. *Psychiatry* 27: 316–331.

Scheflen, A.E. 1965. Quasi-Courtship Behaviors in Psychotherapy. *Psychiatry* 28: 245–256.

Scheidlinger, S. 1974. On the Concept of Mother-Group. *Int. J. Group Psychother.* 24: 417–428.

Schutz, W.C. 1958. *Firo.* New York: Rinehart.

Slater, P.E. 1966. *Microcosm: Structural, Psychological, and Religious Evolution in Groups.* New York: John Wiley.

Slavinska-Holy, N. 1983. Combining Individual and Homogeneous Group Psychotherapies for Borderline Conditions. *Int. J. Group Psychother.* 33: 297–312.

Slavson, S.R. 1950. *Analytic Group Psychotherapy.* New York: Columbia University Press.

Slavson, S.R. 1957. Are There Group Dynamics in Therapy Groups? *Int. J. Group Psychother.* 7: 131–154.

Solomon, A., Loeffler, F.J., and Frank, G.H. 1953. An Analysis of Co-therapist Interaction in Group Psychotherapy. *Int. J. Group Psychother.* 3: 174–188.

Stein, A. 1963. Indications for Group Psychotherapy and the Selection of Patients. *J. Hillside Hospital* 12: 145–155.

Stein, A. 1964. The Nature of Transference in Combined Therapy. *Int. J. Group Psychother.* 14: 413.

Stone, W.N. 1975. Dynamics of the Recorder-Observer in Group Psychotherapy. *Compr. Psychiatry* 16: 49–54.

Stone, W.N. 1983. The Curative Fantasy in Group Psychotherapy. In *Group Therapy Monograph, No. 10.* New York: The Washington Square Institute.

Stone, W.N., Blase, M., and Bozzuto, J. 1980. Late Dropouts from Group Psychotherapy. *Am. J. Psychother.* 34: 401–413.

Stone, W.N, and Gustafson, J.P. 1982. Technique in Group Psychotherapy of Narcissistic and Borderline Patients. *Int. J. Group Psychother.* 32: 29–47.

Stone, W.N., and Rutan, J.S. 1984. Duration of Group Psychotherapy. *Int. J. Group Psychother.* 34: 93–110.

Stone, W.N., Schengber, J.S., and Seifried, F.S. 1966. The Treatment of a Homosexual Woman in a Mixed Group. *Int. J. Group Psychother.* 16: 425–433.

Stone, W.N., and Whitman, R.M. 1977. Contributions of the Psychology of Self to Group Process and Group Therapy. *Int. J. Group Psychother.* 27: 343–359.

Stone, W.N., and Whitman, R.M. 1980. Observations on Empathy in Group Psychotherapy. In *Group and Family Therapy 1980,* edited by L.R. Wolberg and M.L. Aronson. New York: Brunner/Mazel, pp. 102–117.

Sullivan, H.S. 1953. *The Collected Works of Harry Stack Sullivan.* New York: W.W. Norton.

Toffler, A. 1970. *Future Shock.* New York: Random House.

Toker, E. 1972. The Scapegoat as an Essential Group Phenomenon. *Int. J. Group Psychother.* 22: 320–332.

Truax, C.B., and Wargo, D.G. 1969. Effects of Vicarious Therapy Pretraining and Alternate Sessions on Outcome in Group Psychotherapy with Outpatients. *J. Consult. Clin. Psychol.* 33: 440–447.

Tuckman, B.W. 1965. Developmental Sequence in Small Groups. *Psychol. Bull.* 63: 384–399.

Whitaker, D.S., and Lieberman, M.A. 1964. *Psychotherapy Through the Group Process.* New York: Atherton.

Whitman, R.M. 1973. Dreams about the Group: An Approach to the Problems of Group Psychology. *Int. J. Group Psychother.* 23: 408–420.

Whitman, R.M., and Stock, D. 1958. The Group Focal Conflict. *Psychiatry* 21: 269–276.

Winick, C., Kadis, A.L., and Krasner, J.D. 1961. Training and Professional Practice of American Group Therapists. *Int. J. Group Psychother.* 11: 419–430.

Wogan, M., Getter, H., Anidur, M.J., Nichols, M.F., and Okman, G. 1977. Influencing Interaction and Outcome in Group Psychotherapy. *Small Group Behav.* 8: 26–46.

Wolf, A., and Schwartz, E. 1962. *Psychoanalysis in Groups.* New York: Grune and Stratton.

Wolf, A., and Schwartz, E.K. 1971. Psychoanalysis in Groups. In *Comprehensive Group Psychotherapy,* edited by H.I. Kaplan and B.J. Sadock. Baltimore: Williams and Wilkins, pp. 241–291.

Wolf, A., and Schwartz, E.K. 1975. The Role of the Leader's Values. In *The Leader in the Group,* edited by Z.A. Liff. New York: Jason Aronson, pp. 13–30.

Wong, N. 1979. Clinical Considerations in Group Treatment of Narcissistic Disorders. *Int. J. Group Psychother.* 29: 325–345.

Wong, N. 1980. Combined Group and Individual Treatment of Borderline and Narcissistic Patients: Heterogeneous versus Homogeneous Groups. *Int. J. Group Psychother.* 30: 389–404.

Wong, N. 1983. Combined Individual and Group Psychotherapy. In *Comprehensive Group Psychotherapy.* 2nd ed., edited by H.I. Kaplan and B.J. Sadock. Baltimore: Williams and Wilkins, pp. 73–83.

Wright, M.A. 1981. Assumptions and Concepts Fundamental to Kohut's Psychology of the Self. Unpublished manuscript, Smith College.

Yalom, I.D. 1966. A Study of Group Therapy Dropouts. *Arch. Gen. Psychiatry* 14: 393–414.

Yalom, I.D. 1970. *The Theory and Practice of Group Psychotherapy.* New York: Basic Books, pp. 233–244.

Yalom, I.D. 1975. *The Theory and Practice of Group Psychotherapy.* 2nd ed. New York: Basic Books.

Yalom, I.D., Bond, G., Bloch, S., Zimmerman, D., and Friedman, L. 1977. The Impact of a Weekend Group Experience on Individual Therapy. *Arch. Gen. Psychiatry* 34: 399–418.

Zetzel, E. 1956. Current Concepts of Transference, *Int. J. Psychoanal.* 37: 369–376.

Zimmerman, D. 1967. Some Characteristics of Dreams in Group Analytic Psychotherapy. *Int. J. Group Psychother.* 17: 524–535.

Zimmerman, D. 1976. Indications and Counterindications for Analytic Group Psychotherapy—A Study of Group Factors. In *Group Therapy 1976: An Overview,* edited by L.R. Wolberg, M.L. Aronson, and A.R. Wolberg. New York: Stratton Intercontinental Medical Book.

Index

217